ADAPTATION AND APPROPRIATION

From the apparently simple adaptation of a text into film, theatre or a new literary work, to the more complex appropriation of style or meaning, it is arguable that all texts are somehow connected to a network of existing texts and art forms. In this new edition *Adaptation and Appropriation* explores:

- multiple definitions and practices of adaptation and appropriation
- the cultural and aesthetic politics behind the impulse to adapt
- the global and local dimensions of adaptation
- the impact of new digital technologies on ideas of making, originality and customization
- diverse ways in which contemporary literature, theatre, television and film adapt, revise and reimagine other works of art
- the impact on adaptation and appropriation of theoretical movements, including structuralism, post-structuralism, postcolonialism, postmodernism, feminism and gender studies
- the appropriation across time and across cultures of specific canonical texts, by Shakespeare, Dickens and others, but also of literary archetypes such as myth or fairy tale.

Ranging across genres and harnessing concepts from fields as diverse as musicology and the natural sciences, this volume brings clarity to the complex debates around adaptation and appropriation, offering a much-needed resource for those studying literature, film, media or culture.

Julie Sanders is Professor of English and Pro-Vice-Chancellor for Humanities and Social Sciences at Newcastle University, UK.

THE NEW CRITICAL IDIOM

SERIES EDITOR: JOHN DRAKAKIS, UNIVERSITY OF STIRLING

The New Critical Idiom is an invaluable series of introductory guides to today's critical terminology. Each book:

- provides a handy, explanatory guide to the use (and abuse) of the term;
- offers an original and distinctive overview by a leading literary and cultural critic;
- relates the term to the larger field of cultural representation.

With a strong emphasis on clarity, lively debate and the widest possible breadth of examples, *The New Critical Idiom* is an indispensable approach to key topics in literary studies.

Also available in this series:

ADAPTATION AND APPROPRIATION

Second edition

Julie Sanders

Routledge
Taylor & Francis Group

LONDON AND NEW YORK

First published 2016
by Routledge
2 Park Square, Milton Park, Abingdon, Oxon OX14 4RN

and by Routledge
711 Third Avenue, New York, NY 10017

Routledge is an imprint of the Taylor & Francis Group, an informa business

British Library Cataloguing in Publication Data
A catalogue record for this book is available from the British Library

Library of Congress Cataloging in Publication Data
Sanders, Julie, 1968-
Adaptation and appropriation / Julie Sanders. -- 2nd edition.
pages cm
Includes bibliographical references and index.
1. Literature--Adaptations. I. Title.
PN171.A33S26 2015
801--dc23
2015023188

ISBN: 978-1-138-82898-8 (hbk)
ISBN: 978-1-138-82899-5 (pbk)
ISBN: 978-1-315-73794-2 (ebk)

Typeset in Times New Roman
by Taylor & Francis Books

For Gaynor Macfarlane, again, still, always.

CONTENTS

SERIES EDITOR'S PREFACE

The New Critical Idiom is a series of introductory books which seeks to extend the lexicon of literary terms, in order to address the radical changes which have taken place in the study of literature during the last decades of the twentieth century. The aim is to provide clear, well-illustrated accounts of the full range of terminology currently in use and to evolve histories of its changing usage.

The current state of the discipline of literary studies is one where there is considerable debate concerning basic questions of terminology. This involves, among other things, the boundaries which distinguish the literary from the non-literary; the position of literature within the larger sphere of culture; the relationship between literatures of different cultures; and questions concerning the relation of literary to other cultural forms within the context of interdisciplinary studies.

It is clear that the field of literary criticism and theory is a dynamic and heterogeneous one. The present need is for individual volumes on terms which combine clarity of exposition with an adventurousness of perspective and a breadth of application. Each volume will contain as part of its apparatus some indication of the direction in which the definition of particular terms is likely to move, as well as expanding the disciplinary boundaries within which some of these terms have been traditionally contained. This will involve some re-situation of terms within the larger field of cultural representation, and will introduce examples from the area of film and the modern media in addition to examples from a variety of literary texts.

ACKNOWLEDGEMENTS

FIRST EDITION

As this volume evidences, few stories or books ever stand alone and with that in mind I would like to acknowledge those who have contributed to this volume. Fred Botting read and commented on the original proposal with great insight and made the final outline much stronger. Many others have offered help and ideas along the way; special thanks to Kate Chedgzoy, Davina Cooper, Mark Dooley, Finn Fordham, Daniel Grimley, Dominic Head, Barbra Kelly, Máire ní Fhlathúin, Mark Robson, Kiernan Ryan, Michael Sanders, Lauren Shohet and Tory Young, as well as all the students at Keele and Nottingham who have offered their various perspectives and enthusiasms on this topic. The University of Teesside provided a valuable audience for some of this work in its earliest stages and I am grateful to all who attended on that occasion. I underwent my own process of professional adaptation while writing this volume and I thank my new colleagues at the University of Nottingham for making me feel so very welcome. Though they will probably never know it, the Quadriga Consort and the virtuoso musicianship of Andrew Manze were my joint inspiration for the baroque musical theories deployed in these pages and I am endlessly indebted both to the intelligence of their sleeve-notes and the beauty of their playing. Richard Powers's remarkable novel, *The Gold Bug Variations*, first gifted me by my father, and Glenn Gould's haunting 1955 and 1981 interpretations of Bach's *Goldberg Variations* provided the literary and musical soundtrack to much of the thinking laid out here.

My series editor John Drakakis has been a model of sound advice, good readership and great wit, and Liz Thompson at Routledge shaped the volume in several crucial ways; I only hope the final version does them justice. John Higham has been my other, and better, half throughout the enterprise; during that time he has performed for real the acts of grafting that I can only invoke as metaphor, bringing things to fruition with a very tangible beauty and, as ever, I thank him.

The book is dedicated to Gaynor, my best pal, with love and thanks for sharing the journey over many years.

SECOND EDITION

My thanks to Routledge and to Ruth Hilsdon and John Drakakis for the opportunity to reflect on and adapt my own critical work ten years hence. In the intervening decade I have benefited hugely from the engagement of readers with this book and from the opportunity to present and refine research in a global context. Special thanks to the University of Alabama, University of Auckland, University of Calgary, University of Copenhagen, City University of Hong Kong, Flinders University, Universiteit Ghent, University of Queensland, University of Notre Dame, Sogang University, and communities of scholars and colleagues at the University of Nottingham Ningbo China and Malaysia for their contributions; to my students Makenzi Crouch, Klaudia Lee, Donglai Shi and Jason Ward, whose projects on cultural adaptation have helped to keep me thinking hard along the way. And to inspirational colleagues around the world, in particular: Susan Bennett, John Bryant, Christy Carson, Deborah Cartmell, Christine Geraghty, Anne Gjelsvik, Lyn Innes, Li Jun, Tai-Won Kim, Katja Krebs, Derek 'Mac' McAuley, Jo Robinson, Minami Ryuta, Imelda Whelehan and, last but certainly not least, Maggie Yang. I began this book in my first summer at the University of Nottingham and I adapted it in my final summer there before joining Newcastle University on the next big adventure. Thank you to colleagues past and present for your support and belief in me. And thank you to the Quadriga Consort, who, amazingly enough, did find the acknowledgement in the first edition and took the time to get in touch. Only connect.

Some things, though, despite inevitable change and despite the new versions of older arguments presented here, thankfully remain the same. John is still there making sense of it all. And this book, second time around, is still for Gaynor, still my best pal, now with additions and adaptations all of her own – Gregor, Sean and Leo. This one is for all of you, then, with love.

'One who really loves texts must wish from time to time to love (at least) two together ...'

Gérard Genette, *Palimpsests*

'There were, as in all crooked businesses, two sets of books ...'

Peter Carey, *Jack Maggs*

INTRODUCTION
GOING ON (AND ON)

'art never improves, but ... the material of art is never quite the same.'

T. S. Eliot, 'Tradition and the Individual Talent'

This book is concerned with the literariness of literature but also the presence of the literary in many other forms, mediums and genres. It is a book about connections. Any exploration of inter-textuality, and its specific manifestation in the forms of adaptation and appropriation, is inevitably interested in how art creates art, or how literature is made by literature. There is a danger, of course, that this activity of investigating or 'reading' adaptations proves self-serving, merely stimulating the afterlife both of texts and of literary criticism as a scholarly pursuit. The literary, media or cultural studies academic or student reads or watches many 'texts' (and for 'texts' here read alternately: films, creations, compositions, events and performances) throughout their learning career, and the more of this activity they pursue the more echoes, parallels and points of comparison they identify. The notion that the tracing of intertextual reference and allusion is a self-confirming exercise is reasonable enough; for example, Robert Weimann writes persuasively of the 'reproductive dimension of appropriation' (1983: 14), suggesting the manifold ways in which texts feed off and create other texts. But as readers, spectators and critics, we also need to recognize that adaptation and appropriation are fundamental to the practice and, indeed, to the enjoyment of literature and the arts more generally.

The late twentieth century made a particular virtue out of querying the ability to be or even the necessity of being 'original', not least in the arts. Edward Said suggested in 'On Originality' that 'the writer thinks less of writing originally, and more of rewriting' (1983: 135); Jacques Derrida noted that 'the desire to write is the desire to launch things that come back to you as much as possible' (1985: 157). The 'rewriting' impulse, which is much more than simple imitation, is often articulated in theoretical terms such as intertextuality, and many of the early prominent theorists of this practice emerge from the structuralist and post-structuralist movements of the 1960s, especially in France. In the field of anthropology, Claude Lévi-Strauss conducted many of his researches in terms of identifying repeating structures across cultures and cultural forms (2001 [1978]). In the literary sphere, Roland Barthes declared that 'any text is an intertext' (1981: 39), suggesting that the works of previous and surrounding cultures are always present in literature. Barthes also highlighted the ways in which texts were not solely dependent on their authors for the production of meaning, indicating how they benefited from readers who created their own intertextual networks and connections. Julia Kristeva, herself a product of a scientific and anthropological training under Lévi-Strauss, formulated the term *intertextualité* in her essay 'The Bounded Text' to describe the process by which any text was 'a permutation of texts, an intertextuality' (1980: 36). Kristeva's focus was driven by semiotics; she was interested in how texts were permeated by the signs, signifiers and utterances of the culture in which they participated, or from which they derived. Intertextuality as a term has, however, come to refer to a far more textual as opposed to utterance-driven notion of how texts encompass and respond to other texts both during the process of their creation and composition and in terms of any subsequent individual or collective reader or spectator response.

In the new Web 2.0 era we have been exposed to new modes of intertextuality in operation not least through the collective creativity and personalized customizations of the user-maker generation of platforms and sites such as YouTube and YouKu. In this context terms like remix and remediation, along with mash-up, have entered our everyday vocabulary and have in turn posed their own challenges to ideas of authorship and intellectual property versus creativity and open access (Bolter and Grusin 2000). The 'newness' of all this can of course be overestimated as the historical depth of adaptation across art forms referred to in this study confirms; what might be more accurate to state, however, is that technology has made us much more aware of this availability of art in its broadest terms for customization, hyper-conscious perhaps of these digital and indeed textual affordances and the social and cultural values they perform. As novelist Tom McCarthy has put it: 'Technology reveals us to ourselves as we always in fact were: networked, distributed, laced with code' (McCarthy 2011).

In this dispersed and distributed context, it is fair to say that adaptations and appropriations (or mediations and remediations) can vary in how explicitly they state their intertextual or connective purpose. Many of the film, television or theatre adaptations of canonical works of literature that we look at in this volume openly declare themselves as an interpretation or re-reading of a canonical precursor. Sometimes this will involve a director's personal vision, and it may or may not involve cultural relocation or updating of some form; sometimes this interpretative act will also involve the movement into a new generic mode or context. In appropriations the intertextual relationship may be less explicit, more embedded, but what is often inescapable is the fact that a political or ethical commitment shapes a writer's, director's or performer's decision to reinterpret a source text. In this respect, in any study of adaptation and appropriation the creative import of the author cannot be as easily dismissed as Roland Barthes's or Michel Foucault's influential theories of the 'death of the author' might suggest (Barthes 1988; Foucault 1979). Nevertheless the ability of these theories to destabilize the authority of the so-called original text does enable multiple and sometimes conflicting productions of meaning, a fact that will prove important for our analyses. The inherent intertextuality of literature/art forms encourages the ongoing, evolving production of meaning and an ever-expanding network of textual relations and value-systems.

Returning to my earlier points about Web 2.0 contexts, our attention has now been drawn to whole new communities of practice engaged in adaptive work, not least the fan communities who fashion themselves as makers and producers of new kinds of stories and texts (often in the guise of sequels or continuations). Henry Jenkins has produced impressive ethnographic studies of a number of these communities and subcultures in his research into participatory culture and stresses that we can no longer draw a clear line between producer and consumer (1992: 275). In this context, then, the notion of an 'original' or source begins to be rescaled in a discussion of networked distribution and collective interpretation. As texts develop their own incremental history across time and undergo multiple, often multimodal, and sometimes intercultural forms of adaptation and reinterpretation, it also becomes important to consider how a reader or spectator or indeed 'prod-user' (to use Axel Bruns's suggestive phrase, which consciously blurs the idea of usage and production to create a new model of content creation (Bruns 2008)) encounters the so-called original. The perceived original or source might not in fact be first in the sequence. A point of entry for younger people today to canonical texts such as Shakespeare's *Romeo and Juliet* or Lewis Carroll's *Alice in Wonderland* might well be via film adaptations or indeed Walt Disney animated versions of so-called classics. As Linda Hutcheon has stressed, in this new environment 'multiple versions exist laterally not vertically' (2013: xv). How might that order of encounter or point of entry alter the terms in which we understand or describe the adaptive experience from the vantage point of the end-user? We will return to these interpretive challenges throughout.

Literary texts 'are built from systems, codes and traditions established by previous works of literature' (Allen 2000: 1). But they are also built from systems, codes and traditions derived from companion art forms and media. If Kristeva is credited with formulating the theory of intertextuality, hers was a theory that was far from exclusive in its application to literature. She viewed art, music, drama, dance and literature in terms of a living mosaic, a dynamic intersection of textual surfaces. We might wish to add film and now digital culture and computer science to this list, and indeed the terminology deployed throughout this study derives from this diverse set of practices as well as from the natural sciences.

The vocabulary of adaptation is highly labile: Adrian Poole has offered an extensive list of terms to represent the Victorian era's interest in reworking its artistic past: '(in no particular order) ... borrowing, stealing, appropriating, inheriting, assimilating ... being influenced, inspired, dependent, indebted, haunted, possessed ... homage, mimicry, travesty, echo, allusion, and intertextuality' (2004: 2). We can easily continue the linguistic riff, adding into the mix: variation, version, interpretation, imitation, proximation, supplement, increment, improvisation, prequel, sequel, continuation, afterlife, addition, paratext, hypertext, palimpsest, graft, rewriting, reworking, refashioning, re-vision, re-evaluation. And new digital cultures and technologies have further expanded the lexicon with concepts such as remediation and specific concepts such as the mash-up, remix, hack and sample. The glossary at the back of this volume grapples with a small selection of these terms but embedded within the pages of this book the reader will encounter many more. I make no apologies for this proliferation, for the profusion rather than fixity of terms offered: the idiom in which adaptation and appropriation theory functions is rich and various and any study of the same should surely reflect this fact.

J. Hillis Miller has explored various permutations of the paratextual, the peritextual and the hypertextual in his critical writings, delineating the multifarious ways in which a literary text can be 'inhabited ... by a long chain of parasitical presences, echoes, allusions, guests, ghosts of previous texts' (Gilbert and Gubar 2000 [1979]: 46). This volume concerns itself, at various turns with these textual ghosts and hauntings, both literal and metaphorical. In turn, questions of dependency and derivation are broached. Studies of adaptation and appropriation invariably abut with questions of ownership and attendant legal discourses of intellectual property and copyright. Following on from Barthes's destabilization of textual meaning and authority, however, adaptation and appropriation, as both procedure and process, are celebratory of the cooperative and collaborative model of creativity.

Certain distinctions remain, nevertheless, crucial to understanding the operations of adaptation and appropriation. There is a need, for example, to distinguish between direct quotation and acts of citation. Quotation can be deferential or critical, supportive or questioning; it depends on the context in which the quotation takes place. Citation, however, presumes a more deferential relationship; it is frequently self-authenticating, even reverential, in its reference to the canon of 'authoritative', culturally validated texts. Many nineteenth-century novels, those of Thomas Hardy, the Brontë sisters and George Eliot, for example, deployed Shakespearean citations in their work in this manner. But citation is different again from adaptation, which constitutes a more sustained and deeper engagement usually with a single text or source, than the more glancing act of allusion or quotation, even citation, allows. Beyond that, appropriation carries out the same sustained engagement of adaptation but frequently adopts a posture of critique, overt commentary and even sometimes assault or attack.

Adaptation and appropriation are inevitably involved in the performance of textual echo and allusion, but this does not usually equate to the fragmentary *bricolage* of quotation more commonly associated with postmodern intertextuality. In French, *bricolage* is the term for 'do-it-yourself' (DIY), which helps to explain its application in a literary context to those texts that assemble a range of quotations, allusions and citations from an often diverse range of existent works of art. A parallel form in fine art is the creation of *collage* by assembling found items to create a new aesthetic object, or in contemporary music the creative act of 'sampling'. The purposeful reassembly of fragments to form a new whole is, undoubtedly, an active element in many of the postmodern texts explored in the course of this study. There are also important ways in which the act of *bricolage* shades into the literary practice of pastiche. Pastiche is another term of French derivation which, in the musical sphere, refers to a medley of references, a composition made up of fragments pieced together (Dentith 2000: 194). In the domains of art and literature, however, pastiche has undergone a further shift or extension of reference, being applied most often to those works which carry out an extended imitation of the style of a single artist or writer. There are, undoubtedly, some current novelists who are exponents of the medley style of pastiche – Jonathan Coe, for example, in his richly allusive *What a Carve Up!* (1994), which mimics everything from journalism to James Joyce in the course of its narrative – but frequently it is the more sustained act of artistic imitation which is accorded the label of pastiche in contemporary literature. Pastiche is often assumed to have a satiric undertow or a parodic intention, although there are exceptions to this rule. In some respects there is often a complicated blend of admiration and satire at play in pastiches of particular authors or literary styles. J. M. Coetzee's *Foe*, discussed in detail in Chapter 6, reworks with both celebratory and satiric intent the aesthetics of eighteenth-century prose, and the writings of Daniel Defoe in particular, in its version of novels written in the epistolary or journalistic style; Peter Carey effects something similar in his self-conscious revisiting of the tropes and idioms of nineteenth-century fiction, and in particular Dickensian narrative, in *Jack Maggs*, explored in Chapter 7. There are also, in both these novels, moments when *bricolage* and pastiche are jointly in play, but, on the whole, when assigning a political or ethical commitment to acts of literary appropriation such as these postcolonial rewritings of canonical texts (*Robinson Crusoe* and *Great Expectations*, respectively) we acknowledge that stylistic imitation is neither the essence nor the sole purpose of the approach to the source text, even though it may be a defining feature.

James Joyce's 1922 novel *Ulysses* could be viewed as the archetype of the adaptive text. The title alone indicates a structuring relationship with Homer's Ancient Greek epic of the wandering and journeying Ulysses (also known as Odysseus). That relationship was even more apparent in the pre-publication instalments of Joyce's novel, where each chapter heading signified a specific relationship with an event or character in the Homeric narrative: 'Telemachus'; 'Lotus Eaters'; 'Scylla and Charybdis'; 'Sirens'; 'Circe'; 'Penelope'. Joyce's decision to suppress these referential chapter headings in the final published version of the novel raises the question as to whether we required expert knowledge of *The Odyssey* to understand in any comprehensive sense his Dublin narrative. What this question highlights, however, is the fundamental contradictory impulse towards dependence and liberation implicit in the majority of the adaptations and appropriations that will be invoked in the course of this volume. Gérard Genette has categorized *Ulysses* as 'the very type of the self-proclaimed hypertext' and yet as 'an extreme case of emancipation from the hypotext' (1997: 309), with 'hypertext' here equating to the adaptation and 'hypotext' to the source. Joyce's novel can undoubtedly be read alone and appreciated as a narrative in its own right, free of any Homeric associations. It is a remarkable vignette of a day in the life of an ensemble of Dublin inhabitants in 1904: this is by no means a failed or insufficient reading of *Ulysses*. And yet a reading of that narrative alongside an informing awareness of the events of Homer's epic (and Joyce's title surely invites us to perform that action of reading the two alongside each other, to read intertextually in this active way) clearly enriches the potential for the production of meaning. In doing this we see, as Jennifer Levine has noted, the quasi-father–son relationship that emerges between Stephen Daedalus and Leopold Bloom in the novel as suggestive in its own right and yet simultaneously register how it 'sharpens our senses of the potentially filial relationship between them to see them also as Telemachus and Odysseus' (1990: 32). Of course, the intertextuality of Joyce's characters doesn't rest solely with the Homeric comparisons, since Stephen and Leopold's relationship also suggests that of Hamlet and Old Hamlet from Shakespeare's play, and *Ulysses* resonates throughout with Shakespearean echoes and refrains (Putz 2013). If Leopold's wife Molly, who speaks the infamous orgasmic closing monologue of *Ulysses*, is a 1904 Dublin version of Odysseus's wife, Penelope, patiently awaiting her wandering husband's return from epic adventures, there is also a self-conscious rewriting of the informing source text in that Molly proves to be an adulterous version of the loyal Penelope. Joyce expands that particular frame of reference even further by evoking Shakespeare's wife, Ann Hathaway, as another Penelope, since she was left behind in Stratford-upon-Avon when the playwright moved to London to make his name: 'We begin to be interested in Mrs S' (Joyce 1986 [1922]: 165). Joyce here prefigures by some decades the interest of feminist biographers and critics such as Germaine Greer in the elusive Ann (Greer 2008).

There is often humour as well as intellectual richness at work in the parallels and consonances that Joyce evokes. This resolutely Irish epic compresses the decades and continents of the Homeric text into a single Dublin day, punctuated by pub gatherings and cooking on the stove. Cyclops becomes an obstructive drinker in Barney Kiernan's bar, Circe a brothel owner. There is undoubtedly an element of parody and pastiche in this, a version of 'mock-epic' comparable to Alexander Pope's eighteenth-century reduction of the vast scope of the Homeric epic to the micro-geography of a woman's dressing table in his poem 'The Rape of the Lock'. In this respect, *Ulysses* embodies the reduction and compression that Genette has identified as a common impulse in some hypertextual literature, and yet in its verbal complexity, and twisting web-like narrative, the novel also deserves recognition for its deployment of the art of amplification: of making the quotidian lives of its Dublin community epic in scope. An intertextual reading of *Ulysses*, then – one mindful of its adaptive processes – draws the reader's imaginations into the supplementary realms of Homer and Shakespeare, stretching far beyond its self-proclaimed urban environs and cultural geography. The signifying field appears vast as a result.

By introducing so early in this study a text as complex and voluminous in its references as *Ulysses* the aim is in part to move us away immediately from any rigid concepts of fidelity or infidelity in the adaptive process and towards more malleable and productive concepts of creativity. Recent work in translation studies, an important cognate field to adaptation studies, is helpful here in suggesting that even in the context of translation of one text into another language, where the process is in part expected to retain aspects of plot, narrative and form in ways that adaptation palpably need not, the concept of strict fidelity is unhelpful. Susan Basnett argues that all translation is a 'form of rewriting' and cultural negotiation even though the originating text must still be present and visible in the end product (Basnett 2014: 3). All adapters are translators, then, and all translators are creative writers of a sort.

When discussion of adaptation moves into the more globalized spheres of adaptation and interpretation – I am thinking, for example, of a significant industry in global Shakespeare over recent decades – translation theory must come into play, but it is, perhaps, to these more embracing and inclusive ideas of the creative translator that Basnett invokes, from Jorge Luis Borges, to Walter Benjamin, to Octavio Paz, that we should turn (see Basnett 2014: 13, 51, 117, 165).

Joyce's *Ulysses* is a potent reminder, then, of the rich possibilities of the adaptive technique and of readings alert to the politics of rewriting and appropriation. But it is also a fine example of the sense of play that many theorists have stressed as central to the adaptive instinct. Paul Ricoeur describes appropriation as 'the "playful" transposition of the text, and play itself … as the modality appropriate to the reader *potentialis*, that is to anyone who can read' (1991: 87). As this volume will stress, there is frequently heartfelt political commitment standing behind acts of literary appropriation or 're-vision'. Adrienne Rich's coining of this phrase, with its crucial inserted hyphen, was a product of her personal feminist and lesbian politics (Rich 1992 [1971]). But the political aspect of 're-visionary' writing should never occlude the simultaneously pleasurable aspects of reading into such texts their intertextual and allusive relationship with other texts, tracing and activating the networks of association that we have been describing. As Genette observes: 'one who really loves texts must wish from time to time to love (at least) two together' (1997 [1982]: 399). Such statements encourage us to categorize and define adaptation and appropriation and their cultural histories while at the same time taking care to ensure that these elements of pleasure are neither lost nor underestimated.

T. S. Eliot's 1919 essay 'Tradition and the Individual Talent' has been described as 'perhaps the single most formative work in twentieth-century Anglo-American criticism' (Widdowson 1999: 49). Eliot's essay is certainly essential reading for students of adaptation and appropriation. Eliot sought to rethink notions of originality and value, querying the 'tendency to insist, when we praise a poet, upon those aspects of his work in which he least resembles anyone else' (Eliot 1984 [1919]: 37). The unapologetic masculinist emphasis aside, Eliot's comments are pertinent to this project. Suggesting an alternative literary value-system in which the reworking and response to the texts of the past would take centre-stage, Eliot questioned why originality was valued over 'repetition': 'No poet, no artist, of any art, has his complete meaning alone' (38). He was not advocating blind adherence to precursor texts or ages, an action that would after all be little more than literary plagiarism: his notion of the 'individual talent' was that it created new material upon the surface and foundation of the literary past.

Peter Widdowson is correct to acknowledge that Eliot's case for an historical awareness of literary tradition served to justify his own intertextual, discursive style and the aims of the Modernist movement (1999: 49). Modernist poetry, not least Eliot's own, practised intertextuality in the form of quotation, allusion, collage, *bricolage* and fragment. As already stressed, in this study we are looking at something rather different, a more sustained engagement between texts and their creators. We are seeking to theorize an interrelation between texts which is fundamental to their existence and which at times seems to get to the heart of the literary, and especially the reading, experience. Eliot's delineation of the 'historical sense' (1984 (1919): 38) is helpful; he suggests that meaning stems from the relationships between texts, relationships which encourage contrast and comparison. As the close readings conducted here underscore, this is exactly what an aesthetic and historicized critical study of adaptation is concerned with.

Eliot's essay has sometimes been attacked on the grounds that it assumes a stable literary canon, a series of validated texts that are (re)turned to and consulted by subsequent ages (Eagleton 1994 [1981]: 54). The debate that has raged around canon formation in literary studies in recent decades is inescapable in this context. Adaptation appears both to require and to perpetuate the existence of a canon, although it may in turn contribute to its ongoing reformulation and expansion. As Derek Attridge has astutely observed, 'The perpetuation of any canon is dependent in part on the references made to its earlier members by its later members (or would-be members) ...' (1996: 169). The required 'reading alongside' of source and adaptation, the signifiers, respectively, of 'tradition' and 'individual talent' in Eliot's formulation, demands a knowledge on the part of the reader (or spectator) of the source when encountering the derivative or responsive text. In this respect, adaptation becomes a veritable marker of canonical status; citation infers authority.

To this end, adaptation could be defined as an inherently conservative genre. As Attridge continues: 'through their frequently overt *allusiveness* ... novels offer themselves not as challenges to the canon but as canonic ... as already canonized, one might say. They appear to locate themselves within an established literary culture, rather than presenting themselves as an assault on that culture' (1996: 169). Yet, as the notion of hostile takeover present in an embedded sense at least in a term such as 'appropriation' implies, adaptation can be oppositional, even subversive. There are as many opportunities for divergence as adherence, for assault as well as homage.

Another influential essay for studies of appropriation is Adrienne Rich's 'When We Dead Awaken: Writing as Re-vision', first published in 1971. In that essay she made the much-cited observation that for women writers it was essential to take on the writing of the past in order to move beyond it into a creative space of their own: 'Re-vision, the act of looking back, of seeing with fresh eyes, of entering an old text from a new critical direction ... We need to know the writing of the past and know it differently than we have ever known it; not to pass on a tradition but to break its hold over us' (Rich 1992 [1971]: 369). The suggestion is in some sense similar to Eliot's in that it invokes the literary past but insists on an historical understanding to foster creativity both in the present and in the future, but it is also entirely antithetical in that it simultaneously advocates a radical break with that same tradition, a dissonant and dissident rupturing of its value-systems and hierarchies. This critical perspective on the relationship between tradition and the individual talent is one shared by writers producing work from feminist, gay and lesbian, and postcolonial subject-positions. A further theorist of literature's relationship to its own past whose work is frequently both acknowledged and challenged by those subject-positions is Harold Bloom. His seminal work *The Anxiety of Influence*, first published in 1973, considered the fraught relationship between writers and their literary inheritance, constructing it in self-consciously Freudian terms as an Oedipal struggle between young 'sons' and their literary forefathers. Several flaws in this argument have subsequently been exposed, not least its exclusively masculinist position. Bloom constructs a very singular version of literary history, one with an emphasis on the individual creator or literary 'genius', and therefore one that unduly privileges the Romantic era, when a special stress on the individual creative mind emerged. Several critics have since traced alternative teleologies of literary influence, indicating, for example, the impact of the classics on early modern writers such as Shakespeare (Bate 1993), and acknowledging a strong female presence within the communities of influence (Gilbert and Gubar 2000 [1979]). Nevertheless, Bloom's central thesis of 'misprision', the often happenstance or inevitable reinterpretation of texts during the process of adoption, translation and reworking them into new contexts, remains a highly suggestive one for appropriation studies and one which has influenced the vocabulary with which many scholars operate in this field.

The central problem with any tradition is the ability to recognize not only those who constitute that tradition but those who are at various times excluded from it, or, at the very least, consigned to its margins. Henry Louis Gates Jr has examined this phenomenon in relation to African-American writing, a literary domain that in its desire to assert its own methodologies and ways of operating, nevertheless found a need to confront the white literary tradition within its pages; this is what Graham Allen has described as the 'struggle of black subjects to enter into Western literary culture' (2000: 168). Gates's most expansive discussion of these ideas takes place in *The Signifying Monkey* (1988), and invokes the crucial analogue of jazz music and the improvisational yet allusive techniques it deploys: 'In the jazz tradition, compositions by Count Basie ("signify") and Oscar Peterson ("signifyin'") are structured around the idea of formal revision and implication' (Gates 1988: 123). This discussion of adaptation and appropriation will invoke the example of jazz on several occasions, and of musicology on several more. But the specific relevance to African-American writing of 'signifying' and its relationship to jazz deserves notice.

As James Andreas Sr acknowledges, 'To signify in African and African-American cultures is to improvise upon a given *topos*, narrative, or joke the way a jazz musician improvises on a progression of chords, melodic structure, or spontaneous riff in the previous musician's solo' (1999: 107). Andreas's specific example of this in action is the work of Gloria Naylor. Her novels have been much studied due to their intertextuality with Shakespeare, Faulkner, Dante, Chaucer, and the Bible, among others (Erickson 1996). In *Baileys Café*, the signifying practice is played out through a complex series of layers, allusions and shaping influences. The café of the title is a literal space in the novel but one that appears able to cross geographical and temporal borders. The characters who visit the café each have a tale to tell and their tales are reworkings of biblical ones, including those of Eve and Mariam. The intertextuality does not stop there, for the name of the café, as well as the characters' tale-telling, involves a seminal work of English medieval literature: in Chaucer's *The Canterbury Tales*, the host of the Tabard Inn, where the pilgrims gather before their journey to Canterbury, and who proposes that they tell their individual stories en route, was called Harry Bailey.

Shakespeare, a familiar hypotext throughout Naylor's *oeuvre*, is present in the novel's evocation of *The Tempest*, among other texts (Sanders 2001: 170–90), but it is the manner in which the narrative structure is shaped by movements more familiar from the musical domains of blues and jazz that seems most overtly to acknowledge Gates's theories. Sections entitled 'Mood Indigo' and 'Miss Maple's Blues' explicitly acknowledge the literary riffs and improvisations being effected by Naylor on a diverse range of influences and sources. Naylor is a writer steeped in the words of others and yet her literary voice remains distinctly her own; Gates suggests this is typical of African-American writing, which consciously positions itself in relation to canonical (white) Western culture and the companion productions of fellow African-American writers. As Andreas Sr notes in his discussion of Naylor's *Tempest*-soaked novel *Mama Day*, her work embodies the familiar African-American practice of 'playful but wilful manipulation of the signified [that] alters perception of the signified' (1999: 107).

In all of the instances discussed in this Introduction, the 'rewrite', be it in the form of novel, play, poem, or film, invariably transcends mere imitation, serving instead in the capacity of incremental literature (Zabus 2002: 4), adding, supplementing, improvising, innovating, amplifying. The aim is not replication as such, but rather complication, expansion rather than contraction (Andreas 1999: 107). In scientific terms, we might speak about the crucial difference between a clone and a genetic adaptation. And if musicology offers us one highly applicable and suggestive set of metaphors and idioms for conducting discussion of literary adaptation and appropriation within these pages, it will also be registered that the scientific domain of genetics, stretching from the nineteenth-century horticultural experiments of Gregor Mendel and Charles Darwin's controversial theory of natural selection and environmental adaptation through to the research into DNA in the twentieth century, provides a further set of productive correspondences.

Deploying a separate field of terminology derived from the world of horticulture, Genette has written at length about the 'palimpsestuous nature of texts', observing that 'Any text is a hypertext, grafting itself onto a hypotext, an earlier text that it imitates or transforms' (1997 [1982]: ix). Grafting is just one of several creative metaphors for the adaptive process favoured by this volume. As Chapter 2 explores further, there is a need to establish a more diverse lexicon for discussing and describing the relationships between text and hypertext, source and appropriation, than those labels at present enable. In these phrases the relationship is often viewed as linear and reductive; the appropriation is always in the secondary, belated position and the discussion will therefore always be couched in terms of difference, lack or loss. Travel can change for the better, though, so the metaphor of the journey may still be helpful, even if it implies a linear movement from A to B.

By eschewing a linear epistemology altogether, however, phrases such as 'grafting' or models derived from musicology which allow for greater dynamic impetus in the new composition serve us well. To quote Genette: 'In music, the range of transformational possibilities is probably broader than in painting, broader than in literature certainly, given the complexity of musical discourse, which, unlike the literary text, is unhampered by the strict "linearity" of the verbal signifier' (1997 [1982]: 386). Chapter 2 investigates further the potential of phrases themselves appropriated from the discipline of music – terms such as variation and sampling – to revivify our understanding and appreciation of the kinetic processes of adaptation.

As my endless ruminating over terminology even at the outset suggests, this is a study sympathetic to theories of pluralism rather than fixity. To this ends the volume is divided into three parts. Part I, 'Defining terms', offers a series of definitions for, and ways of thinking about, adaptation and appropriation as both practice and process. The aim here is to open out and widen the range of applicable terms rather than ossifying one specific definition or concept. Part II, on 'Literary archetypes', examines the recurring interests of adaptation and appropriation in many of the central texts and genres of Western culture: myth, fairy tale, folklore and Shakespeare. The latter playwright, of course, reworks in his drama many of the structures and storylines of myth and fairy tale, indicating the cultural osmosis that regularly occurs between adaptation, writers, texts and forms. It will be witnessed on countless occasions in this study how frequently adaptations adapt other adaptations. There is, then, a filtration effect taking place, a cross-pollination; we are observing mediations and remediations taking place across time and across cultures.

The final part, Part III, stretches the parameters of considerations even further to consider 'Alternative perspectives'. As well as Daniel Defoe, Charlotte Brontë, and Virginia Woolf, this section considers the ongoing fascination with re-creating and critiquing the Victorian era via various performances of rewriting and pastiche (see Heilmann and Llewellyn 2010). From a detailed focus on appropriations of fictional writing from the period, the later chapters of this study focus on the appropriation of historical 'fact' and so-called real-life subjects as well as the adaptation of alternative art forms and paradigms from scientific research. What becomes clear as these parts progress is how frequently adaptations and appropriations are impacted as much by movements in and readings produced by the theoretical and intellectual arena as by their explicit source or inspiration text. Many of the texts and films studied here are produced as much by the tenets of feminism, post-structuralism, postcolonialism, queer theory and postmodernism as by the literary canon *per se*. As the critical anxieties and the Robert Weimann quotation at the beginning of this Introduction indicated (see p. 2), the reproductive capacity of both adaptation and the study of adaptation and appropriation should not be underestimated. Texts feed off each other and create other texts, as well as other critical studies; literature creates more literature, art creates more art. Part of the sheer pleasure of the reading or spectating experience where adaptation is concerned – and I make no apologies for introducing pleasure into the equation at the outset of this study – must be the tension between the familiar and the new, and the recognition of both similarity and differences, both between texts and between us as readers and receivers; this is what Linda Hutcheon has termed recently the 'doubled pleasure of the palimpsest' (Hutcheon 2013: 116). The pleasure exists, and persists, then, in the act of reading in, around, through and on (and on).

PART I

DEFINING TERMS

1

WHAT IS ADAPTATION?

'All matter is translated into other matter.'
Kate Atkinson, *Not the End of the World*

The processes of adaptation and appropriation that are the concern of this book are, as already indicated, strongly linked to work in cognate areas and practices such as intertextuality and translation studies. As mentioned in the Introduction, ideas of intertextuality are most readily associated with Julia Kristeva, who, invoking examples from literature, art and music, made her case, in essays such as 'The Bounded Text' (1980) and 'Word, Dialogue and Novel' (1986), that all texts invoke and rework other texts in a rich and ever-evolving cultural mosaic. The impulse towards inter-textuality, and the narrative and architectural *bricolage* that can result, is regarded by many as a central tenet of postmodernism (Allen 2000).

The interleaving of different texts and textual traditions, which is manifest in that intertextual impulse, has also been linked to the now-contested postcolonial theory of 'hybridity'. Homi Bhabha's account of hybridity suggests how things and ideas are 'repeated, relocated, and translated in the name of tradition' (1995: 207), but also how this process of relocation can stimulate new utterances and creativity. For Bhabha, however, only hybridity that respects essential difference enables innovation, whereas the cultural synthesis or homogenization of multiculturalism proves stifling (208). Science-led notions of hybridization regard cultural artefacts as irrevocably changed by the process of interaction. In the case of colonial cultures this is particularly problematic, since if the scientific notion of dominant and recessive factors (or genes) holds true for cultures, then the colonial or imperial tradition dominates over the indigenous in any hybridized form. This notion of the dominant and the recessive was an idea first posited by Gregor Mendel in the mid-nineteenth century (Tudge 2002), but in the literary field it has been adopted to articulate a debate about dominance and suppression that is crucial for any consideration of intertextual relationships. Studies of adaptation and appropriation intersect in this way not only with scientific idiom, which T. S. Eliot deployed in his essay 'Tradition and the Individual Talent' when he wrote of the chemical reaction that takes place between literary inheritance and the artist that creates a wholly new 'compound' (Eliot 1984: 41), but also with the critical and cultural movements of postmodernism and postcolonialism; indeed, as a result, the effort to write a history of adaptation necessarily transmutes at various points into a history of critical theory.

Adaptation studies throws up a rich lexicon of terms: version, variation, interpretation, continuation, transformation, imitation, pastiche, parody, forgery, travesty, transposition, revaluation, revision, rewriting, echo. But, as this list suggests, texts that come under this heading can possess starkly different, even opposing, aims and intentions; as a result adaptation studies necessarily favours a kind of 'open structuralism' along the lines proposed by Genette in *Palimpsests* (1997: ix). Readings in this context are invested not in proving a text's closure to alternatives but rather in exploring, even celebrating, ongoing interactions. Sequels, prequels, compression and amplification all have roles to play at different times in the adaptive mode.

Adaptation can be a transpositional practice, casting a specific genre into another generic mode, an act of re-vision in itself. It can parallel editorial practice in some respects, indulging in the exercise of trimming and pruning: yet it can also be an amplificatory procedure engaged in addition, expansion, accretion and interpolation (compare, for example, Deppman *et al.* 2004 on 'genetic criticism'). Adaptation is nevertheless frequently involved in offering commentary on a source text. This is achieved most often by offering a revised point of view from the 'original', adding hypothetical motivation or voicing what the text silences or marginalizes. Yet adaptation can also continue a simpler attempt to make texts 'relevant' or easily comprehensible to new audiences and readerships via the processes of proximation and updating. This might, for example, be aimed at engaging with youth audiences or, through translation in its broadest sense, linguistic and interpretative, in global, intercultural contexts. This can certainly be seen as an artistic drive in many adaptations of so-called 'classic' novels for television and cinema. Shakespeare has also been a particular focus, beneficiary even, of these proximations or updatings. Providing the scaffolding for these approaches is, of course, the role of literature in educational contexts and this introduces the social as well as economic rationales for adaptation, themes and topics to which we will return.

The relevance of particular terms to a specific text and the moment in time when these become active culturally can provide some very focussed clues as to a text's possible meanings and its cultural impact, intended or otherwise, and the purpose behind an act of adaptation. As Robert Weimann stresses, appropriation as an activity 'is not closed to the forces of social struggle and political power or to acts of historical consciousness' (1988: 433). The intention here is to examine in detail these specific impulses and ideologies, personal and historical, at play in various adaptations. It seems useful therefore to begin by unpacking in some detail what we might understand by such umbrella terms as adaptation and appropriation, and to consider the different modes and methodologies involved. This will in turn connect us with a variety of disciplinary engagements behind literary studies, not least film studies, performance studies and translation studies, but also with musicology, computer science and digital humanities, law and economics, not least in the realm of intellectual property and copyright, cultural geography and the natural sciences.

In his richly informative study of 'hypertextuality', Genette described the act of writing a text, in whatever genre, with other texts in mind as a 'transgeneric practice' (Genette 1997 [1982]: 395). As any reading of this book will make clear, a vast range of genres and sub-genres are regularly involved in the kinds of hypertextual activity Genette interrogates. Adaptation is, however, frequently a highly specific process involving the transition from one genre to another: novels into film; drama into musical; the dramatization of prose narrative and prose fiction; or the inverse movement of making drama into prose narrative. It can also involve the making of computer games or graphic novels or be dispersed into modes such as music or dance.

We have already established that when we discuss adaptation in these pages we are often (though admittedly not always) working with reinterpretations of established (canonical or perhaps just well-known) texts in new generic contexts or perhaps with relocations of an 'original' or source text's cultural and/or temporal setting, which may or may not invoke a generic shift. And it is impossible to avoid the question of value or taste in this context. Modules on higher education programmes which examine the transition of literature into other forms, not least film, are now fairly commonplace and any student engaged in studying and theorizing adaptation is involved in thinking critically about what it means to adapt and appropriate, and sometimes is even engaging in creative work of their own as part of the assessment process or the learning outcomes. Intellectual or scholarly examinations of this kind are quite deliberately not aimed at identifying 'good' or 'bad' adaptations. On what grounds, after all, should such a judgement be made? Nor are they engaged in identifying where an adaptation has been faithful or unfaithful to its source, at least in the context of any value judgement. As I hope this volume demonstrates, my argument would be that it is at the very point of infidelity or departure that the most creative acts of adaptation take place. The sheer impossibility of testing fidelity in any tangible way comes to mind when we recognize that many of the so-called 'original' texts we are handling in such circumstances, Shakespeare's plays most obviously, are highly labile, adaptive patchworks themselves. Adaptation studies needs to be understood as a field engaged with process, ideology and methodology rather than encouraging polarized value judgements.

Establishing some useful templates for studying cinematic interpretations of well-known novels, Deborah Cartmell argues for three broad categories of adaptation:

  i   transposition
  ii   commentary
  iii analogue.

(Cartmell and Whelehan 1999: 24)

On the surface, all screen versions of novels are transpositions in the sense that they take a text from one genre and deliver it into a new modality and potentially to different or additional audiences. But many adaptations, of novels and other generic forms, contain further layers of transposition, relocating their source texts not just generically but in cultural, geographic and temporal terms. Baz Luhrmann's 1996 *William Shakespeare's Romeo + Juliet* is a useful example: updating Shakespeare's early modern Veronese tragedy to a contemporary North American setting, Luhrmann retains the play-text's sense of urban gang feuding but accords it a troublingly immediate and topical resonance. Famously, the much-mentioned swords and rapiers of Shakespeare's play-script become in Luhrmann's vividly realized Verona Beach the engraved monikers for the modern era's weapon of choice, the handgun. Genette would describe this as 'movement of proximation' (1997: 304) and it is extremely common as an approach in screen adaptations of classic novels.

As mentioned, Shakespeare's *oeuvre* has proven to be a particularly rich seam to mine for such proximations: in 1999 Kenneth Branagh remade *Love's Labour's Lost* as a 1930s Hollywood film musical, embedding Shakespeare's competition of courtly wit and sonneteering within a *faux*-Oxbridge setting. The events of the film unfurl on the eve of the Second World War, providing audiences with a more recent (and therefore perhaps more accessible?) context for conflict than Shakespeare's late sixteenth-century interactions with the French Wars of Religion. Branagh added a deliberately nostalgic soundtrack of songs by George and Ira Gershwin and

Cole Porter to appeal to those audience members who would share the film's cultural associations. In a different move, Michael Almereyda's millennial *Hamlet* (2000) re-envisioned Elsinore as a Manhattan financial corporation with Claudius as a corrupt CEO. In an interesting twist, the disaffected young prince in this version was an anti-establishment art student, who created his 'play within a play' as a video montage to be submitted as a course assignment. There is an interestingly predictive aspect to this since the decade following the release of Almereyda's film witnessed the creation of YouTube, now home for many thousands of such assignments and short film versions of Shakespeare (Desmet 2014; O'Neill 2014).

The motive or compulsion behind this and many other updatings is fairly self-evident: the 'movement of proximation' brings the text closer to the audience's personal frame of reference, allowing always for variation between local contexts and audiences (cf. Burnett 2013: 11). Not all transpositional adaptations that make temporal shifts move forward towards the present day, however – Franco Zeffirelli's 1990 film *Hamlet* opted for a Gothic medieval setting – but it is certainly a common approach. In the example of Zeffirelli's *Hamlet* it could be argued that his casting was an embedded form of proximation since it brought to bear a self-conscious act of intertextuality with the world of contemporary film by casting Mel Gibson, best known for the *Mad Max* action movies (dir. George Miller, 1979, 1981, 1985), as a very particular kind of Hamlet, and playing on the associations of Glenn Close as Gertrude with the box office success of the film *Fatal Attraction* (dir. Adrian Lyne, 1987), with its particular emphasis upon female sexual desire.

Shakespeare is not the sole focus of transpositional adaptation, although, as we will see in Chapter 3, his works do provide a cultural barometer for the historically contingent process of adaptation. In 1998, director Alfonso Cuarón effected a similar shift of setting and context with Charles Dickens's *Bildungsroman Great Expectations*, relocating it to contemporary New York, with his Pip (Finn Bell) as a struggling artist. Comparable transpositions can be found being performed on the work of Henrik Ibsen, Jane Austen, Anton Chekhov and Joseph Conrad, among others. There is a case to be made that in some instances the

process of adaptation starts to move away from simple proximation towards something more culturally loaded. This constitutes
Cartmell's second category of commentary, or adaptations that
comment on the politics of the source text, or those of the new
mise-en-scène, or both, usually by means of alteration or addition.
Film versions of Shakespeare's *The Tempest*, for example, which
bring the Algerian witch Sycorax visibly onscreen, comment by
means of this action on her absence from the play. In Shakespeare's
text she is constructed solely by means of Prospero's negative
word-portraits. Derek Jarman's 1979 film *The Tempest* and Peter
Greenaway's *Prospero's Books* (1991) both featured an onscreen
Sycorax. One film version of Jane Austen's *Mansfield Park* (dir.
Patricia Rozema, 2000) made explicit that novel's minimally
articulated contextual setting in the history of British colonialism
and the practice of slavery on Antiguan plantations. Rozema
made visible facts that the novel represses. In both these instances,
the absence or gap in the original narrative being commented on
in the transpositional films was one that had previously been
highlighted by the work of postcolonial critics. Adaptation might
in this instance be seen as responding directly to the work of critical
theory.

In all these examples it can be argued that the full impact of
the film adaptation depends upon an audience's awareness of an
explicit relationship to a source text. In expectation of this the
most formal adaptations carry the same title as their source or
informing text. Shared titles mobilize complex understandings of
similarity and difference and might seem to invite comparative
analysis, and it is certainly true that the majority of reviews of a
film adaptation of Thomas Hardy's *Far from the Madding Crowd*
would likely make some direct reference back to the novel and
perhaps point out similarities and difference, but an enjoyment of
the film is not necessarily dependent upon knowing the novel at
all. Indeed, such is the accretive nature of adaptation that reviews
of a film adaptation in 2015 of that same novel (dir. Thomas
Vinterburg and starring Carey Mulligan as Bathsheba Everdene)
have more often seized the opportunity to draw comparison with
a 1967 film adaptation directed by John Schlesinger and starring
Julie Christie as Bathsheba which had become canonical in its

own right. So we learn from this example that the notion of the 'source' might actually shift over time or might fashion a multi-layered entity rather than a single original.

Knowledge of the adaptational work is not necessary for a satisfying experience of viewing such a film, then, but we might argue that such knowledge brought into play in the process of understanding could enrich the spectator's experience and may indeed enhance or complicate the pleasures involved. The 2007 adaptation of Ian McEwan's 2001 novel *Atonement*, itself a masterful pastiche of the work of Jane Austen, Elizabeth Bowen and twentieth-century wartime memoirs, made some brilliant generic shifts from the book's knowing and intricate explorations of textuality (and the unreliable nature of the same) to a series of knowing visual effects that drew as much upon the history of cinema (1940s films, war movies, documentary footage) as from direct textual prompts or cues in the book (Geraghty 2009: 107). This particular set of readings or understandings was not necessary to appreciate or even enjoy the film but it certainly made the knowing spectator approach the achievements of director Joe Wright and screenplay writer Christopher Hampton in a different way. Hampton is an established writer in his own right, and here we are introduced to another way in which adaptation can work in an accretive manner as we may start to see an interesting hybrid of both McEwan's novel and Hampton's style in the finished screenplay. It also confirms the collaborative work that film constitutes, with writer and director, alongside actors and technical team, bringing the complex whole to the screen. Similar multiplicity exists when we look at a film such as *The Hours* (dir. Stephen Daldry, 2002), adapted by playwright David Hare from Michael Cunningham's 1998 novel of the same name, which is itself a complex adaptation of Virginia Woolf's biography, her 1923 novel *Mrs Dalloway* and new creative input by Cunningham himself which brings into play contemporary queer politics and the AIDS epidemic (for a fuller discussion see Chapter 6).

Is there particular or distinct pleasure involved for those spectators who can mobilize these nuanced understandings of similarity and difference? There is a danger of over-complicating the sensations involved and there may be equal pleasure simply in seeing a story on the screen that you have previously enjoyed reading in book format. Philip Cox has suggested something akin to this in relation to the huge popularity of stage adaptations of Charles Dickens's novels in the nineteenth century. These productions consciously staged tableaux, images of famous moments from the novels: 'The use of the illustration-tableau would suggest the expectation of audience familiarity with the serial instalments of the novels themselves; the pleasure to be gained through such acts of mimicry could only be brought about by an instant recognition of the similarities' (Cox 2000: 43–4). It is, of course, in this way among others that adaptations prove complicit in activating and in some cases reactivating the profile and popularity of certain texts, participating in canon formation in some respects. Similar mobilization of familiarity worked itself out in David Edgar's remarkable stage adaptation of Dickens's *Nicholas Nickleby* which premiered in the 1980s at the Royal Shakespeare Company; the onstage references were as knowing in their allusion to those earlier stage adaptations and tableaux as to the canonical novel. In none of these instances is familiarity with the source necessary, but the experience is certainly altered by that stance of familiarity.

In Cartmell's third and final category of adaptation, analogue, the case is more similar than it might at first seem. While it may deepen our understanding of the new cultural product to be aware of shaping intertexts, it may not be entirely necessary in order to enjoy the work independently. Examples of stand-alone works that nevertheless gain layers of meaning when their status as analogue is revealed might include: Amy Heckerling's *Clueless* (1995), a Valley-Girl variation on Jane Austen's *Emma*; Francis Ford Coppola's Vietnam film *Apocalypse Now* (1979) and its recontextualization of Joseph Conrad's dark nineteenth-century exploration of the colonial enterprise in the Congo, *Heart of Darkness*; and Michael Winterbottom's *The Claim* (2001), in which Thomas Hardy's 1886 *The Mayor of Casterbridge* is re-envisioned as a subtle variation on the Hollywood genre of the western, relocating the action to gold-rush America in the 1860s. Another example which actually exhibits a two-stage process of adaptation is William Reilly's *Men of Respect* (1990), a late twentieth-century US film about the Mafia, which reworks both a 1955 film about the British gangland scene,

Joe Macbeth (dir. Ken Hughes), and that film's own Shakespearean dramatic precursor, *Macbeth*. The complex question provoked by these examples as to whether or not knowledge of a source text is required or is merely enriching will recur throughout the readings proffered in this volume.

Globalization, as both cultural phenomenon and practice, further complicates this question of familiarity when the adapted text is translated not only into a different genre but into a different language from the perceived original. Mark Thornton Burnett (2013), writing on Shakespearean adaptations in the contemporary global cinematic context, rightly emphasizes the need for criticism to move away from labels such as 'foreign' and to think instead in terms of local and global and, indeed, in terms of channels of access. In this domain the understanding of adaptation becomes as much about social and cultural politics as about literary analysis. Linda Hutcheon has proposed the use of the term 'indigenization' to explore 'how meaning and impact shift radically' in trans-cultural adaptation processes and to register the dialogue that takes place between societies as a result (2013: xviii, 148–9). As we consider adaptations of Shakespearean plays that speak to new cultural geographies such as the Venezuelan Andes or contemporary Singapore (*Sangrador*, dir. Leonardo Henríquez, 2000, a reimagining of *Macbeth; Chicken Rice War*, dir. Chee Kong Cheah, 2000, a reworking of *Romeo and Juliet*), we are invited to attend to issues surrounding the 'current inequities of space and place' (Burnett 2013: 13). While questions persist about what 'kind' of Shakespeare is being circulated or promulgated by these non-Anglophone interpretations, Burnett stresses that we need a more capacious form of criticism that accepts there is 'no fixed hierarchy between a play and its surrogate language or languages' (Burnett 2013: 3, 4).

It would, of course, be misleading to apply adaptation studies theory solely to cinematic versions of canonical plays and novels, although that is perhaps its most common and easily understood manifestation. Another genre that is engaged in self-conscious adaptation on a regular basis is the stage and film musical. Intriguingly Shakespeare once again appears as a facilitating presence: as well as *The Boys from Syracuse*, which made *The Comedy of*

Errors into musical theatre, there is Jerome Robbins's and Robert Wise's *West Side Story*, with music by Leonard Bernstein and lyrics by Stephen Sondheim, which reimagined *Romeo and Juliet* as a 1950s tale of gang violence in the streets and concrete playgrounds of New York. This in turn influenced Luhrmann's previously mentioned 1996 film adaptation of Shakespeare's romantic tragedy. And *Kiss Me Kate* famously riffs on *The Taming of the Shrew* by means of the songs of Cole Porter, perhaps an informing fact when Branagh turned to his songbook when translating *Love's Labour's Lost* into a film musical.

The musical genre finds much of its source material in the literary canon and now increasingly also the cinematic one: from Victor Hugo's epic novel *Les Misérables* to T. S. Eliot's *Old Possum's Book of Practical Cats* (which became the Andrew Lloyd Webber–Tim Rice blockbuster *Cats*); from *Billy Elliot* (initially a Stephen Daldry directed film in 2000, and now a long-running stage musical) to *Wicked* (a stage reimagining of Gregory Maguire's 1995 novel of the same name, which is itself a retelling, from the vantage point of the witches, of the 1939 movie of *The Wizard of Oz* and L. Frank Baum's 1900 novel). One musical which has achieved its own canonical status, both in its stage format and by means of George Cukor's 1964 film version, is *My Fair Lady*, Alan Lerner's version of George Bernard Shaw's play *Pygmalion*, which in its title glances even further back into the literary past for its influences, to the shape-shifting stories of Ovid's *Metamorphoses*, where Pygmalion creates a statue with which he falls in love. We will explore other Ovidian adaptations in Chapter 4, but what already begins to emerge in the more kinetic account of adaptation argued for in the Introduction is that these texts rework texts that often themselves rework other texts. The process of adaptation is constant and ongoing.

A kinetic or dynamic account of adaptation is enhanced and exacerbated by what Henry Jenkins has described as the convergence culture in which we now operate, which brings old and new media into a new relationality and deliberately eschews conventional notions of hierarchies in favour of a new more conjoined participatory cultural politics (Jenkins 2006: 282). In this more fluid and relational context we are asked to rethink the dynamics between so-called source and adaptation, and to read less in a linear than in a networked and connective mode. One of the best working examples of this comes from contemporary childhood, where, in Cathlena Martin's words, 'Adapted texts saturate children's culture – lining toy stores, pervading bookshelves, filling television time slots and permeating internet websites' (2009: 85). In her astute account, a young person playing the computer game version of E.B. White's *Charlotte's Web* (1952) may well not understand that experience in terms of a derivative or secondary adaptation but as simply one action or set of actions in a broader field of trans-media storytelling and experience. As André Bazin foretold as early as 2000, in the new convergence culture, texts or encounters may well be understood not in a linear or historicized hierarchy of original and adaptation but rather in terms of a single work refracted through different art forms, all of which are conceivably perceived as equal in the eyes of the user (Martin 2009: 88; Bazin 2000: 26). As Jim Collins has noted, shifts in cultural authority take place as a result, and we encounter new cues, codes and rituals of reception, many of which are no longer spatially defined by sites and institutions such as the library or even the university (2010: 79). Our ideas and concepts of adaptation are themselves necessarily adapting in the new technological era.

It is not entirely unconnected that some of the disciplinary domains in which the term 'adaptation' has been perhaps most resonant are from the natural sciences: biology, zoology, ecology and environmental science. Ever since Charles Darwin's presenta-tion of his controversial theories of evolution in the nineteenth century, the scientific community has been fascinated by the complex processes of environmental and genetic adaptation, from Darwin's famous finches on the Galápagos Islands, whose variation in bill and beak type was an indicator of the different foodstuffs they had adapted to eat in competition with one another; to the peppered moth in British industrial cities, a melanism or darker variation on the traditional species thought to have developed to blend in with the black surfaces caused by heavy industry in those areas. Adaptation proves in these examples to be a far from neutral, indeed a highly active, mode, far removed from the blander notion of substandard copying or repetition with which it is too often allied. Adaptation has, perhaps, suffered from an over-emphasis in post-Romantic Western culture on a highly singular notion of creativity and genius but is finding new purchase in the era of global circulations and the digital age of reproduction and re-makings. Adaptation and appropriation now provide their own intertexts such that they often perform in cultural dialogue with one another, so perhaps it will increasingly serve us better to think in terms of complex filtration, and in terms of networks, webs and signifying fields, rather than simplistic one-way lines of movement from source to adaptation. In the latter model, certainly, the importance of audience, reception and contextualized production of meaning is made properly visible.

In all of these categorizations and definitions of adaptation, it remains crucial to keep in sight the pleasure principle. In a very suggestive account of film's impact upon our experience of canonical literature, John Ellis argues that adaptation enables a prolonging or extension of pleasure connected to memory: 'Adaptation into another medium becomes a means of prolonging the pleasure of the original presentation, and repeating the production of a memory' (1982: 4–5). Ellis's thesis is equally resonant in its application to the recent vogue for television adaptations of classic texts, perhaps best exemplified by the genre of BBC period drama in the UK: examples would include adaptations of Jane Austen's *Pride and Prejudice*, Elizabeth Gaskell's *North and South* or Charles Dickens's *Bleak House* (cf. Cardwell 2002). The practice extends beyond the realms of the nineteenth-century novel and into the domain of contemporary fiction with adaptations of Jonathan Coe's *The Rotters' Club* (2001) or Alan Hollinghurst's *The Line of Beauty* (2004). The latter examples proved as loving a reconstruction of Britain in the 1970s and 1980s, respectively, as the previous more overtly historically informed adaptations.

By prolonging the pleasure of the initial encounter with a text, Ellis suggests that 'adaptation trades upon the memory of [that text], a memory that can derive from actual reading, or, as is more likely with a classic of literature, a generally circulated memory' (1982: 3). He continues, 'This adaptation consumes this memory, attempting to efface it with the presence of its own images' (3). It is at this point that I part company with his otherwise persuasive argument. For consumption need not always be the intended endpoint of adaptation: the adapting text does not necessarily seek to consume or efface the informing source or intertext. Indeed, as I will suggest, it is the very endurance and survival of the source text, alongside the various versions and interpretations that it stimulates or provokes, that enables the ongoing process of juxtaposed readings that are crucial to the cultural operations of adaptation, and the ongoing experiences of pleasure for the reader or spectator in tracing the intertextual relationships. It is this inherent sense of mutually informing play, produced in part by the activation of our informed sense of similarity and difference between the texts being invoked, and the connected interplay of expectation and surprise, that for me lies at the heart of the experience of adaptation and appropriation.

2

WHAT IS APPROPRIATION?

There are many ways in which both the practice and the effects of adaptation and appropriation intersect and are interrelated, yet it is equally important to maintain some clear distinctions between them as creative activities. An adaptation most often signals a relationship with an informing source text either through its title or through more embedded references; an Anglophone cinematic version of Shakespeare's *Hamlet*, although clearly reinterpreted by the collaborative efforts of director, scriptwriter, actors and the generic demands of the movement from staged drama to film, remains ostensibly *Hamlet*. Building on the subcategory of adaptation categorized by Deborah Cartmell as analogue, which we began to consider in Chapter 1 (Cartmell and Whelehan 1999: 24), appropriation frequently effects a more decisive journey away from the informing text into a wholly new cultural product and domain, often through the actions of interpolation and critique as much as through the movement from one genre to others. Indeed, appropriation may or may not involve a generic shift and it may certainly still require the kinds of 'readings alongside' or comparative approaches that juxtapose (at least) one text against another, which we have begun to delineate as central to the reception of adaptations. But certainly appropriations tend to have a more complicated, intricate and sometimes embedded relationship to their intertexts than a straightforward film version of a canonical or well-known text would suggest. The relationship can therefore seem more sideways or deflected, further along the spectrum of distance than a straightforward generic transposition. This chapter aims to unpack some of the diverse modes and operations of appropriation. In order to ease the discussion, the examples have been divided into two broad categories: embedded texts and sustained appropriations.

EMBEDDED TEXTS AND INTERPLAY

The stage and film musical has already been cited as an inherently adaptational form, often reworking canonical plays, novels and even poems into a mode that uses song and dance to deliver its narrative. *West Side Story* and *Kiss Me Kate*, two previously mentioned Shakespeare-informed musicals, are intriguing examples of this practice since they go one stage further by also operating as proximations: modern reworkings of the Shakespearean play-source. *West Side Story* would certainly not exist without *Romeo and Juliet*: Tony and Maria are clearly modern reimaginings of Shakespeare's 'star-crossed' lovers in a 1950s New York context. Their story of a love denied by feuding urban communities, and in particular the musical's two presiding gangs, the Jets and the Sharks, finds its origins in the Montague–Capulet rivalry, the 'ancient grudge' that drives the prejudice and violence of Shakespeare's stage Verona. The film's carefully realized *mise-en-scène* highlighted what was a topical issue of race conflict in New York at the time when the musical was first written and performed, and which manifested itself in violence against the immigrant Puerto Rican community.

There is much pleasure to be had in tracing the interrelationships and overlaps between the two texts, musical and early modern drama. The iconic fire escapes of the West Side provide a striking counterpart to the balcony scene of Shakespeare's play. Romeo's quasi-patriarch and confidante, the Friar, first seen in the play collecting herbs, is transformed into the gentle 'Doc', owner of the local drugstore where many of the Jets meet but also someone keen to act as a bridge between the rival communities. In a production working in a 'teenage' idiom – the late 1950s being the moment when teenage culture was formalized in both cultural and commercial terms at least in a US–UK context – 'Doc' is the sole parental figure we see on stage or on the screen (the musical was made into a film in 1961). Maria's parents are heard, but only as voices off; authority is effectively sidelined, removed from the centre. There are other supposed figures of authority who have a physical presence, in particular Officer Krupke and his colleagues from the NYPD, and the dance hall compere, but they are either laughably corrupt or inept in their handling of the tense situation. In Shakespeare's play Juliet has a counterpart confidante to Romeo's in the comic figure of the Nurse. In *West Side Story* the comic aspects of that relationship are downplayed in favour of the sisterly attentions of Anita, fiancée to Maria's gang-leader brother Bernardo. One unforgettable sequence depicts a choreographed sexual assault performed on Anita by Jets members when she tries, and fails, to deliver a message from Maria to Tony, with tragic results. This moment is another suggestive reworking of *Romeo and Juliet*, collapsing into one scene both Mercutio's bawdy misogynistic banter with the Nurse and the plotline of the mis-delivered letter, something Jacques Derrida and others have identified as the crucial turning point of the play.

This is still adaptation then but it is adaptation in another mode or key. *West Side Story* does stand alone as a successful musical without particular need of *Romeo and Juliet*, but I would maintain that audiences of the musical who possessed an intertextual awareness of Shakespeare in play had their experience deepened and enriched by a wider range of possible responses. Lyrics such as 'There's a place for us' undoubtedly return us to issues of spatial confinement in the tragedy, and the Jets' much reiterated gang tag 'Womb to Tomb' is a witty allusion to the tragic confinement of the play's young protagonists by the final scene of the play. This is a good example of the more sustained imaginative (and sometimes politically left-leaning) reworking of the source text which I am identifying here as intrinsic to appropriation: rather than the movements of proximation or cross-generic interpretation that we identified as central to adaptation, here we have a more wholesale redrafting, or indeed recrafting, of the intertext.

Kiss Me Kate has Shakespeare's misogynist comedy *The Taming of the Shrew* literally at its core: in a classic meta-theatrical move, the musical (filmed in 1953) is about a group of performers staging a musical version of *The Taming of the Shrew*. Audiences register two levels of adaptation and appropriation taking place here. The embedded musical of '*The Shrew*' is on the surface a more straightforward adaptation, reworking the characters and events of Shakespeare's play into a song and dance format with Katherina's societal resistance translated into songs such as 'I Hate Men' (though it must be said that rethinking Biancha's flirtatious playing off her suitors into the song 'Tom, Dick and Harry' represents a considerable leap of imagination). The format of a musical 'play within a play' is itself Shakespearean in resonance, recalling the meta-theatrical framework of *The Taming of the Shrew* itself but also *Hamlet, Love's Labour's Lost* and *A Midsummer Night's Dream*, among others. *Shrew* opens with the 'Induction', which establishes that the whole play of Katherina and Petruchio's embattled relationship is a performance by a troupe of travelling actors who have tricked the inebriated Christopher Sly into thinking he is a lord watching household theatricals on his aristocratic estate. *Kiss Me Kate* frames its *Shrew* musical with a plotline of embattled theatre stars, once married but now divorced. There are obvious, hilarious ways in which their offstage temperaments mirror their onstage performances; Lilli Vanessi, for example, is outspoken and hot-headed in a manner appropriate to her character Katherine. While the musical's untroubled manifestations of early twentieth-century US sexual politics, including the beatings and confinements visited upon the forceful Lilli, may no longer be acceptable as comic fodder in an era alert to domestic violence, the point remains that *Kiss Me Kate* is both an adaptation and an appropriation at the same time. If the pure adaptation rests in the embedded musical, then the appropriative aspect is found in the wider framework story of the US theatre performers and in the related subplot of the Mafia henchmen seeking debt repayments from the production's Hortensio, Bill Calhoun. The gangsters deliver one of the show's most famous songs, whose title has itself almost reached the status of comic by-line for the act of Shakespearean adaptation: 'Brush Up Your Shakespeare'. When Angela Carter chose this as one of the three epigraphs to her late novel on theatre, Shakespeare and the musical, *Wise Children* (1992), she was surely anticipating a readership with a vivid cultural memory of *Kiss Me Kate*.

Kiss Me Kate can obviously be viewed and understood in the context of Shakespearean appropriation more generally, which, as we will see in Chapter 3, is a veritable cultural field in its own right, but it also relates to a tradition that can best be described as 'backstage dramas'. These are texts interested in going behind the scenes of performances of particular plays or shows. This can be achieved in self-reflexive ways on the stage, as in *Kiss Me Kate* or Michael Frayn's play about English repertory theatre, *Noises Off* (1982). *Shakespeare in Love* (dir. John Madden, 1998) also exploits this motif, exploring an offstage relationship between Will Shakespeare and his star performer Thomas Kent (a disguised Viola de Lesseps) via suggestive cinematic cross-cutting between their 'real' life and their onstage performance in an embryonic *Romeo and Juliet*.

Backstage drama of this kind has also been developed in a prose fiction context. Australian author Thomas Keneally's 1987 novel *The Playmaker* recounts the rehearsals and performance of a production of George Farquhar's 1706 play *The Recruiting Officer*. The play is performed by a group of convict actors who have been assembled for the purpose by Lieutenant Ralph Clark, a British military officer who is overseeing the penal colony established in Sydney, Australia, in the late eighteenth century. In a funny and touching account of the rehearsal period, Keneally draws on resonant echoes between the events of Farquhar's play, which depicts the sexual shenanigans of a group of recruiting officers in the provincial shire town of Shrewsbury, and daily life in the penal colony, where site-specific hierarchies prevail and where many of the women convicts are the sexual property of the military officers and overseers.

Lieutenant Clark falls in love with his lead actor, Mary Brenham, a convicted clothes thief who performs the part of the cross-dressing Silvia in *The Recruiting Officer*, but we are always aware of the geographical and temporal parameters of this love story. Keneally structures his narrative in the form of five chapters and an epilogue, self-consciously recalling dramatic structure, and in the epilogue we learn of Ralph's return to his English fiancée. Mary Brenham, along with the majority of convicts whose lives we have followed, slips from the historical record. Keneally's purpose in writing this novel stretches in resonance far beyond the 1789 setting of the events it purports to recall; shadowing the world of the penal community represented in the novel stand the lives of the displaced aboriginal and First Nation communities of Australia. For all the play-within-the-novel's claims to be the 'first' theatre production in this 'new' land, the reader is made all too aware that the Sydney penal colony is far from being the 'original' existence in this space and place. Behind the deployment of the surface appropriation of Farquhar's play to explore the world of the penal colony (Keneally worked extensively with historical archives), the author is concerned to make visible another more hostile act of cultural appropriation, the seizure of the land rights and cultural claims of the indigenous societies. The novel is tellingly dedicated to 'Arabanoo and his brethren, still dispossessed', and Keneally has continued to be a prominent campaigner against Australia's restrictive immigration laws for related reasons. Appropriation, then, as with adaptation, shades in important ways into the discursive domains of other disciplines, here the legal discourse of land property and human rights.

Intriguingly, Keneally's novel underwent a further process of adaptation when playwright Timberlake Wertenbaker re-created *The Playmaker* as a stage drama, *Our Country's Good*, in 1988. Following the practice of adaptation outlined in the previous chapters, Wertenbaker altered, condensed and redirected the focus of Keneally's novel for the purposes of her play. She chose to commence the play with a scene on board the convict ship that transports the prisoners to Australia, whereas in the novel this experience is only ever recalled in flashback and by means of collective memory. Adding in the specific character, and in some sense narrative mouthpiece, of the Governor-in-Chief of New South Wales, Arthur Philip, Wertenbaker embeds in her play several extended justifications for the rehabilitative and socially constructive power of theatre and the arts. She had her own political motives for this in the late 1980s. The debates conducted in the play about the sociocultural importance of the arts had a highly topical resonance in an era of UK Arts Council funding cuts. In an interesting twist, *Our Country's Good* has in turn proved an extremely popular play for staging and performance by prison drama groups, continuing the active case for drama as socially therapeutic. Reading the accounts of prison actors of the inspirational effect of the experience of staging *Our Country's Good*, there exists a sense in which the events described in Keneally's novel have come full circle (Wertenbaker 1991 [1988]: vi–xvi).

Wertenbaker's play was first staged by the Royal Court Theatre in London, playing in repertory alongside *The Recruiting Officer*, which invited audiences to experience the texts in a comparative way. To further emphasize their connections, both productions shared the same company of actors so that for audiences attending both performances there was an interesting read-across from one to the other. On one night spectators might see a particular actor playing Justice Balance in *The Recruiting Officer* and then the next day that same actor playing Keith Freeman in *Our Country's Good*, the public hangman who assumes the role of Balance in the Australian convict production. Another double-handed play frequently staged by theatre companies for similar reasons and with similar read-across effects is Alan Ayckbourn's *A Chorus of Disapproval* (1984). This play is also about a company rehearsing a production, this time a provincial amateur British theatre group staging a production of John Gay's eighteenth-century operatic musical *The Beggar's Opera*. Gay's text has been subject to numerous adaptations and acts of cultural filtration, famously providing the template for Bertolt Brecht and Kurt Weil's *Three-penny Opera*. Ayckbourn ensures that his audiences are alert to the particular connection between his play and Gay's by commencing *A Chorus of Disapproval* at the end, as it were, as the curtain falls on the successful performance and the actors take their bows. As a consequence of this, when the play lurches back in time to the start of the audition and rehearsal process the audience already knows that it is tracing Guy Jones's ascent from theatre hopeful to leading man. Of course, the humour also resides in the fact that Guy becomes far too easily identified with his part as Gay's womanizing criminal protagonist Macheath, upsetting various female members of the company in the process. Much of the comedy of *A Chorus* derives from the audience's active engagement with the embedded text and resonance of *The Beggar's Opera*, playing as it does on similarity and difference in ways that we have already seen are central to the adaptive process. Ayckbourn highlights the continuity of actor and part but also the discontinuities between Guy's privileged provincial existence and the eighteenth-century underworld of Gay's comic opera. When *Beggar's Opera* plays in repertory with Ayckbourn's play these connections and contrasts are drawn out for audiences in a highly explicit fashion.

The methodology of immersive theatre company Punchdrunk, whose work has found particular purchase with audiences in the UK and the US during the past decade, again appears to rely on the prior knowledges that audiences bring to the experience of their experimental stagings of canonical plays and operas. In their 2010 collaboration with ENO (English National Opera), they staged John Webster's *The Duchess of Malfi* (1612–13) in such a way that audiences could choose the sequence in which to experience the scenes staged in different rooms; in this way the idea of personalized experience was heightened but the randomness of the experience suggested that those with a prior understanding of the play and its linear or incremental sequence of events would experience the enforced fragmentation in very particular ways, reconnecting in their own heads the relationships between discrete events. In another remarkable collaboration in 2013, the company staged *The Borough*, which was an audio-directed personal navigation of the Suffolk town of Aldeburgh in which the listener-walker confronted elements of George Crabbe's Aldeburgh-based collection of poems, first published in 1810, and *Peter Grimes*, the Benjamin Britten opera created out of Crabbe's poem (specifically from Letter XXII) in the early twentieth century. Since on the midsummer weekend when I experienced *The Borough* there had also been a site-specific beach performance of the opera, the same beach on whose crunchy pebbles the audio experience hauntingly began, provided a clear indication of the overlap and cross-referentiality of the immersive experience. That the experience itself invited the hearer-walker to consider the feeling of rejection that Grimes undergoes, and how a community can act as threat as well as a space of welcome, placed the participant at the centre of the adaptive process, at one point quite literally hiding in a wardrobe in the bedroom of a terraced house near the seafront. Immersion, but also the role of the personalized response to adaptations, is brought strikingly into view by this particular participatory experience.

Encouraged interplay between appropriations and their sources begins to figure here as a fundamental aspect of the reading or spectating experience, one productive of new meanings and applications. But, as already stressed, appropriations do not always make their founding relationships and interrelationships explicit. The gesture towards the source text can be wholly more shadowy than in the above examples, and this brings into play, sometimes in controversial ways, questions of intellectual property, proper acknowledgement and, at its worst, the charge of plagiarism.

SUSTAINED APPROPRIATION: HOMAGE, PLAGIARISM AND TRAVELLING TALES

When Graham Swift won the Booker Prize in 1996 for his novel *Last Orders*, a controversy over the award soon emerged. As Pamela Cooper has recorded, connections were identified between Swift's novel and William Faulkner's 1939 American classic *As I Lay Dying*:

> In a letter to the book review supplement of the newspaper *The Australian* John Flow of the University of Queensland underlined some very close similarities in structure and subject-matter, including a monologue given to the dead person, a monologue consisting of numbered points, and a monologue made up of a single sentence.
>
> (Cooper 2002: 17)

Flow's accusation was that the provable line of influence from Faulkner rendered Swift's book secondary, a substandard derivation of *As I Lay Dying* and therefore unworthy of a prize, in conferring which the judges had praised its originality. Charges and counter-charges flew in the British press, with several of the Booker judges, including Jonathan Coe, admitting that they had never read the Faulkner novel (Cooper 2002: 60) and with Julian Barnes defending Swift on the grounds that the novelist himself called *Last Orders* an 'homage' to Faulkner. In the final analysis the argument appeared to pivot on whether Swift had sought to suppress or obscure the relationship between the two novels. Had he declared *Last Orders* as an adaptation, though, would the Booker judges have made the same decision? Was the assumption of originality the driving factor? We can never know for sure, but the situation highlights the assumption by some at least (Flow for sure) that adaptations are second rate, not worthy of major literary prizes. It is for this reason that adaptation studies theorists often feel the need to go on the defensive, and assert the right of an adaptation to be considered a new work, a work of creativity in its own right: 'an adaptation is derivation that is not derivative – a work that is second without being secondary' (Hutcheon 2006: 9). A close reading of Swift's richly textured and hyper-British narrative convinces me that the adaptive relationship only heightens its literary achievements and enhances its capacity to produce profound responses in the self-aware reader.

It should be stressed that earlier work by Swift had been compared to Faulkner's, not least *Waterland* (1983), in both style and the way that it approached land as character. As Flow's critique of *Last Orders* identified, there are several notable structural overlaps between Faulkner's tale of a Mississippi family group transporting the corpse of their dead wife/mother to the town of Jefferson for burial and Swift's story of four male companions transporting the ashes of their late friend, the butcher Jack Dodds, to scatter them off the end of Margate Pier. Faulkner's novel is shaped by means of a series of juxtaposed monologues, both from family members, including the highly poetic but increasingly mentally troubled and estranged Darl, who in some sense provides the novel's central narrative consciousness, and onlookers to the grotesque comedy of the strongly smelling coffin being carried through floods and townships to its final resting place. Swift's novel shares the same sense of grim comedy and the same structural monologues. At one point we have a single-sentence monologue from a character in the Faulkner novel – the child Vardaman – and Swift has Vince's exclamation 'Old buggers' voiced at the Chatham naval memorial, one of several poignant staging points on the grieving friends' Margate pilgrimage in *Last Orders* (Swift 1996: 130). Faulkner's corpse Addie Bundren speaks a single monologue, delivered, as it were, from beyond the grave, and Swift's Jack does the same (1996: 285). In both novels, readers are party to monologues delivered by women left behind: Cora Tull in *As I Lay Dying* and Amy, Jack's widow, in *Last Orders*. In one remarkable sequence in the Faulkner narrative, Cash, the eldest Bundren son, recounts the obsessive care with which he fashioned the coffin in which his mother's rotting corpse is now being transported; the nailing together of the coffin was the action that began the novel. In Swift's novel this narrative touch has been transformed into Ray Johnson's 'rules' for betting on horses. In both novels, though, these seemingly practical and prosaic lists, both strongly tied to their place of origin, have metaphorical application.

In a manner akin to Faulkner's Darl and Cash, whose distinct voices and world-views provide the centre to the juxtaposed monologues of *As I Lay Dying*, Ray's monologues place him as the central consciousness of *Last Orders*. Between the lines of what Ray tells us we learn of his love for Jack's wife Amy and his estrangement from his own wife and daughter, as well as the past history of this complicated set of friends and associates (many of their relationships dating back to wartime experiences). Swift's historical and geographical context and even the idioms within which he writes are acutely his own; what the reader's awareness of Faulkner's novel does, however, is to deepen the understanding of the themes of mortality and friendship and of the significance of the environments which we ourselves inhabit to the story Swift is telling. What is both interesting and troubling in the case of *Last Orders* and its homage to Faulkner (declared or not), however, is that what in the case of Shakespeare studies might be termed an examination of creative borrowings, citing allusions in his *oeuvre* to Ovid, Plutarch, Thomas Lodge, the Roman comedies and so on, becomes in the case of a modern novel a reductive discussion of plagiarism and 'inauthenticity'. Robert Weimann states that 'In precapitalist societies the distance between the poet's act of appropriating a given text or theme and his or her own intellectual product and property is much smaller: the extent to which his *matière* is given, the extent to which "source", genre, plot, patterns, topoi, and so on are pre-ordained is much greater' (1988: 434). Modern legal notions of copyright have complicated the freedom with which writers seek to engage explicitly with the work of others, but it is worth adding that in his volume on *Literature* in this series Peter Widdowson asserted that 'revisionary' writing is a fundamental sub-set of what we might categorize as the literary (Widdowson 1999).

The consonances between the two works under the spotlight, Faulkner's and Swift's, are inescapable, but what is of particular interest in this context is the specific charge of indebtedness. Flow seemed to devalue Swift's novel because it was 'unoriginal', but how sustainable is that position in an era of postmodernist borrowing and *bricolage*? What also concerned critics and readers responding to Flow's initial observations was the lack of explicit acknowledgement of these borrowings by Swift. Could *Last Orders* have regained cultural status if there had been a prefatory note declaring the homage publicly? James Joyce's *Ulysses* may have signalled its Homeric debts in its title but its Shakespearean allusions are almost as plentiful, yet they tend to be mentioned in non-accusative ways. Does that render Joyce's novel somehow inauthentic? Surely not. The *Last Orders* controversy raises important questions as to whether a novelist needs to 'adequately' acknowledge intertextuality and allusiveness. If we adhere to Genette's theories of palimpsestuous writing as discussed in Chapter 1, then surely part of the pleasure of response for readers in these instances consists in tracing these relationships for themselves and according to their own reading experience. Without wishing to reduce the act of reading to a game of 'spot the appropriation' it is important to recognize that explicit soundings of intertextual relationships may close down, as much as open up, the possibility for interpretation.

Swift's novel is in many respects all about the search for family and a sense of home, and, like so many novels of travel, its ultimate focus is really on the starting point or origin as much as the stated destination. The generous or intertextually alert reader might

then have seen early on in Swift's approach an acknowledgement
of the importance of predecessors. In the novel Swift alludes to
several literary archetypes. The device of the journey is an ancient
one in Western and other literatures, as is the topic of death. Swift
himself has registered: 'The story about the pressure of the dead
on the living, in the wake of death, is as old as Homer' (cited in
Cooper 2002: 17). The novelist has always been a deeply allusive
writer. *Waterland* opens with a highly suggestive epigraph from
Dickens's *Great Expectations*: 'Ours was the marsh country ...';
Ever After (1992) carries resonances of *Hamlet*, as discussed in
Chapter 3, and, as discussed in Chapter 4, *The Light of Day*
(2003) rewrites the genre of detective fiction (filtered through a
specific Graham Greene intertext, *The End of the Affair*) alongside the classical myth of Orpheus. Pamela Cooper has identified
further links between *Last Orders* and the poetry of T. S. Eliot, in
particular his 1922 poem 'The Waste Land', with its London
public house refrain of 'Hurry up please it's time', which seems to
replay itself in the opening location of the novel and its punning
title; and the third part of which was written – by Eliot's own
assertion in personal correspondence – in the Nayland Rock
shelter on the Margate promenade (now a listed building due to
its literary associations; see Thorpe 2009). Eliot's bleak rumination
on post-war society gives an added resonance to the ruminations
of Swift's wartime friends. As they stand on the pier at the close
of the novel, overlooking the same Margate Sands alluded to by
'The Waste Land', a tone of nihilism is introduced into a novel
that in other ways is threaded through with the hopefulness of
connection:

> On Margate Sands
> I can connect
> Nothing with nothing.
> (Eliot 1969)

Eliot's poem has several rich intertexts of its own, but one
which strikes a reader early on is that of Geoffrey Chaucer's
seminal medieval work *The Canterbury Tales*, whose positive
hopeful opening in springtime – 'Whan that Aprill with his

shoures soote / The droghte of March hath perced to the roote'
(Chaucer 1986: 'General Prologue', ll. 1–16) – Eliot inverts to
'April is the cruellest month'. This might alert us in turn to a
parallel set of allusions to Chaucer's story of pilgrimage in Swift's
novel as the grieving friends make their way to the south of
England to scatter their friend's ashes. The narrative appears
almost to enjoy this intertextual game: 'Look out for signs to
Canterbury' (Swift 1996: 181). There is even a significant detour
to Canterbury Cathedral.

By appropriating Chaucer's *Canterbury Tales* fused with Eliot's
modernist rewriting, Swift adopts and adapts the ancient literary
strategy of paralleling an actual journey with an inner or spiritual
one. All of this is glancingly alluded to in the opening pages of
Last Orders: Ray is sitting in a Bermondsey public house – the
jokingly named 'Coach and Horses' since, as the characters keep
reflecting 'it ain't never gone nowhere' (6). This, of course, parallels
Chaucer's Southwark inn, the Tabard, where his twenty-nine
pilgrims first encounter one another and decide to travel together,
passing the time by telling stories at the suggestion of Harry
Bailey, the tavern host. At the start of *Last Orders*, Ray is awaiting
his companions for the Margate Pier trip. As in Faulkner's *As I
Lay Dying*, there is a grimly comic element to this gathering and
the journey, a fact emphasized by the container for Jack's ashes,
which, instead of being a holy grail, more prosaically resembles
an instant coffee jar. Yet, at its heart, the 'pilgrimage' to Margate
proves to be a deeply epiphanic experience for the four men involved.
If *Last Orders* is structured through monologues in a manner akin
to *As I Lay Dying*, this 'polyphonic' structure also echoes at a
deeper level Chaucer's poem with its embedded stories (Phillips
2000: 2). In a manner that is aesthetic as much as linguistic, Swift
transports Faulkner's style into a very mixed English idiom.

Chaucer's pilgrims travelled on horseback; Faulkner's grotesque
funeral procession moved forward by a stumbling combination of
horse and wagon; Swift's protagonists travel in a royal blue Mercedes
or 'Merc', provided by Vince, who is a used-car salesman. The
car thus becomes in *Last Orders* emblematic of the new mobility,
social and actual, of South Londoners; a mobility that pulls figures
like Vince away from the family business in butchery and which

renders trips to Kent simple and (almost) insignificant in a way unimaginable to Chaucer's pilgrims and perhaps even to the much remembered seasonal hop-pickers of these particular Londoners' past. The four men begin their journey in April when there are 'daffs out on the verges' (Swift 1996: 30), and with a sense of promise akin to Chaucer's pilgrims. But *Last Orders* is, as its title indicates, also deeply elegiac in tone. The novel is a journey through post-imperial England; the narrative refrain reflects on how things have changed for the British male in particular, for this journey is undoubtedly a masculine quest. The wife figure in this novel, Amy, is, however, no travelling Wife of Bath; she chooses to stay behind, resisting the grim irony of going to Margate with Jack's ashes when it was the journey she had planned to make with him in life in their retirement. Amy's travel in the novel is far more restricted: the circular No. 44 bus journey she makes to see her and Jack's mentally impaired daughter June in the hospital. The England depicted in *Last Orders* is both oddly resilient and on its last legs, mutable and yet with a rich sense of historical legacy.

Similarly to *As I Lay Dying*, but also like the organized pilgrimages of the Middle Ages, the route, actual and psychological, of *Last Orders* is mapped out by means of various specifically named places, way-stations and sites which carry meanings for both the past and the present: 'The four men, compelled by a common errand, travel together across a small part of England, making discoveries about themselves, each other, their world, time, and history' (Cooper 2002: 23). Part of considering the role of historical process for Swift involves a strong engagement with a specific English past. A further crucial intertext in that work is a cinematic one: Michael Powell and Emeric Pressburger's wartime rumination (from an immigrant perspective) on English identity, *A Canterbury Tale* (1944), in which four people make a journey to Canterbury that is itself strongly suggestive of pilgrimage. My point in tracing these complex allusive networks in Swift's novel is to suggest that the Faulkner appropriation is just one of a series of homages and responses and that the act of appropriation involves an anglicizing of the themes and approach in quite self-conscious ways to explore the topic of national identity and inheritance. Flow was clearly right in identifying the Faulknerian legacy in *Last Orders* but a debate about originality misses the point when encountering such a deeply intertextual novel.

Critics have identified yet further allusions in *Last Orders* to the Old English poems *Wanderer* and *Seafarer* (Cooper 2002: 32), not least in the narrative's engagement with different landscapes, environments and habitats: land, sea, *terra firma*. Most obviously, Margate pier in the novel offers us a version of 'land's end' and we have desert and sea settings at play in the wartime remembrances of our four travellers. Dee Dyas (2001: 23) has indicated how *Wanderer* and *Seafarer* deploy biblical parallels and Cooper has rightly traced elements of the Edenic storyline in Swift's novel, not least in the Cain and Abel struggle between Lenny and Vince. The novel's extended funeral procession both is and is not a secular version of the medieval pilgrimage, just as Chaucer's pilgrims are a mix of the mercantilist, the romantic, the self-serving and the pious. The movement is both familiar and new each time it is made.

VARIATIONS ON A THEME

If a working knowledge of Swift's Faulknerian intertext is crucial, revealing, and often moving, in highlighting for us distinctly South London analogues to the Mississippi of the 1930s that informed *As I Lay Dying*, we must also acknowledge that we are dealing in *Last Orders* with, in Pamela Cooper's words, a 'symphony of intertexts' and that it is how these play off against each other that provides the truly meaningful reading experience (2002: 37). The musical metaphors of symphony and polyphony that seem to attach themselves to Swift's novel are instructive since it is one of the major contentions of this volume that when searching for ways to articulate the processes of adaptation and appropriation we need a more active vocabulary, and one derived from the performing arts as much as from the biological sciences is illuminating. A kinetic vocabulary is one that is dynamic, enabling adaptation studies to constantly move forward as much as it is backward looking, and one that embraces ideas of composition and creativity. Music allows us access to less linear understandings than the motif of the journey so obviously deployed by Swift in *Last Orders*, and was interestingly one of the forms to which T. S. Eliot was most drawn when trying to create a new poetry rooted in fragmentation. It is, then, in musicology that some of the more enabling metaphors for the adaptation process might be located.

Much European baroque music in the sixteenth and seventeenth centuries derived its performative impetus from improvising upon dance music and patternings, working with such forms as the *bergamasca*, the *folia* and the *passamezzo*. Improvisation, or variation upon a firm foundation, is therefore fundamental to the composition and structure of baroque tunes. Musical creations by Diego Ortiz, Marco Uccellini and Henry Purcell, in Spain, Italy and England, respectively, were commonly structured in terms of 'grounds', repeated harmonic base instrumental patterns, often played by lute, harpsichord or cello, or a combination of both, on the surface of which the more improvisational lines of instrumentation are performed by flute, recorder, bass, viol or violin. We have in this a rather alluring model for the way in which an intertext in a novel such as *Last Orders* might function as the base or 'ground', informing the top note that constitutes the creative turn. The way in which Faulkner's chapter structure for *As I Lay Dying* became the formulaic scaffold for Swift's rumination on Englishness is newly appreciated from this vantage point and Eliot's notion of 'Tradition and the Individual Talent' finds new aesthetic purchase in this context.

Perhaps one of the most well-recognized musical contexts in which this ongoing yet circular process of innovation upon a base ground takes place is Johann Sebastian Bach's *Aria mit verschiedenen Veränderungen* ('Aria with Different Variations'), better known as *The Goldberg Variations*. There are thirty variations framed by an opening and closing performance of the base aria. As novelist Richard Powers so eloquently describes in *The Gold Bug Variations* (discussed further in Chapter 9):

> The set is built around a scheme of infinitely supple, proliferating relations. Each of the thirty is a complete ontogeny, unfolding until it denies that it differs at its conception from all siblings by only the smallest mutation ... an imperceptibly vast *chaconne*, an evolutionary *passacaglia* built on the repetition and recycling of this Base.
>
> (Powers 1991: 578)

Powers's own metaphorical point of reference here is the genetic patterning revealed by research into DNA in the 1940s and 1950s, and the identification of the intertwined double helix by Francis Crick and James Watson; but what his prose gives us is an invaluable set of terms for reconceptualizing the process of adaptation, moving away from a purely static or linear approach. Unfoldings, mutations, repetitions, evolutions, variations: the possibilities are endless and exciting.

A modern musical counterpart to baroque music's deployment of grounds can be found in the improvisational qualities of jazz. Jazz riffs, themselves a model of repetition with variation, frequently make reference or pay homage to base canonical works (see also McClary 2001). A potent example of this in action is Duke Ellington's suite *Such Sweet Thunder*, based on several Shakespearean plays and sonnets (1999 [1957]). Ellington's virtuoso interpretation of the Shakespearean base texts perfectly exemplifies Henry Louis Gates Jr's theory of 'signifying' in African-American culture, as cited in the Introduction, which Gates actually adopted from the practice and example of prominent jazz musicians: 'In the jazz tradition, compositions by Count Basie ("signify") and Oscar Peterson ("signifying") are structured around the ideas of formal revision and implication' (1988: 123).

Even more recently we have the working example of sampling in musical genres such as rap and hip-hop, and now more generally in digital composition and electronic music contexts. Desmond Hesmondhalgh has provocatively described this as plagiarism, but more so as a cultural tactic or interventionist act, indicating ways in which debates about plagiarism and intellectual and literary property rights need to be demobilized in more positive, socially productive and empowering ways. Exploring what he describes as the 'tangled' sounds of rap, Hesmondhalgh queries the extent to which rap's interest in appropriation, intertextuality and 'recontextualization' can be subjected to conventional copyright law: 'To what extent does the act of recontextualisation, the placing of the sample next to the other sounds, mean that authorship (and the resultant financial rewards) should be attributed to those sampling rather than sampled?' (2000: 280). That 2015 has witnessed the largest settlement against music deemed by the courts to have 'sampled' the work of Marvin Gaye suggests that this moment in legal terms is still some way away. As with the furore over *Last Orders* (and other literary homage cases which ended up in the courtroom rather than in the press) we are dealing with a complex ethics of indebtedness, although with the added complication, as pointed out by David Sanjek (1994: 349), that in the music industry musical language doesn't carry quotation marks. Perhaps in a more celebratory recognition of richness and potential we need to view literary adaptation and appropriation from a vantage point that sees them as actively creating a new cultural and aesthetic product, one that stands alongside the texts that have provided inspiration, and, in the process, enriches rather than 'robs' them. This would provide 'grounds' perhaps for exonerating Graham Swift of all charges, and establishing in the process a more vibrant methodology for exploring the appropriative instinct.

PART II

LITERARY ARCHETYPES

3

'HERE'S A STRANGE ALTERATION'
SHAKESPEAREAN APPROPRIATIONS

Adaptation and appropriation are dependent on the literary canon for the provision of a shared repository of storylines, themes, characters and ideas upon which their creative variations can be made. The spectator or reader must be able to participate in the play of similarity and difference between the original sources or inspiration to appreciate fully the reshaping or rewriting undertaken by the adaptive text, though an experience in and of itself of the adaptation need not require these prior knowledges. There are, however, particular bodies of texts and source material, such as myth, fairy tale and folklore, which by their very nature seem to depend on this communality of shared understanding and access. These forms and genres have cross-cultural, often cross-historical, readerships and audiences; they are stories and tales which appear across the boundaries of cultural difference and which are handed down, albeit in transmuted and translated forms, through the generations. In this sense they participate in a very active way in a shared community of knowledge, and they have therefore proved rich sources for adaptation and reworking. The following two chapters will consider myth and fairy tale in greater detail, but before turning to them it seems crucial for any historicized study of the adaptive process to touch base with the playwright whose *oeuvre* functions in a remarkably similar way to those communal, shared, transactional, transcultural and frequently transnational art forms of myth and fairy tale: William Shakespeare.

It is no coincidence that the Shakespearean canon has provided a crucial touchstone for the scholarship of appropriation as a literary practice. Several book-length studies have considered adaptation and appropriation from a Shakespearean perspective (see, for example, Marsden 1991; Chedgzoy 1995; Novy 1999; Desmet and Sawyer 1999; Fischlin and Fortier 2000; Sanders 2001, 2007; Zabus 2002; Massai 2005; Kidnie 2008; Fischlin 2014; Huang and Rivlin 2014). To cite Daniel Fischlin and Mark Fortier in the valuable overview essay that accompanied their anthology of dramatic adaptations of Shakespearean plays: 'As long as there have been plays by Shakespeare, there have been adaptations of those plays' (2000: 1). Dramatic adaptation of Shakespearean play-texts had become routine by as early as the Restoration period in England. From 1660 onwards, playwrights such as Nahum Tate and William Davenant altered plotlines, added scenes and characters, and set aspects to music (Clark 1997). And it does not stop at plays: poetry, novels, films, animations, television advertisements and computer games have all engaged with Shakespeare as both global icon and author and through specific texts. As Fischlin and Fortier point out, the Latin root of the word 'adapt', *adaptare*, means 'to make fit' (2000: 3). The adaptation of Shakespeare invariably makes him 'fit' for new cultural contexts and political ideologies different from those of his own age. As a result, a historiographical approach to Shakespearean appropriation becomes also in part a study of theoretical movements; many theories which have had their intellectual foundation in recent decades, such as feminism, postmodernism, structuralism, gay, lesbian and transgender theory, postcolonialism and now, increasingly, the new digital humanities, have all had a profound effect on the modes and methodologies of adapting Shakespeare.

The ongoing adaptation of central figures of Western culture such as Shakespeare raises all kinds of questions about originality, authority and intellectual property rights. Some authors are accused of seeking to authenticate their own activities by attaching Shakespeare's name to their writing. In such cases an honorific approach is assumed. Others are seen to be less deferential, iconoclastic even, in their intent, rewriting and 'talking back' to Shakespeare from an overtly political position. Whatever the ideological stance(s) of his adapters, the inescapable fact is that Shakespeare was himself an adapter and imitator, an appropriator of myth, fairy tale, folklore, the historical chronicles of Holinshed, and the prose fiction and poetry of his day, as well as classical texts by Ovid and Plutarch. The early twentieth century witnessed a veritable academic trade in Shakespearean source-spotting: Geoffrey Bullough's influential eight-volume series *Narrative and Dramatic Sources of Shakespeare* was, and still is, a standard presence in any university reference library. The organization of Bullough's volumes proves insightful (Fischlin and Fortier 2000: 9). He divides his chapters in accordance with the following categories: direct source, analogue, translation, possible source and probable source. The direct sources include Cinthio's prose text about a jealous Moor reworked as *Othello*, the story of 'Pyramus and Thisbe' from Ovid's *Metamorphoses*, which is performed by the mechanicals in *A Midsummer Night's Dream*'s play-within-a-play, and Thomas Lodge's *Rosalynd*, incorporated into *As You Like It*. In many of these instances whole plotlines are lifted, assimilated and recontextualized by Shakespeare. Elsewhere sustained allusion and analogues figure in the mix, such as Prospero's delivery of a speech in *The Tempest*, which is translated from Ovid by Arthur Golding and then adapted again into dramatic verse by Shakespeare. Through this mechanism Prospero voices words originally spoken by the sorceress Medea with all of the complicated connections that they might provoke in a knowing spectator, not least aligning the onstage magus with the offstage Algerian witch Sycorax (5.1.33–56).

All of the diverse methods of adaptation that we have been exploring in this volume apply to Shakespeare's varied personal practice of appropriation. Much recent scholarship has stressed the collaborative writing environments in which he worked and the influence this had on his eclectic style and approach. He co-authored several plays such as *The Two Noble Kinsmen* and

Henry VIII, or All Is True with John Fletcher, for example. Perhaps a useful way of thinking about adaptation is as a form of collaborative writing across time, and sometimes across culture or language. Shakespeare's age had a far more open approach to literary borrowing and imitation than the modern era of copyright and property law encourages or even allows. Imitation was learned and practised in schools and continued into adult writing careers; Shakespeare would perhaps have expected to be adapted by future ages and writers for this very reason. Jean Marsden has suggested that Ben Jonson's famous poetic observation that Shakespeare was 'not of an age but for all time' need not be taken to endorse the hoary old claims to his 'universality' but rather as an indication that he remains available to subsequent ages to adapt and adopt as they wish. Shakespeare's cultural value, then, lies in part in his availability (McLuskie and Rumbold 2014); as Marsden notes, 'each new generation attempts to redefine Shakespeare's genius in contemporary terms, projecting its desires and anxieties onto his work' (1991: 1).

Returning to issues of the canon already broached by efforts to define terms in this study, Shakespeare is so frequently adapted in part because he is a major author (Fischlin and Fortier 2000: 6). His global currency in recent decades seems to further fuel that adaptability, recognizable as his 'brand' is in Asia, Latin America, West Africa and elsewhere. There are also undoubtedly economic and legal factors at play: Shakespeare is helpfully outside copyright law, making him both safe and cheap, as well as fascinating, to adapt. And adaptation as an art, as we have already seen, feeds other adaptation, so the 'Shakespeare industry' is a self-generating force in this regard. Shakespeare is constantly being made new, remade, by this process: 'if adaptations of Shakespeare somehow reinforce Shakespeare's position in the canon … it is a different Shakespeare that is at work' (Fischlin and Fortier 2000: 6). In the twentieth century, for example, *Henry V* was re-envisioned as a play about the Second World War, the Falklands Crisis and the First Gulf War.

Performance is in itself an inherently adaptive art; we might even argue that each individual performance is an adaptation. If drama embodies within its own conventions an invitation to reinvention, so the movement into a different generic mode can encourage a reading of the Shakespearean text from a new or revised point of view. Stage plays more usually offer a broader perspective on events than the camera in close-up or a first-person narrator. There are of course exceptions to the rule, such as the heightened moment of soliloquy which Shakespeare deployed to such effect in his drama, but this focus can rarely be sustained across an entire performance. A novel written from a specific point of view can therefore radically recast a play by choosing to focus in on a single character and their reaction or version of events. The transformation involved in seeing things from a different point of view is a driving force in many non-Shakespearean appropriations of classics texts, as we shall see in Part III of this volume. In Jean Rhys's *Wide Sargasso Sea* (an appropriation of Charlotte Brontë's *Jane Eyre*) or Peter Carey's *Jack Maggs* (an Australian re-visioning of Dickens's *Great Expectations*) the narrative is voiced wholly or in part by marginalized characters from the source text, offering a commentary on the canonical source in the process, not least from a postcolonial perspective. J. M. Coetzee's *Foe* reimagines Daniel Defoe's *Robinson Crusoe* from a female perspective entirely absent from the original text. In all of these instances an informed knowledge of the hypotext or source is crucial to appreciating the full force of the twists and turns of the adaptive text and the political impulse that lies behind each of them: 'The hypertext invites us to engage in a relational reading' (Genette 1997 [1982]: 399). Christy Desmet and Robert Sawyer make the intriguing point in respect of Shakespearean appropriation that this interest in entering a story from the perspective of a particular character, and therefore point of view, can seem to reintroduce a very outmoded form of 'character criticism' (1999: 10); but there is also often a wilful misreading of the 'parent' text implicit in these rewritings such as would suggest a more politicized stance on the part of these 'offspring' than mere character criticism would imply.

Novels in the late twentieth century which sought to reshape Shakespeare certainly exhibited a strong interest in first-person narrative. Jane Smiley's *A Thousand Acres* not only relocates the family struggle for control of land and emotions in *King Lear* to the American Mid West of the 1980s, but chooses to view events from the perspective of Ginny, the eldest daughter of Larry Cook, the farmer-patriarch whose division of his land promotes the internal jealousies and ruptures in the family that promulgate events in the novel. If Larry is a direct analogue for Lear, the king's madness mirrored here in encroaching dementia, then Ginny stands for Goneril. By allowing Ginny a developed voice and personal history, one which eventually exposes supposed incest at the heart of this close-knit family, Smiley is able to 'flesh out' Goneril's violent actions as they appear in the play and to offer some empathy for her situation. This is an example of the process of revaluation outlined by Genette in *Palimpsests*: 'The revaluation of a character consists in investing him or her – by way of pragmatic or psychological transformation – with a more significant and/or more "attractive" role in the value system of the hypertext than was the case in the hypotext' (1997 [1982]: 343).

If in *King Lear* Goneril's limited stage time and lines reduce her actions to a tragicomic grotesque version of villainy, such as when she poisons her sister Regan in a fight for the sexual attentions of Edmund, Smiley at least accords Ginny narrative time and considerable motivation for her actions. The poisoning plotline resurfaces in the novel and now constitutes a failed attempt by Ginny to wreak revenge on her sister Rose for a shared relationship with Jess Cook, their neighbour (the novel's Edmund). The Cook family storyline provides the novel's analogue to the Duke of Gloucester subplot in the play, the rivalry between his two sons and his eventual blinding. It is a mark of the detailed relocation of the events of the play that Smiley effects that in *A Thousand Acres* the blinding occurs as a result of an agricultural accident rather than the random torture witnessed onstage in productions of Shakespeare's play. Smiley's purpose in this rewriting of *King Lear* is multiple. She clearly felt a need to 'write back' to Shakespeare's demonization of female characters such as Goneril and Regan and to consider what might have caused their behaviour; to achieve this she retrieves female experience from a male-authored narrative (Zabus 2002: 6). But she also writes from a late twentieth-century eco-feminist standpoint in terms of the novel's supplementary political and ecological concerns with pollution of the land by so-called conventional farming techniques and the heavy use of pesticides and the materialistic aims of modern capitalist business practices (Mathieson 1999: 127–44; Sanders 2001: 191–216).

Marina Warner's novel *Indigo, or Mapping the Waters* exhibits a similar interest in retrieving the woman's story from a male-centred text. This time the focus is Shakespeare's late romance *The Tempest*. Warner's narrative, which will also be examined in Chapter 5 in terms of its engagement with fairy tale, offers an extended voice to two of that play's marginalized characters, Miranda and Sycorax. If Miranda is subject to her father's controlling presence throughout the play, then Sycorax is reduced to the accounts provided by others: she is only talked of, never seen. Warner's novel interweaves a double time scheme to depict Miranda in the twentieth century and Sycorax in the early modern period. In doing so she is able to resist any simplistic linearities in her account. *Indigo* challenges the stability of the historical account by subjecting it to the patterns of storytelling and multiple textualities, which in turn allows a feminist viewpoint to be articulated.

Framing the entire narrative is the storytelling of Serafine Killabree, a figure who connects both Sycorax and Miranda, thereby drawing the novel into more circular modes of being than the linear teleology of standard 'History' would allow. In turn, a critical, post-feminist, and postcolonial reading of *The Tempest* is incorporated into this revisionist text (Chedgzoy 1995: 94–134). It is an example of what Steven Connor has called 'fidelity-in-betrayal', 'more of an improvisation upon its original than an attempt to translate it' (1996: 186):

> If rewriting of this kind compromises the cultural authority of the original text, then this never amounts to a simple denial of it; in its attention to its rewritten original, its fidelity-in-betrayal, the rewritten text must always submit to the authority of an imperative that is at once ethical and historical.
>
> (Connor 1996: 167)

No simple denial or rejection of Shakespeare's play is made in *Indigo*, since it is by no means as straightforward a 'rewriting' as this would require, but its tenets and themes are re-viewed through a postcolonial lens. As Warner's acknowledgements to scholars such as Peter Hulme in the foreword indicate, this novel is a further instance of appropriation informed by critical history and literary theory.

If the claim that we made earlier that Shakespearean appropriation serves as a cultural barometer of changing tastes, issues and values stands, then we might expect different plays to surface in their importance to adapters at different times. A statistical analysis of adaptations undertaken of Shakespeare in the late twentieth century would most likely have identified *The Tempest* as a key focus. There was a raft of film adaptations and several novels responding to the play during the closing decades of that century, a marker perhaps of the prominence of postcolonial issues and theory at the time (Zabus 2002). The play became a standard presence in postcolonial studies, which in turn drove an interest in performance, which in turn fed more radical rewritings and adaptations in film versions and in novels and poetry written from the former colonies that strove to 'talk back' to the colonizing contexts of Shakespeare's drama. We are acknowledging in this a force that is not solely literary and which cannot be explained by literary analysis alone; as Simone Murray has argued, it is important to materialize adaptation studies as well, to recognize the economic and social imperatives that in part explain the adaptational impulse and, at a very simple level, the choice of text (Murray 2012: 12).

The global turn at the beginning of the twenty-first century is changing the picture once more as plays that have greater resonance in countries of rising power (and cultural buying power) rise to the fore: this means, not least in Asia, plays such as *Romeo and Juliet*. Mark Thornton Burnett records no less than 28 world cinema versions of that play from the 1980s onwards (2013: 195). That particular dominant presence both in cinematic and digitized contexts and platforms might also be attributed in part at least to the global influence of Baz Luhrmann's 1996 film; content drives further content, as we have seen (O'Neill 2014: loc. 109). *Hamlet*, perhaps because of a strong presence in school and university curricula on several continents, continues to score highly in terms of adaptational responses, a fact likely to be further enhanced by the Globe Theatre's decision to 'export' the play to

205 countries in 2014–16 as part of what is billed, in rock star terms, as a 'world tour'. If adaptation requires foreknowledge of the source for the system of analogue and juxtaposition to succeed fully, then Shakespeare does become a reliable shared cultural referent (even for stances of opposition), a language which for complex geopolitical, educational and sometimes economic reasons we all 'understand'.

Othello is also a text that features high on the list of analytics-driven studies of Shakespearean adaptation. As a text dealing with racism within its themes and action it has proved a rich source for adapters seeking to examine the tensions of multi-cultural societies in the modern era. In a 2001 film appropriation of the play, '*O*', director Tim Blake Nelson relocated the storyline to a US college. Odin James (Othello) is a top-flight basketball player on the college team and engaged in a passionate relationship with a fellow student who is also the dean's daughter, Desi (Desdemona). The coach's son Hugo (Iago) is jealous on every level. In the hothouse atmosphere and highly competitive world of college sports, Blake Nelson finds a perfect analogue for the complicated military allegiances and rivalries of the play, but also speaks to very contemporary concerns about campus drug use and fraternity house sexual violence. It is no coincidence, either, that Odin's initials, OJ, recall another high profile African-American sports star accused of murdering his white wife, O. J. Simpson. By exploring contemporary US issues via the filtering lens of a Shakespearean tragedy, Blake Nelson exposes the class rivalries and racism embedded in the US education system. With bitter irony the film suffered a lengthy delay in its public release due to retrospective parallels found with the college shootings that happened in Columbine High School in 1999.

The 1995 trial of O. J. Simpson was recalled in another modern variation on *Othello*, Djanet Sears's play *Harlem Duet* (1997). With each scene framed by audio recordings of significant events and speeches for and within the black community, including Martin Luther King's 1963 Washington, DC address 'I have a dream ...', Malcolm X, Louis Farakhan and the Million Man March of 1995, Simpson's trial and the sexual harassment hearings that involved academic Anita Hill and Supreme Court judge Clarence

Thomas in 1991, the play enjoys a triple time scheme. Juxtaposed scenes depict Harlem in the 1850s and 1860s, that is to say the years leading up to the American Civil War, and then again in the 1920s, and finally in the 1990s, the years that were contemporary to the play's first production. The events actually serve as a prequel to those of Shakespeare's play in the sense that the modern Othello in this text is a Columbia University Literature professor who has left his partner for a white colleague, Mona. Audiences are invited to 'read in' the future for these characters using their memory of the Shakespearean tragedy: Mona is Desdemona, Chris Yago, the jealous colleague, is Iago, and the summer school position that Othello accepts in Cyprus during the course of the action bodes ill for his relationship with Mona.

This play is a complex meditation on the history of black representation in society and in the theatre as well as a clever appropriation of *Othello*. It is telling that Mona is only represented in performance by a disembodied arm and voice, and there are numerous inversions of the Shakespearean original as well as its conventional expectations. Fischlin and Fortier suggest that 'Shakespeare's text remains a barely visible (but nonetheless significant) backdrop' (2000: 287). Sears's production is also evocatively devised around musical signifiers. It has an aesthetic structure derived in part from jazz and the blues. The 'duet' of the title is performed not only by the various allusive intertextual partnerships we read into the play but also by the paired instrumentation of cello and double bass. A black contribution to musical culture and arts in the US is underscored by this decision but the frame also serves to perform Sears's own improvisational approach to her Shakespearean intertext. Henry Louis Gates Jr's notions of 'signifyin'' are once again relevant (1988; Andreas 1999: 107), and once again we see a wider frame of reference in which Shakespeare is just one component at play in the new work.

Hamlet has canonical standing in any study of Shakespearean reception and appropriation. This is for a combination of often changing reasons due to context. Ophelia's tragic trajectory has proved of considerable interest to feminist adapters, male and female alike; Angela Carter's novels and short fiction are haunted by the image of Ophelia, often filtered through subsequent adaptational gestures, not least Pre-Raphaelite painting and cinematic interpretations (Sage 1994: 33; see also Peterson and Williams 2012). If feminism has found relational associations with *Hamlet* in more recent decades in the early twentieth century, it was the work of Sigmund Freud and the influence of theories of psychoanalysis that placed the play at the heart of the literary canon. As the exploration of a mind in crisis, the play attracted numerous commentators and respondents, not least T. S. Eliot, whose essays and wider interests in this area proved influential both in the shaping of the canon and in the discipline of English Literature itself (Di Pietro 2006; Corcoran 2010: 61–119).

One factor that has amplified and extended the canonicity of *Hamlet* is that the Prince of Denmark has come to be regarded as the culminating role for any aspiring young actor. It serves as a career touchstone as much as a literary one. The 'actor of the day' is almost obliged to engage with the role in some format: in the twentieth century Sir John Gielgud, Sir Laurence Olivier, Richard Burton and Kenneth Branagh among them. In the early twenty-first century prime examples of this phenomenon would be *Dr Who* star David Tennant, globally successful *Sherlock* actor and Oscar nominee Benedict Cumberbatch or indeed Maxine Peake, one of the most renowned stage and television actors of her generation, all of whom have embraced the role in high profile productions in recent years. In a related vein, film adaptations, both Anglophone and non-Anglophone have burgeoned. These range from Laurence Olivier's Freud-imbued 1948 black-and-white rendition, which carried the voiceover declaration that this was the tragedy of 'a man who could not make up his mind' (Rothwell 1999: 59), through Franco Zeffirelli's Gothic rendition of the 1990s taste for the action movie genre, starring Mel Gibson in the main role, to Kenneth Branagh's epic wide-screen, so-called 'full text' version in 1996. Non-English-speaking variants striking examples from China, including *The Banquet* (dir. Xiaogang Feng, 2006), which had epic credentials akin to Branagh's version and which in a manner akin to the Zeffirelli film benefited from a global vogue for martial arts action movies at the time of release, and a Chinese–Tibetan collaboration, *Prince of the Himalayas* (dir. Sherwood Hu, 2006) (see Burnett 2013: 125–6).

As mentioned in Chapter 1, in 2000 Michael Almereyda produced his *Hamlet* set in a millennial Manhattan. The corporate values of the late twentieth century here substituted for the early modern play's plotlines of dynastic rivalry and cross-border battles for territory. The Castle of Elsinore was replaced by the Denmark Corporation, with Claudius as a manipulative CEO. In this version – which drew on many independent filmmaking tropes, including its casting of Ethan Hawke as the melancholic prince – both Hamlet and Ophelia are arts students, enabling some suggestive (post) modern substitutions in the play's iconic moments: Ophelia's distribution of symbolic flowers in her madness at Act 4, Scene 5, becomes the giving of photographic representations of the same; 'The Mousetrap', *Hamlet*'s play-within-a-play, which, as we observed earlier, becomes a short film montage shot on 16mm by Hawke's media studies 'prince'. The latter proved wonderfully proleptic of the YouTube era of short film Shakespeares (see O'Neill 2014). Once again the filtration effect of adaptations influencing other adaptations cannot be ignored. A chronological study of Shakespearean adaptation uncovers all manner of cross-fertilization: in this case, Almereyda's acknowledged debt in creating a corporate *mise-en-scène* to Japanese director Akira Kurosawa's 1960 film *The Bad Sleep Well*, which relocated the play to the Tokyo Stock Exchange. Similar interactions can be explored between William Reilly's previously cited *Men of Respect* and its UK precursor *Joe Macbeth*, and in a very rich sense between Orson Welles's *Chimes at Midnight* (1966), a film reworking of the collated *Henry IV* plays, and Gus Van Sant's remarkable transposition of the Hal–Falstaff relationship and the Eastcheap scenes of those plays to contemporary Portland, Oregon, in *My Own Private Idaho* (1991).

GRAFTING, OR READING BETWEEN THE LINES

Film adaptation is one important sub-set of adaptation and appropriation that often signals its relationship to the precursor Shakespearean play-text in a fairly straightforward manner (though less so in the non-Anglophone variants and certainly in a more refracted manner in examples such as *Idaho*). But there are further sub-groups which deploy a source text as a creative springboard for an often wholly different text, a move often signified by a radical shift in title. This creative move is sometimes achieved by extrapolating a particular storyline or character's trajectory from the original and relocating that to a new context, historical, geographical and/or cultural. The relationship to the original remains present and relevant but it is as if a grafting has taken place of a segment, or rootstock, of the original text. The rootstock is conjoined to a new textual form, or scion, to create an entirely new literary artefact. I am deploying these metaphors of grafting quite self-consciously; not only did Shakespeare deploy the metaphor in his late romance *The Winter's Tale* (4.4.87–97) but Genette uses this exact phrase to describe the adaptive relationship between hypotext (original) and hypertext (re-creation) (1997 [1982]: ix). In this notion of rootstock and scion being brought together by the grafting process to create a new plant (pear trees, for example, are always grown on quince rooting stocks) literature has long found a rich source of metaphor for the creative process. Shakespeare's sonnets in particular abound with the imagery of grafting, and Eliot's notion of tradition and the individual talent finds an intriguing analogue in this horticultural practice.

Perhaps one of the most influential 'grafts' of Shakespearean drama is Tom Stoppard's 1967 play *Rosencrantz and Guildenstern Are Dead*. This play melds an appropriative reading of *Hamlet*, one which seeks to imagine a back-story for two minor characters who are the prince's former friends and attendant lords, with a quasi-parodic approach using the absurdist theatrical practices which were in the ascendant when Stoppard created his drama. Another clear intertext for *Rosencrantz and Guildenstern Are Dead* is Samuel Beckett's ground-breaking 1952 play *Waiting for Godot*. Stoppard creates his attendant lords in the image of Beckett's endlessly philosophizing vagrants, Vladimir and Estragon, who for the majority of their play wait on a largely bare stage for something to happen. Stoppard's opening stage direction makes this connection overt: '*Two Elizabethans passing the time in a place without any visible character*' (Stoppard 1990 [1967]: 9). The joke is that the audience, unlike Rosencrantz and Guildenstern, know what will happen if they know the script of *Hamlet*. Hence, as the title informs us, Rosencrantz and Guildenstern are in effect already dead, even before they have started the play; aficionados of Shakespeare know only too well their plotline of the sea journey and the redirected letters which send the two attendant lords to their death in England instead of the prince. Stoppard's play exploits the idea of 'every exit being an entrance somewhere else' (22). We witness Rosencrantz and Guildenstern in their 'downtime' or offstage moments from *Hamlet*; that offstage becomes this play's onstage. Stoppard does not simply impose his themes on a Shakespearean scaffold or framework. In many instances he finds direct precedent for his dramaturgical decisions in the Shakespearean sources. For example, Elizabethan and Jacobean plays often commence with attendant lords in discussion (see, for example, *Antony and Cleopatra, The Winter's Tale* and *King Lear*), and *Hamlet*, like *Rosencrantz and Guildenstern Are Dead*, is interested in the themes of broken or ruptured ritual and ceremony ('maimèd rites', *Hamlet* 5.1.214) and metatheatre (Sale 1978: 83).

Stoppard's play was hugely influential in that it chose to re-view *Hamlet* from the theatrical sidelines, and through the eyes of minor characters. This serves to render the play's tragic events and the prince in particular as slightly absurd. Aspects, events, lines and characters from Shakespeare's play are all present in Stoppard's drama but creatively decentred, reduced to dumb-show or comic fragment. In the process the play's tragic 'hero' is reduced to a somewhat histrionic and risible figure. Many critics have, as a result, labelled this as an exercise in postmodernism, fragmenting, defamiliarizing as it does, one of the most canonical texts of English literature and Western culture; Roger Sales has also suggested that it is an act of depoliticization, although a flipside to that argument might be to see the play as a viewpoint from the marginalized serving classes on the aristocratic and noble centre of tragic form (1978: 83).

Seeing things from marginal or even offstage characters' points of view is a common drive in many adaptations and appropriations. In *Longbourn*, for example, Jo Baker rethinks Jane Austen's *Pride and Prejudice* from the viewpoint of the servants in the Bennett household. As her 'Author's Note' states:

> The main characters in *Longbourn* are ghostly presences in *Pride and Prejudice*: they exist to serve the family and the story. They deliver notes and drive carriages; they run errands when nobody else will step out of doors – they are the 'proxy' by which the shoes for the Netherfield Ball are fetched in the pouring rain. But they are – at least in my head – people too.
>
> (Baker 2013: loc. 5361)

And in a structural ploy directly akin to Stoppard's in *Rosencrantz and Guildenstern Are Dead*, *Longbourn* presents in carefully scripted fashion the offstage of the novel, engaging in class politics in the process: 'When a meal is served in *Pride and Prejudice*, it has been prepared in *Longbourn*' (loc. 5361) and in this way a footman who appears on just one page of Austen's novel is given narrative life and a story to go with it.

When the dramatic genre is reworked into prose fiction a particularly intriguing equivalent for dramatic soliloquy is often found in the extended form of first-person narrative. Postmodernist fiction, with its investment in highlighting the mode of unreliable narration, draws attention to the bias implicit in the singular point of view, but of course what a biased perspective allows in the rewriting of Shakespeare is the ability to see things from a particular character's angle. Novelists are drawn to the idea of seeing from a marginalized or disenfranchised character's point of view to enable fresh and often politicized readings of the original to emerge, and we can see immediately how this would appeal to postmodern or indeed postcolonial writers engaged with theories of class, gender or ethnicity. An ideological purpose to the act of re-vision is almost inevitable in this context and so we observe that many Shakespearean appropriations are motivated by a political commitment. Smiley's eco-feminist rethinking of *King Lear* in *A Thousand Acres* is a very vibrant example of this kind of activity at work, or indeed Caryl Phillips's *The Nature of Blood* (1997), which engages with both the protagonists of *Othello* and *The Merchant of Venice* from the vantage points of others as well as in a rethinking of their own subjectivity, in a thoughtful rumination on identity, ethnicity and faith (see Chapter 6 for a more extended discussion of the latter novel in particular and of alternative points of view in general).

US novelist John Updike indicated in an afterword to his *Gertrude and Claudius* (2000) that a renewed awareness of 'off-stage characters' in *Hamlet* came about for him not from experiencing Stoppard's play in performance but rather at a screening of Branagh's 1996 film version. Updike does not choose to write from a first-person perspective but his text is sympathetic to the situation of Hamlet's mother Gertrude in particular, who marries the brother-in-law who has murdered her husband. The novelist achieves this by means of a timeframe which functions for the first two sections of the text as a prequel to Shakespeare's play. We see how the young Gertrude, or Gerutha as she is called in Part 1 of the novel, was subject to the dynastic ambitions of her father when choosing her husband: 'And I am to be the plunder in exchange' (Updike 2000: 5). In this arranged marriage, her husband Horwendil the Jute (the Old Hamlet of the play) proves to be a committed warrior but a rough lover. In this way, and in a manner akin to Smiley's re-creation of *King Lear*'s Goneril as her sexually abused narrator Ginny, Updike imputes a motive to Gertrude's adultery which is not present in the Shakespearean precursor (a back story if you like). This ascription of motive encourages the reader to respond with understanding to Gertrude's predicament when she is seduced by the tender attentions of Horwendil's brother Feng (Claudius).

The variant, and indeed variable, nomenclature of Updike's novel makes several important points in its own right. The novel has a tri-partite structure and although the events portrayed in each section are continuous in chronological terms, the main players' names alter from section to section. The protagonists' names in Part 1 derive from the ancient *Hamlet* legend as detailed in Saxo Grammaticus's *Historia Dania* (1514): Gerutha, Horwendil the Jute, Feng his brother, Corambus (the Polonius precursor) and Amleth (Hamlet). In Part 2 they derive from François de Belleforest's *Histoires tragiques* (Paris, 1576): Geruthe, Horvendile, Fengon, Corambis and Hamblet. It is not until the third and final part of the novel that we encounter more familiar Shakespearean nomenclature: Gertrude, King Hamlet, Claudius, Polonius and Hamlet. Updike adds a further textual layer in that Polonius is called Corambis in the quarto edition of Shakespeare's play. This slippage between signifying names is an indication that *Hamlet*, and the Hamlet story, has multiple provenance and that Shakespeare's play comes quite late in the line of adaptation and interpretation. That Shakespeare's drama is a variation on a much older theme is further emphasized by Updike's decision to open each section with the same sentence: 'The King was irate'; as with Bach's *Goldberg Variations*, as discussed in Chapter 2, we are given the central aria (or in this instance plotline) on which many adapters have ruminated and offered their own textual variants.

A fixed or stable reading of a canonical Shakespeare play-text is effectively challenged by Updike; the rich textual provenance of *Hamlet* justifies the author's speculation with regard to motivation for the play's events. Part 2 of *Gertrude and Claudius* ends with a brother's murder of a brother while he sleeps in an orchard, an event recalled in flashback in Shakespeare's play by the Ghost (1.5.59–79). In Part 3, events as well as names offer a more familiar signification to readers; we get direct quotation from the play as well as recognizable events, not least the court celebrations for the 'o'erhasty' marriage of Gertrude and Claudius, and Hamlet's 'muttered puns' (Updike 2000: 208) in response to his uncle's elaborate performance of duty in front of the other Elsinore courtiers. But, as the Shakespeare-alert reader will register, this is only the first act of *Hamlet* that we are witnessing here: much lies ahead beyond the novel's closing pages for those familiar with the play. The tragic impetus is what feeds the reader's imagination and expectation, in contradistinction to Claudius's thoughts as they appear on the page:

> The era of Claudius had dawned; it would shine in Denmark's annals. He might, with moderation of his carousals, last another decade on the throne. Hamlet would be the perfect age of forty when the crown descended. He and Ophelia would have the royal heirs lined up like ducklings ... He had gotten away with it. All would be well.
>
> (Updike 2000: 210)

The last phrase is an allusion to Claudius's prayer scene at 3.4. of *Hamlet*, though with a notable shift from the subjunctive mode ('All may be well', 3.4.72) to one of (misplaced) certainty. The further juxtaposition of the Shakespearean frame of reference with a contemporary US idiom ('gotten away with it') points up the playfulness and irony of Updike's approach to his multiple sources.

The film adaptations of *Hamlet* and the appropriative grafts of Stoppard and Updike discussed here have an explicit relationship with their Shakespearean precursor and seem therefore to invite, even demand, comparative readings, but appropriation, as we saw in Chapter 2, need not always signal its intertextual relations in an explicit way. A range of relations from 'direct contact to indirect absorption' (Miola 1992: 7) might exist. Nevertheless in situations where the relationship is not necessarily directly sounded, or is sounded in a deliberately tangential way, perhaps through comic allusion or more embedded moves or by means of glancing references, there might still be the case of a 'deep source' (7) in operation. A 1992 novel by Graham Swift, *Ever After*, and a 1996 comic novel by Alan Isler, *The Prince of West End Avenue*, will form the closing case studies to this chapter in an effort to highlight the operations of 'deep source'.

Swift's novel has a deeply introspective first-person narrator who is both haunted by the suicides of his (supposed) father and wife and has suicidal tendencies of his own; this in itself offers a parallel with Shakespeare's introspective protagonist, a point directly made by the narrator: 'for a large part of my life ... I have imagined myself – surreptitiously, presumptuously, appropriately, perversely – as Hamlet. And you all know one of his tendencies' (Swift 1992: 4). The narrative style offers a further analogue to Hamlet's multiple self-analytical soliloquies as well as highlighting the thin line between fact and fiction which the play is concerned with: 'One may smile and smile and be a villain'. *Ever After*'s narrator, Bill Unwin, whose name we only learn halfway through the novel – an indication of the extent to which his life and personality are repressed and determined by those around him – is an academic researcher. Despite his crippling self-doubt, compounded by the fact that his research fellowship is dependent upon the patronage of his step-father, Unwin is researching a set of family notebooks dating from the 1850s. These manuscripts record the crisis in faith experienced by his ancestor Matthew

Pearce, who, in the wake of evolutionary theory and the doubts it cast on a religious understanding of the world at this time, sacrificed his marriage and family life to a growing state of 'unbelief'.

In Chapter 7, we will investigate a series of novels that find their source material in the 1850s and 1860s and what might be deemed the 'Darwinian moment'. Charles Darwin published *The Origin of Species* in 1859. That text is directly cited in *Ever After*, and in working with this material as well as the Shakespearean intertexts – as well as *Hamlet*, the text has recourse to *Love's Labour's Lost* and *Antony and Cleopatra* at crucial moments – Swift also pays homage to late twentieth-century fiction's interest and investment in the impact of Darwin's findings. One particular focus of Swift's wider intertextuality in this regard is John Fowles's postmodern re-creation of the Victorian novel as a genre or recognized form, *The French Lieutenant's Woman*, which, like *Ever After*, features an 1850s geologist working in Lyme Regis (Fowles's novel is discussed in detail in Chapter 7). As discussed in Chapter 2, Swift is a writer deeply aware of the literary foundations of his writing and one whose narratives are self-consciously steeped in a subtle and pervasive form of allusion and adaptation. He seems to positively encourage this understanding of his narrative technique via Bill Unwin's analysis of academic research as a complicated blend of fact and hypothesis, and of the supplementation of available material: 'let's read between the lines' (Swift 1992: 211). Appropriation, but also the reading of appropriative texts, is frequently involved in a process of reading between the lines, offering analogues or supplements to what is available in a source text, and drawing attentions to its gaps and absences. Swift's title, after all, is one that we inevitably supplement with a missing word – 'happy' – to evoke the fairy tale fiction of a life or story that is 'happy ever after'.

We have in action before our eyes here the role of the reader in the text that reader-response theorists such as Wolfgang Iser and Hans-Robert Jauss delineated. For Iser, the act of reading was a dynamic and participatory process, one in which meaning was produced in a 'convergence of text and reader', and via the reader's engagement with the 'unwritten' parts of the text (Iser 1972: 279, 280). For Iser, this rendered not only the initial reading of a text but any subsequent (re-)readings unique and innovative. The idea of 'filling in the gaps' (285) and the active role of the reader or spectator in the adaptational experience is a very compelling one that once again points us towards the pleasures, cognitive and emotional, involved in engaging with adaptations and appropriations.

Gaps in the narrative and reading between the lines also help to define the complex textual operations of Alan Isler's *The Prince of West End Avenue*. This is a novel that ironically acknowledges an indebtedness to *Hamlet* not least in its deliberately bathetic or disjunctive title. Set in a New York Jewish nursing home and narrated by an unreliable narrator, Otto Korner, the narrative is couched as a memoir, although, in a manner akin to Unwin's circuitous narrative in *Ever After*, some of the most confessional revelations are withheld until near the very end of the reading experience. Despite his claim, 'I want to set the record straight' (Isler 1996: 2), Korner's narrative is in reality full of suppression and evasion, and it is here that the tragic impulse starts to invade the comic surface of the novel. Like Unwin (and indeed Hamlet), Korner is haunted by ghosts from the past, not least memories of the Holocaust, which might naturally lead us as readers towards a position of empathy, but there is also a deep and potentially offensive narcissism in his determination to place himself at the centre of twentieth-century historical events. We learn that he met Lenin and Joyce, that he is the forgotten founder of Dadaism (albeit, in a wonderfully Dadaist move, by accident), and he even at one point takes on personal responsibility for Jewish deaths in the Nazi internment camps because he failed to see the gravity of events in the 1930s and therefore persuaded his family to remain in Berlin. Undoubtedly at a family level this led to the deaths of his wife and child and the subsequent suicide of his guilt-ridden sister Lola, but, even so, the extrapolation to wider responsibility leaves the reader uncomfortable.

The reader response to Korner is, then, a strange blend of sympathy and yet an apprehensive feeling about his egotism. That egotism, the desire to place himself at the very centre of things, becomes comprehensible largely through the novel's intertextual relationship with *Hamlet*. In one of the novel's knowingly ironic gestures, the octogenarians in the residential home stage their own version of *Hamlet*, a 'play-within-the-novel' as it were. This encourages a whole series of comic comparisons and oddly dissonant juxtapositions: elderly and infirm Ophelias, for example, and several ironic linguistic echoes. In one instance, Hamlet's 'sea of troubles' from the 'To be or not to be' soliloquy (3.1.58–90 [61]) is reduced to refer to Otto's constipation, another example of bathos at the heart of this novel's technique: 'My troubles, it seems, may be solved by valium, a muscle relaxant, and, inevitably, stewed fruit' (Isler 1996: 216). Yet for all this comic irony, there is a deeply serious subtext to this Jewish-American appropriation of *Hamlet*, one in which the ghosts of public history are all too chilling and real.

Our questioning, as readers, of Otto's insistence on placing himself at the heart of public history is in part negotiated by his attitude to, and our understanding of, Shakespeare's tragedy. Otto desperately wants to play Hamlet in the nursing home production, to be at the centre of the play and the performance; as he observes in another moment of unchecked quasi-Coleridgean arrogance: 'in the Prince of Denmark I see much of myself' (Isler 1996: 44). Initially, he is, to his chagrin, cast as the Ghost, though this is perhaps entirely fitting for someone so haunted by remembrances of things past. But then, due to the untimely deaths of other cast members, he is 'promoted' to First Gravedigger. His response at this point is to conceive of that role as one equal in importance as that of the prince: '*the Gravemaker and the Prince are two faces of a single coin*' (98); 'May we not say, therefore, that it is the Gravedigger who leads Hamlet to his identity?' (99). There may be a further playful allusion in the coin reference to the opening scene of Stoppard's *Rosencrantz and Guildenstern Are Dead*, where the attendant lords are seen flipping a coin, but Korner's reading of *Hamlet* and his understanding of his own position in history has a further intertextual referent, one which he also directly cites: 'As Prufrock puts it, "I am not Prince Hamlet, nor was meant to be"' (22). The allusion here is to T. S. Eliot's poem 'The Love Song of J. Alfred Prufrock', in which the ageing speaker of Eliot's dramatic monologue considers his own marginal role on the social stage by means of comparison to the *dramatis personae* of *Hamlet*: 'No! I am not Prince Hamlet, nor was meant to be;/

Am an attendant lord ...' (Eliot 1969: 16). On the surface, as with Korner's declaration, there is a resignation here to performing a marginal role onstage or indeed in society, and yet the reader who is in full command of the nuances and complexities of Eliot's poetic meditation on ageing and Shakespearean drama, who is filling in the gaps as it were, and reading between the lines, can reach some very different conclusions. For the role that Prufrock eventually assigns himself is as the 'Fool' ('Almost, at times, the Fool'); seen from a Shakespearean perspective and alert to the use of the higher case (Fool, not fool, we note), we might think of wise, all-seeing characters such as Feste in *Twelfth Night* or the king's Fool in *King Lear* and deduce that Prufrock has actually assigned himself considerable importance in the scheme of things, not least as a social commentator. What a participatory reading of *The Prince of West End Avenue*, one that actively seeks to fill in the gaps in Isler's terms through a parallel reading of *Hamlet*, releases is not only the comic-ironic material at play in the narrative, achieved, as already noted, through a series of puncturing juxtapositions and bathetic moves, but new depths to the twists and turns of Korner's unreliable narration.

A brief word at the end of these close readings about methodology and the broader practices of adaptation studies as a field might be deemed necessary. Simone Murray has recently criticized adaptation studies for exercising a method that is overly dependent on literary close reading and a one-to-one positioning of adaptation against text. It might be said that I have done exactly that in the preceding case studies and it is unashamedly a method I will deploy elsewhere in this volume (Murray 2012: 7). My response would be that close reading is not pursued in adaptation studies at the expense of the consideration of the material context and 'textualizing' process that both Murray and film scholar Thomas Leitch have argued for in other contexts (Murray 2012: 12; Leitch 2007: 302), but rather as an active complement to those understandings and dynamics.

Studies of Shakespearean adaptation and appropriation have in themselves become a complex means of measuring and recording multiple acts of mediation and filtration, as well as considering global, economic and social factors at work in the circulation and recirculation of these texts. As with the body of postcolonial texts responding to *The Tempest* or *Othello* mentioned earlier, appropriations are often as much in dialogue with each other in this process as with the Shakespearean source text. This, perhaps, is the essence of literary archetypes: their availability for rewriting means that they are texts constantly in flux, constantly metamorphosing in the process of adaptation and retelling. Literary archetypes persistently enact and re-enact the activity of storytelling, and Shakespeare has provided a repository of some of the most familiar stories of Western culture. This is also the case with the two literary forms considered in detail over the next two chapters: myth and fairy tale.

4

'IT'S A VERY OLD STORY'
MYTH AND METAMORPHOSIS

A culture's mythology is its body of traditional narratives.
Mythical literature depends upon, incites even, perpetual acts of
reinterpretation in new contexts, a process that embodies the very
idea of appropriation. In the Introduction to this volume, Joyce's
exploitation of mythic structures in *Ulysses* to evoke age-old, even
universal, themes alongside time- and place-specific issues of Irish
politics and language was identified. Myth it seems, lends itself to
this dual plane of exploitation. As Roland Barthes asserts in
Mythologies, 'the fundamental character of the mythical concept
is to be appropriated' (1993 [1972]: 119). Barthes views this process
in terms of a metalanguage communicated across generations and
cultures – 'Mythical speech is made of a material which has
already been worked on so as to make it suitable for communica-
tion' (110) – but which is persistently relocated in a new cultural
geography at each occasion (or site) of adaptation and appropriation. Barthes invokes the specific example of a tree. Mentioned in
a text, this undoubtedly stands for a tree in the literary context, a
cross-cultural and cross-historical object, but it also becomes
loaded with localized and particularized meaning according to its

'social geography', as Barthes calls it; the tree is 'adapted to a certain type of consumption' (109), as, indeed, are myths. This form of adaptation, relocation and recontextualization proves an expansive rather than redactive mode for Barthes; he argues that myths 'ripen' as they spread (149). Genette articulates the related concept of amplification, deploying the specific example of classical drama (1997 [1982]: 262). Tragic drama, he stresses, had its origins in the reworking of a few simple myths.

Each new generation of story-makers adopts familiar mythic templates and outlines for their storytelling projects. Even writers such as Ovid, Aeschylus and Euripides, whom we might consider to be the source of much contemporary literary and cinematic adaptation of myth, were themselves refashioning previous mythic traditions. But a myth is never transported wholesale into its new context; it undergoes its own metamorphoses in the process. Myth is continuously evoked, altered and reworked, across cultures and across generations. To cite Barthes again, 'there is no fixity in mythical concepts; they can come into being, alter, disintegrate, disappear completely' (1993: 120). All of these descriptions and critical formulations gesture at the metamorphic and transformative process of adaptation: the term functions literally as well as metaphorically. It should come as no surprise, then, that Ovid, the prime author of narratives of metamorphosis, has proved a particularly rich and alluring source for contemporary novelists, poets, playwrights, screenwriters and directors. As this chapter will demonstrate, his complex, generically hybrid texts, such as the *Metamorphoses* and the *Heroides*, which knowingly blur the comic and the tragic, appeal to the experimental and metafictional aspects of much modern and postmodern writing. As examples from authors such as Salman Rushdie and Kate Atkinson will indicate, Ovid's stories of metamorphosis provide a template for the artistic and ideological act of adaptation; furthermore, specific stories from the Ovidian *oeuvre*, such as that of the poet-musician Orpheus and his doomed lover Eurydice, will prove to have been a potent repository for re-visionary artists, attracting a creative community as diverse as the Australian director Baz Luhrmann, the Southern US playwright Tennessee Williams and the British novelist Graham Swift.

MODERN METAMORPHOSES

Postmodern writing, we are constantly reminded, is a form in which the reader is asked to be aware of the constructing author, and of the artifice of the work. There is in fact nothing new in this, as any reading of Ovid reveals. In the *Metamorphoses*, Ovid persistently draws attention to the role of the storyteller; many of his best-known accounts of metamorphosis and transformation, such as Pygmalion, Venus and Adonis, Leda and the Swan, and Danaë and the golden shower, are inset narratives, stories contained within the storytelling, singing, or indeed web-weaving, of Orpheus, Arachne and others. What mythical appropriations facilitate, therefore, is a means for contemporary authors to carry out self-conscious investigations into the artistic process itself. But Ovid's tales of shape-shifting and change, narratives that frequently occur under the pressure of particular heightened events such as attempted rape or extreme grief, also find resonant parallels within the themes and concerns of those writers. Myth extracts events from an everyday context into the world of gods and the supernatural, the extraordinary in the fullest sense of that term, and for this reason it has proved an especially attractive resource for magical realist writers, such as Salman Rushdie or indeed Gabriel García Márquez, who seek to lift the quotidian event into spaces of greater possibility (Bowers 2004: 31–62).

Magic realism or mythical appropriation is not a denial of real social issues: Alison Sharrock suggests that, despite its themes of gods and goddesses and worlds other than our own, myth 'allows space ... for the examination of family matters ...' (Hardie 2002: 105). As well as enabling the flights of fantasy associated with magic realism, then, myth is deployed to discuss the most familiar of subjects: families; fathers and daughters; love. This potent blend of the extraordinary and the everyday has proved part of the appeal of Ovid for a cluster of appropriations in recent years. Poets including Seamus Heaney, Simon Armitage, Carol Ann Duffy and Ted Hughes (who went on to write his full-length *Tales from Ovid* in 1997) contributed to the 1994 anthology *After Ovid*; prose writers ranging from A. S. Byatt and Joyce Carol Oates to the Dutch magic realist Cees Nooteboom all wrote short stories for the 2000 *Ovid Metamorphosed* collection. Many of these rewritings bring the mythical frame of reference down to earth. Oates's retelling of the death of Actaeon in 'The Sons of Angus MacElster', for example, recounts the demise of a Cape Breton patriarch; the hounds that tear Actaeon to pieces in the shape of a stag are now MacElster's sons hacking at their father's drunken body in the family barn after he has assaulted their mother (Terry 2000: 72–7). Carol Ann Duffy's 'Mrs Midas' is a contemporary housewife who is distraught to see the objects in her home turning to gold (Hofman and Lasdun 1994: 262).

The double drive apparent in the mythical appropriation process, which is a simultaneous invocation of the marvellous and the everyday, is nowhere more evident than in the early-career writings of Kate Atkinson. Her 1997 novel *Human Croquet* (the title of course an allusion to Lewis Carroll's *Alice in Wonderland*) is a deeply intertextual creation that has been discussed elsewhere in terms of its sustained allusions to Shakespeare (Sanders 2001: 66–83). The novel weaves a complex web of material, ranging from science fiction to children's literature, including, among others, the work of Enid Blyton and E. Nesbit, within a recognizably Ovidian frame. As with the *Metamorphoses*, the novel opens at the point of creation from chaos. Within its pages the specific tales of Daphne being turned into a laurel to escape Apollo's unwanted sexual attentions and of Phaeton's sisters transformed into trees by their excessive grief are alluded to. The novel's first-person narrator, the excitable Isobel Fairfax, is studying Ovid and Shakespeare at school, so it should not surprise us that these writers form the shaping frames of reference for her thoughts. But Isobel is also overwhelmed by grief, like Hamlet or Phaeton's sisters. Their mother's violent death haunts the memories of both Isobel and her brother Charles, who, in a grim reworking of fairy tale, discovered her corpse in the woods on a family outing: 'Absence of Eliza has shaped our lives' (Atkinson 1997: 28).

When Isobel is set the task by a schoolteacher of translating the passage on Phaeton's sisters from Ovid, she produces an emotionally charged version of this tale of uncontrollable grief (163). It is equally apposite that at various points in the narrative Isobel imagines her brother is metamorphosing into a dog; since the

Ovidian parallel is the story of Hecuba, another template of extreme grief. (Hecuba's story in turn informed Shakespeare's *Hamlet*, as it is a role performed by the Player King when the actors visit Elsinore Castle.) Hecuba was transformed into a canine state by her visceral mourning for her husband King Priam, murdered in the siege of Troy:

> His ill-starred wife
> Lost, after all besides, her human shape;
> Her weird new barking terrified the breeze.
>
> (Ovid 1987: 306)

Atkinson returned to Ovid again in her collection of short stories *Not the End of the World* (2002). Here, we encounter metamorphoses and transformations of various kinds, all based in recognizable modern contexts, a fact underlined by Atkinson's easy allusions to brand names and popular television programmes of the day. We meet, for example, Eddie, the product of a transgressive sexual liaison between his mother and Neptune the sea-god during a memorable Cretan summer holiday; this story knowingly recalls those of Pasiphaë and the bull, Leda and the swan, and numerous other tales of Jovean transformation into the shape of fish, animal or fowl to seduce women in the *Metamorphoses*. Enhancing our notion as readers of Atkinson herself as a kind of Arachne, weaving a web of tales together, each story finds resonance and echo in each other: characters recur, family connections are uncovered and, in one story, a car crash is witnessed by a passerby who in a previous tale has revealed to us a gruesome encounter with death in the shape of Hades on the M9 motorway. The entire collection is framed by the tragicomic story of Charlene and Trudi, who find the reliable luxuries of modern life and shopping malls disintegrating before their eyes following what appears to be a nuclear attack.

Atkinson's stories, as the collection's title both indicates and teasingly denies via the deployment of cliché, provide an apocalyptic image of millennial British society. Another writer who has deployed Ovid to a quasi-apocalyptic end is Salman Rushdie in his controversial novel *The Satanic Verses* (1988). For Rushdie, however, metamorphosis becomes the means not just of imagining fantastical transformation, although his novel features many such examples, but rather the specific condition of the late twentieth-century migrant. Sadly, this topic has become ever more pertinent in the wake of a global crisis some twenty-five years or more after the novel's first publication, as thousands of migrants take to the high seas in peril of their lives on a weekly basis. The epigraph to the novel, taken from Daniel Defoe's non-fictional work *The Political History of the Devil* (1726), provides a clue. It describes Satan as a vagabond, recalling in turn the wandering exile of John Milton's canonical epic poem *Paradise Lost* (1667). The parallel with the modern migrant condition becomes clearest in the description of the devil as a person of 'unsettled condition ... without any certain abode'. In the implicitly conservative value assigned by the Defoe quotation to being 'placed', to being of fixed abode and society, Rushdie identifies a partial cause of the misplaced fear of immigrants by those communities they seek to join. Rushdie's magic realism is central to his appropriation of Ovid, and specifically the text of the *Metamorphoses*. He invokes Ovid to create a fantastic world of hybrid shapes and mythical creatures, but then uses these creations to discuss social reality and global issues.

We start the novel with a 'fall'. That phrase has resonance in the Christian theological context, evoking the descent of the bad angels from heaven to hell as well as Eve and Adam's transgression in the Garden of Eden. Rushdie is not afraid to play with these concepts of the fall as both downfall and act of creation. In this sense, the fall is symbolic, and yet the novel's opening is the starkly literal fall of two Bollywood actors from an Air India plane that has been exploded by hijackers (the novel has accrued further resonance following subsequent world events, including 9/11). Describing this moment, Rushdie evokes mythic parallels by referencing the fall of Icarus: 'Just climbed too high, got above themselves, flew too close to the sun, is that it?' (Rushdie 1998 [1988]: 5). It is significant that our protagonists are actors; their trade is one of representation in a novel that suggests that modern life itself has become a simulacrum of reality. The influence here of Jean Baudrillard's theories on Rushdie is palpable. In

Simulacra and Simulation (1981) Baudrillard argued that it was part of the postmodern condition that artificial, constructed worlds such as Disneyland or the cinema would come in time to appear more 'real' than reality. As we now move in the world of virtual reality, avatars and online communities, that suggestion has also accrued resonance.

That Rushdie's actors originate from Bombay and 'Bollywood' filmmaking emphasizes this hyper-real world of Baudrillardian simulacra at play in the novel. Bollywood has fashioned a reputation based on the appropriation of mythic templates and existent stories to create stock plots to great acclaim; even its nickname is an allusion to a supposed US precursor (Hollywood) in this respect. Rushdie finds humour in this: 'Bombay was a culture of re-makes. Its architecture mimicked the skyscraper, its cinema endlessly reinvented *The Magnificent Seven* ...' (1998 [1988]: 64). But his vision is at the same time troubled by this assumption that all Indian artistic creations have a Western 'original' or source. This concern corresponds with much postcolonial writing about the need to challenge or subvert these supposed 'originating sources', as we saw in earlier discussion of Henry Louis Gates Jr's theory of 'signifyin''. In the specific Rushdie quotation the joke is actually on the reader who fails to notice that *The Magnificent Seven* in its 1960 Hollywood version was in fact an intercultural cinematic appropriation of a film of Asian origin, Japanese director Akira Kurosawa's *The Seven Samurai* (1954). This in turn set a precedent for director Sergio Leone, whose 'spaghetti westerns' *A Fistful of Dollars* (1964) and *A Few Dollars More* (1965) were derived from another Kurosawa film, *Yojimbo* (1961), and indeed occasioned protracted legal hearings about the rights to remake the Japanese original.

As the two actors, Gibreel and Saladin, fall through what Rushdie describes as the ultimate modern site of 'air-space' (1998 [1988]: 5), what they witness is Ovidian in quality: 'pushing their way out of the white, came a succession of cloud forms, ceaselessly metamorphosing, gods into bulls, women into spiders, men into wolves' (6). The men land in 1980s London, a place that both is and is not the capital, because it so tangibly fails to live up to their expectations. In *The Satanic Verses*, London and Bombay provide parallel examples of metamorphic, unstable cities. For Saladin Chamcha, formerly Salauddin Chamchawala, whose UK-schooled father was significantly named Changez Chamchawala, the pain of disappointment is particularly deep. To assimilate into British society, Saladin attempts to alter his personality and appearance as well as his name, only succeeding in the process in totally estranging himself from his Indian family and background. In the face of this failed metamorphosis, however, his body seems unable to halt the process of destabilizing change. This results in the comic grotesque episode in the back of a 'Black Maria' or London police van, when Saladin, now in the shape of a satyr – half-man, half-goat – is arrested and brutally beaten by British police officers. What Rushdie finds in this Ovidian image of mutability is a means of suggesting the reduction of men like Chamcha to the status of beasts by the minds of the prejudicial minority who carried out widespread racist attacks in 1980s Great Britain.

Rushdie captures in his mythical appropriation the dehumanized behaviour of those who perpetrate racial violence. Ovid's swirling world of minotaurs, satyrs and centaurs is evoked not as an abstract 'world elsewhere' but as a parable by means of which to address the brutalities and injustices of an equally hybrid contemporary England. Only in the magical night-time escape from the hospital of Saladin and hundreds of fellow 'beasts' – similarly brutalized asylum seekers and detainees – does Rushdie allow himself and the reader a moment of fantastic optimism. This is a striking example of the amplification and ripening of myth advanced by Genette and Barthes. The Ovidian myth of metamorphosis is not lost in the process of adaptation but, rather, much is gained.

The meta-language of myth is deployed in these examples as an accessible code to discuss and communicate complex issues. In turn the persistently adaptable and malleable myth is given a newly relevant social and cultural geography by the adapters. Metamorphosis would seem a particularly apposite concept in this respect, but other Ovidian narratives have offered comparative potential for creative reworking, in particular the tale of Orpheus, the artist whose story persists beyond his narrative ending, beyond death. To an era interested in self-conscious accounts of the artistic process this story has proved especially durable, exhibiting what Linda Hutcheon calls 'narrative persistence' (2013: xxi) across genres and cultures.

ORPHIC NARRATIVES

'Once and for all, it's Orpheus wherever there is song.'
Rainer Maria Rilke, *Sonette an Orpheus* (1928)

Orpheus, a musician of great skill, marries the beautiful nymph Eurydice but she is killed by a fatal snakebite on their wedding day. Stricken with grief, Orpheus descends into the underworld to beg for his dead wife's return to the living. Because his music is so moving the gods of the underworld grant his wish, but on one condition: that when leading Eurydice out of Hades he does not look back at her. Whether out of love, fear or anxiety, Orpheus breaks this condition and Eurydice dies a second time. Barred from further re-entry to the underworld, Orpheus retires to woodland, mad with grief, shunning the company of all women. There, a group of jealous females dismember him in a moment of Bacchic frenzy, and in some versions of the tale Orpheus's decapitated head continues to sing until he can be symbolically reunited with Eurydice in the underworld. Ovid was not the first to recount this story; Virgil had included it in Book 4 of the *Georgics*. Nevertheless, the significance of its placement in the narrative of the *Metamorphoses* has meant that Orpheus's story is inextricably linked with that work. The narrative of Orpheus and Eurydice takes place in Book 10 and his death is related in Book 11. Perhaps most significantly, Ovid's Orpheus is both a subject and a teller of stories. When he retires to the wilderness in his state of grief, he finds solace in singing tales which are warnings to resist 'destructive passion' (Bate 1993: 54). These tales include those of Ganymede, Hyacinth, Pygmalion, Myrrha, Venus and Adonis, and Atalanta. Orpheus's function as an embedded storyteller within the Ovidian narrative partly explains his availability to adapters and appropriators of subsequent centuries and generations. He is a prototype of the artist, be it as musician, painter, storyteller or poet, and this aspect of his story propels allusions to his work across the centuries in the poetry of Milton, Shelley and Browning, among others (Miles 1999: 61–195).

What we are dealing with in much mythic appropriation is an interest in archetypes. If Orpheus is viewed as the prototype of the artist, so his relationship with Eurydice is deployed as literary shorthand for extreme and enduring love. As with Romeo and Juliet, or Tristan and Isolde (or Tristan and Iseult in their Cornish folktale context), Orpheus and Eurydice have become archetypes of passionate love, their story reappearing in diverse cultural and generic contexts from opera to contemporary film, from Brazil to South London. This availability for reworking gestures at the dual potentiality in myth identified by Barthes's transcultural theory of a meta-language, but also by his articulation of the significance of culturally-specific contexts for the consumption of myth. The process of 'universalization', then, a term so often coupled with the notion of archetype, is for Barthes a deeply political and politicized activity (1993 [1972]: 142–5). Myth as archetype concerns itself with themes that endure or persist across cultural and historical boundaries: love, death, family, revenge. These themes might in some context be deemed 'universal', and yet the essence of adaptation and appropriation renders the archetype specific, localized and particular to the moment of (re-)creation.

The 1950s Brazilian film *Orfeu Negro* or *Black Orpheus* (dir. Marcel Camus, 1959) retains character names and the essential plotline of Orpheus and Eurydice's doomed passion but chooses to relocate the Ovidian narrative to the very contemporary setting of the Rio de Janeiro carnival, a 'movement of proximation' in Genette's previously cited terms (1997: 304). The Orpheus of this film is a musician of considerable skill, in addition to being a ticket collector on the Rio tram network. Early on we see him repurchasing his guitar from a pawnshop, one of the film's numerous allusions to the poverty in which this modern mythical hero resides; he lives in a shanty town or *favela* on the hillside overlooking the Brazilian capital. At one point, he persuades two young boys from the *favela*, whose gaze in some sense provides the audience point of view in this film, that his guitar, the equivalent to Orpheus's lyre, has the power to make the sun rise and set. The sartorial association of Orpheus with the sun in this film (this is his carnival costume and *persona*) draws on the suggestion in many versions of the myth that Orpheus was the son of Apollo. At the very end of the film, when, true to his story, as the myth dictates, Orpheus has been murdered by a horde of jealous women, the sun becomes a symbol of regeneration. One of the boys picks up Orpheus's guitar as the sun starts to rise. At that very moment, a young girl dressed all in white joins him and begins to dance, instructing the young guitarist that he is now Orpheus. Eurydice herself was dressed in white when we first saw her, so this visual suggestion here is very much that the lovers live on beyond death through transmission of their love in art, in song, story and film. There is a self-consciousness throughout *Black Orpheus* that we have already identified as a common trope of appropriations: a knowingness about the relationships and similarities to an archetypal source. A marriage registrar jokingly tells Orpheus, persuaded by his fiancée Mira to obtain a marriage licence, that his bride-to-be's name should in fact be Eurydice, and when Orpheus first meets her at her cousin's residence, he laughs: 'Wonderful, I have loved you for a thousand years … it's a very old story.' There is a sense in which their names predestine their tragic fate; this Orpheus and Eurydice cannot escape the fatal outcomes of their literary forebears. This particular story is doomed to repeat itself.

This act of repetition is, however, highly specific in cultural, temporal and geographical terms. The *mise-en-scène* of *Black Orpheus* provides a striking version of the mythic underworld. The entire film revolves around the passion and frenzy of the Rio carnival, as did the Brazilian stage play by Vinicius de Moraes, *Orfeu da Conceição* (1956), on which the film is based. As well as invoking the familiar associations of the carnivalesque in the wake of influential theories by Mikhail Bakhtin (see Bakhtin 1984 [1968]; Dentith 1995) which argue that carnival offers temporary popular release from everyday hierarchies, inequalities and injustices, the day's revelries in Rio provide a dangerous parallel to the Bacchic intoxication of the avenging women in the Orphic myth. The audience becomes swept up in the passion and excitement of the moment as participants, with the soundscape of the film ensuring that, from the opening credits, the penetrating drumbeat of the carnival procession pervades ears and minds. Eurydice is pursued through the crowds and revellers of carnival by a figure in the skeletal costume of Death to the tram terminus where Orpheus usually works and where she first met her now lover at the start of the film. Playing on the word 'terminus', part of the film's texture of verbal puns, further evidence of its knowingness, the tram depot provides the dark space in which she meets her fate: the ominous red lighting and threatening buzz of the electricity cables adding to a sense of foreboding. In the next sequence we witness an ambulance speeding through the city streets with Death riding post. The ambulance enters a road tunnel that is a modern evocation of Charon the ferryman taking people across the River Styx and into the underworld: this is the point of no return, as the Orphic myth makes clear. On the hillsides and slopes of Rio, we see the spread-eagled bodies of drunken post-carnival revellers, and it is no coincidence that they resemble corpses, the lost souls of the mythic underworld. 'Carnival is over', as one police officer informs them.

Black Orpheus is simultaneously strikingly original and highly referential; its urban vision of the 'underworld' owes as much to Jean Cocteau's experimental film version *Orphée* (1950), an earlier reimagining of the Orpheus myth set in a post-war Parisian context, as to classical myth. Cocteau's contribution can be viewed as part of a broader mid-twentieth-century engagement with the Orphic myth across the genres of both stage play and feature film. In 1957 Tennessee Williams's play *Orpheus Descending* was performed for a short run on Broadway. It was itself an adaptation of the playwright's earlier drama *Battle of the Angels*, and tells the story, in Williams's own rich idiom, of 'a wild-spirited boy who wanders into a conventional community in the South of the United States', that is, classic Williams territory, 'and creates the commotion of a fox in a chicken coop' (Williams 2001: 238). Two Rivers is the Mississippi town and Val Xavier the proverbial fox, a Louisiana Orpheus, a snakeskin jacket-wearing guitar player who arrives by train from New Orleans with the scent of sexuality and possibility attached to him. Deeply erotic encounters with two local women and the frenzied suspicions of locals lead to a dramatic climax, with the Torrance dry-goods store torched by an armed Bacchanalian male gathering which has come there to drive Val from town. There are obvious ways in which Williams engages with contemporary politics here, albeit in sideways fashion, with the civil rights agenda in the Deep South at this time and the ever-present peril of the lynch mob and the Ku Klux Klan; though it is also a play about timeless but fated passion: 'A good looking boy like you is always wanted', Val is informed by one of the local men, with an obvious play on the term 'wanted' in this context (Act 2, Scene 2: 326). The fatal 'look back' in this retelling of the Orpheus and Eurydice tale comes towards the close of the second act, when Lady and Val finally give in to the obvious sexual chemistry that exists between them. Val, who has been employed as a temporary night watchman for the store (something of an irony since his presence there will lead to its complete destruction in the closing moments of the drama), steps into the alcove where his bed is made up and begins to draw the curtain: '*he looks back at her*' (314). This will be a fated sexual union that ends in both life and death, since we will later learn that Lady is pregnant, and it was prefigured earlier in a stage direction towards the close of the first act when their relationship is in its embryonic stages: '[*He crosses towards the door as a dog barks with passionate clarity in the distance. He turns to smile back at her.*]' (280).

Echoing the Orphic association with music and song, the entire play is underscored by Val's guitar playing, and the symbolism of that particular loaded artefact onstage is inescapable when in Act One it is with the guitar rather than the man that Lady first makes physical contact: '*He goes out … Then she turns and wonderingly picks up and runs her hand tenderly over his guitar as the curtain falls.*]' (280). The play was re-made just two years later as a film, *The Fugitive Kind* (dir. Sidney Lumet, 1959), starring Marlon Brando in the role of Xavier, with the snakeskin jacket and guitar still to the fore. The casting of screen heartthrob Brando again placed the Orpheus myth at the heart of popular cultural concerns and fashions of the day, and the film version's title was an adapted reference to one of Williams's stage directions, which described Carol Cutrere as having 'an odd fugitive beauty' (254). In 1994 the play and its particular brand of Southern Gothic was reconfigured once again, this time as a two-act opera by Bruce Saylor, in a sense bringing the story full circle back to music.

In *Black Orpheus* it is the aptly named Hermes, the blind man who earlier gave Eurydice directions on her arrival in Rio, who informs Orpheus of his lover's death. In mythological terms, Hermes is a messenger but also the god of transportation, hence his association with the particular space of the tram depot in that film. He is by tradition also the spiritual guide to the underworld, so it is he who takes Orpheus to the local mortuary to find Eurydice. Section 12 of the mortuary proves to be, in a literal sense, the site of 'lost souls'. There are no bodies to be found there, only a janitor drowning in stacks of paperwork. In this way, there is a quiet but disturbing analogy with the anonymous world of modern bureaucracy as well as the sad fate of missing persons in South America throughout much of the twentieth century. Travelling down stairwells lit by a reddish hue, Orpheus passes a barking guard dog; this is Cerberus, the many-headed canine who guards the gates of the underworld. Eventually Orpheus finds himself in a room of white-robed singers and dancers in a state of trance or drug-induced intoxication, a hellish version of a *voodoo* ritual. Orpheus's song is invited to conjure Eurydice, but although he hears her voice, on that fatal turn what he sees is an old woman performing the role of medium for her words. His abject sense of loss is articulated in the terms of social injustice alluded to elsewhere and which pervade the film: 'I am poorer than the poorest negro' is the translation in the 1950s subtitles. Further emphasizing the end of carnival as event and condition, we then observe Orpheus carrying Eurydice's corpse through streets that are being cleaned by refuse trucks, the debris of the night visible everywhere.

Only music seems to provide a means of endurance at the film's close, surviving beyond the end of carnival, and in some ways outlasting or transcending even the fixed stone sculptures of the lovers which return to sight in the closing credits. The story of Orpheus and Eurydice has undoubtedly continued through the ages and crossed cultures. Any claim to 'universality', however, runs the concomitant risk of de-historicizing the particular choices of the individual work of art. The soundtrack of *Black Orpheus* is as located and specific as the Rio carnival that provides its central location and spectacle, and the roots of both in the complex legacy of Portuguese colonialism deserve acknowledgement.

There is, then, certainly a case to be made for the structural adaptability of certain archetypal stories – this is the essence of structuralist readings in literature and anthropology – but we must, as readers and spectators, remain alert to the specific contexts, political, cultural and aesthetic, of each new version. *Black Orpheus* has itself been reworked more recently by the Brazilian director Carlos Diegues as *Orfeu* (1999). In this version the carnival and *favela* settings are retained (as is Jobim's music from the original film) but in the crucial 'movement of proximation' the figure of Death in millennial Brazil becomes a local drug-dealer. The 'universal' love story is once more shockingly recontextualized in order to speak to contemporary social issues.

Yet a further example of this in terms of screen geographies can be found in the Bombay/Mumbai slum communities that are at the heart of the Danny Boyle and Loveleen Tandan-directed 2008 film *Slumdog Millionaire*, itself an adaptation of Vikas Swarup's novel *Q & A* (2005). Ostensibly premised on the television blockbuster game show *Who Wants to Be a Millionaire?*, the film nevertheless interweaves the Orpheus and Eurydice myth into its frame in a number of ways, although this time eventually with a 'happy ending'. Jamal Malik (Dev Patel) searches throughout the film for Latika (Freida Pinto), the girl he met in tragic circumstances during the 1990s Bombay Riots, here played out with fire and violence in the shockingly close confines of the Juhu slum tenements (one of several 'hellish' visions in the film). Latika is left behind in a night-time escape from child abusers by a cruel act of Jamal's brother, who deliberately lets go of her hand rather than lift her up onto the train which is their route out; 'She's history' is what Salim chillingly says to Jamal at this point, though the phrase can also be thought of as signifying that Latika links to other archetypal lost women in tragic love stories. Visually the film signals the link to Jamal's first backward glance to the left-behind Latika wearing a yellow dress by costuming her as an adult with a signature and signifying yellow shawl. Certainly, the film re-creates this moment of Jamal looking back to see Latika left behind in several revised contexts and sequences. But the link to the Eurydice story is made explicit by the decision to deploy a sequence at the Taj Mahal, to where the young brothers have travelled and where they are making a covert living as tour guides, where a production of an eighteenth-century operatic version by Christoph Gluck is being performed. In a film whose soundscape is central to its production of meaning and the cultural geography it depicts, and where a joyous Bollywood pastiche dance number plays over the closing credits, the importance of this piece of product placement to the love story unfolding should not be underestimated.

The role of music in the Orpheus story suggests the transcendence of art. The Bollywood dance sequence that closes *Slumdog Millionaire* or the children dancing to guitar music as the sun rises over Rio in *Black Orpheus* are part of this story, as is Baz Luhrmann's 2001 film musical *Moulin Rouge*. In his magic realist evocation of 1890s Paris and the Pigalle and Montmartre area's infamous Moulin Rouge nightclub, Luhrmann produces a *tour de force* of filmmaking. *Moulin Rouge* is a musical extravaganza which signals its origins in the great Hollywood tradition through knowing visual allusions to Busby Berkeley and Fred Astaire, as well as to more avant-garde contributions to the form such as Bob Fosse's *Cabaret*. But *Moulin Rouge* is also a postmodern reinvention of the genre. Postmodernism, as well as evincing an interest in intertextuality, has exhibited a penchant for pastiche and quotation as simultaneous acts of re-creation and fragmentation (Hoesterey 2001; Sim 2001). Luhrmann carefully researched his *fin-de-siècle* Parisian *mise-en-scène* and the history of the Moulin Rouge but also deliberately ruptured that precise historical re-creation by selecting a soundtrack from his own time of growing up in the 1970s–1990s. In a similarly disjunctive mode, costumes in the film are painstakingly copied from the paintings and sketches of Henri Toulouse-Lautrec of performers from the time, La Goulue and Jane Avril, and yet are worn by singers and dancers performing the works of David Bowie, T-Rex, Nirvana, Elton John and Madonna. There is a deliberate clash of periods and contexts, drawing instructive parallels in the process between the excesses of the late twentieth century and the previous *fin-de-siècle*.

A further diachronic parallel is implicit in Luhrmann's aesthetic: the Bohemian artistes of Montmartre are described as the 'children of the revolution'. Not only does this enable Luhrmann to play Marc Bolan's song of the same name as a kind of refrain, but it also evokes the 1960s peace movement. The Indian and South-East Asian aspects of the play-within-the-film created by the English writer Christian evoke 1890s Paris and its interest in the exotic alongside 1960s flirtation with eastern religion, and the 1990s explosion of Bollywood film aesthetics into the Hollywood main-stream. Bollywood, as noted earlier, is a genre partly determined by processes of adaptation, and its aesthetics are therefore ideally suited to Luhrmann's postmodern and eclectic directorial style. These references, however, carry more than purely artistic reso-nance in the film as they reach out to its investment in the adap-tation of myth and musical for the modern era and to the specific engagement with the 'timeless' yet 'timely' story of Orpheus and Eurydice.

When we first enter the deliberately inauthentic model-world of Paris in the film, Toulouse-Lautrec is singing at the window of the fake windmill that provided the façade to the real Moulin Rouge building. The camera then zooms across the cityscape to the entrance to the village of Montmartre, which is marked by a hell-mouth gateway, resonant of those used on the medieval stages and scaffolds of mystery and morality drama. There are also visual links to the hellish landscapes depicted by the paintings of Hier-onymus Bosch in the fifteenth and sixteenth centuries. Luhrmann's frame of reference is both plural and highly localized since there was a hell-mouth entrance to the aptly-named *Cabaret d'enfer* (Cabaret of Hell) that stood opposite the Moulin Rouge on Place Blanche, with its infamous façade depicting the falling figures of damned souls (Milner 1988: 140). The underworld associations of the nightclub are brilliantly signified by this image, a reading further strengthened by the words of Christian's father, who warns him against entering this dangerous society: 'Turn away from this village of sin, this Sodom and Gomorrah.' Christian's overlaid first-person narrative confirms the connection: 'Moulin Rouge. A nightclub, a dance-hall, and a bordello, ruled over by Harold Zidler, the king-dom of night-time pleasure where the rich and powerful come to play with the young and beautiful creatures of the underworld.' If Christian is our Orpheus, descending into the seductive underworld of Zidler's nightclub – Moulin Rouge's real owner was Charles Zidler (Hanson and Hanson 1956: 128) – where the dominant colour palette is fiery orange and reds, and where the momentarily lit sails of the windmill resemble red pitchforks in the sky, then his Eurydice is the courtesan and performer Satine. Christian and Satine's great passion is expressed through music and song throughout the film and is perhaps best encapsulated in their duet 'Come What May', with its central lyric: 'I will love you till my dying day'. Their love is, however, as the myth instructs us, doomed, as fated and temporary in the material world of the nightclub as the passion of their mythic forebears: Satine, unbeknownst to Christian or herself, is dying of tuberculosis.

The myth of Orpheus and Eurydice is only one of several informing subtexts for *Moulin Rouge*. Giacomo Puccini's *fin-de-siècle* opera *La Bohème* (first performed in 1896), set in the Paris wintertime of the 1840s, is another crucial focus of allusion. In that opera, which Luhrmann went on to direct in New York following the filming of *Moulin Rouge*, a group of students, artists, musicians, singers and writers struggle to survive in a Paris garret. Rodolfo, an author, falls in love with Mimi and the couple form the focus of several duets in a manner akin to Christian and Satine in the film. Mimi too is suffering from tuberculosis and her death provides the opera's poignant finale. The parallels with *Moulin Rouge*, which, as with Luhrmann's *Romeo + Juliet*, signals its indebtedness to opera in general as well as to the musical in the structures and references of its soundtrack, are self-evident. Another opera clearly referenced here is Guiseppe Verdi's *La Traviata* (1852), based in turn on Alexandre Dumas fils's *La Dame aux Camelias* or *The Lady of the Camellias* (1848), which tells another tragic love story and has yet another doomed courtesan as its heroine, Marguerite, who is also dying of consumption.

La Bohème of course shares the nineteenth-century Parisian locale of *Moulin Rouge* in ways that the Orphic underworld can never quite. Nevertheless there are moments in Luhrmann's film when the Orpheus and Eurydice story rises to the surface with real force, nowhere more so than in the culminating play-within-the film, authored by Christian, about a penniless sitar player. Once again the Indian influences are equally strong and meld with the classical inheritances; Luhrmann himself has spoken of the impact on the film's aesthetic of a visit to India and the powerful effects of seeing a Bollywood movie, with its rapid code-switching between comedy and tragedy:

> When I was in India researching *Midsummer Night's Dream*, we went to this huge, icecream picture palace to see a Bollywood movie. Here we were, with 2,000 Indians watching a film in Hindi, and there was the lowest possible comedy and then incredible drama and tragedy and then break out in songs. And it was three-and-a-half-hours! We thought we had suddenly learned Hindi because we understood everything! ... We thought it was incredible. How involved the audience were. How uncool they were – how their coolness had been ripped aside and how they were united in this singular sharing of the story. The thrill of thinking, 'Could we ever do that in the West? Could we ever get past that cerebral cool and perceived cool.' It required this idea of comic-tragedy. Could you make those switches? Fine in Shakespeare – low comedy and then you die in five minutes ... In *Moulin Rouge*, we went further. Our recognizable story, though Orphean in shape, is derived from *Camille, La Boheme* – whether you know those texts or not, you recognize those patterns and character types.
>
> (Andrew 2001)

Luhrmann brilliantly captures here the multiple levels on which audience members might respond to deeply layered and allusive texts of this kind depending on their different code-sharing and on which elements of the story are 'recognizable' to them.

Certainly those viewers alert to the Orphic narrative respond to the film's closing sequences through this lens. Informed by Zidler that she is dying of TB and that her suitor, the duke, intends to kill Christian, Satine casts her lover off in a self-sacrificing effort to save his life. Subsequently we witness his painful attempts to gain re-entry to the underworld of the nightclub from which he has been expelled, only to be cast into the gutter by the duke's henchmen. Finally Christian obtains access and, breaking the frame of the performance, walks onstage to reject Satine in public, since he imagines her to have betrayed him for personal financial gain. As he walks away down the theatre's central aisle, Satine starts to sing their song. In a vital twist on Orpheus's persuasion of the underworld through his power of song, it is Satine who hails him back to her through the power of emotion in her voice. But, of course, he has turned around, and when the curtain falls on the performance, Satine dies in his arms, echoing the endlessly repeated stage deaths of the operatic protagonists of *La Bohème* and *La Traviata*.

Black Orpheus and *Moulin Rouge* appear to embody the truth of Rilke's claim in the epigraph to this section that 'it's Orpheus, whenever there is song'; and another even more recent appropriation, this time in novel form, Richard Powers's *Orfeo* (2014), would seem to bear that out. Powers's novel, a complex rumination on music and mortality, centres on the avant-garde composer Peter Els, now looking back on his life, and several failed but significant relationships. It manages to combine Orphic undertows with a very modern story of bio-terrorism and the power of social media channels. What, though, is a reader to make of a novel that features neither music nor song, and does not signal its Orphic connections or codes in the knowing ways that Camus, Luhrmann and even Powers do?

Graham Swift's *The Light of Day* is, I suggest, an Orpheus appropriation by way of 'critical proxy', as Chantal Zabus terms it (2002: 121). It is not something that the creator has signalled to us in any explicit fashion. As earlier discussions of Swift's intertextual style have indicated, his refusal to cite his sources has troubled some critics (see Chapter 2). Certainly, Swift's work is never so dependent on an informing source that failure to recognize it would render it incomprehensible; lack of foreknowledge of the resonance of the Orpheus story will not prohibit or prevent any satisfactory reading of *The Light of Day*, with its intricately related themes of exile, detection and love. Nevertheless, the reader who approaches the novel with an active sense of the subtextual depth provided by the Orpheus myth has the opportunity for additional production of meaning(s), which can only enrich an experience of the narrative. Swift's decision, for example, to mention only a few chapters from the novel's end the cave network that exists under Chislehurst is reasonable enough in the geographical setting of the novel, but if the reader is aware that, in both Virgil's and Ovid's versions of the myth, Orpheus descends to the underworld by means of a cave, then this simple connection of caves with underworlds, and by extension with the Orpheus and Eurydice story, brings myth into the everyday world of the novel in exciting ways.

What we are doing by recognizing the mythic pull of Swift's novel is expanding the potential network of meanings available to the interactive reader. It is a classic example of the ways in which this form of embedded intertextuality, one that does not signal or demand an intertextual interpretative framework for any reading, as some explicit adaptations might, depends crucially upon the reader's recognition of the subtexts and intertexts involved. It is a working example, then, of Iser's theory of reader-reception: manipulation and control is certainly exerted by the text upon the reader, but the reading process remains reliant upon different and differing modes of collaboration between reader and narrative in the production of meanings (Iser 2001: 179–84).

What Swift's novel ultimately proves is that it is often in the mundane, quotidian world of supermarkets, crematoria and suburban kitchens that the deepest passions are at work. Swift's title, *The Light of Day*, a phrase that contributes the closing words of the novel, has multiple connotations. The first-person narrator is George Webb, a failed policeman turned private detective, regularly charged by suspicious wives with the task of proving their husbands' adultery by bringing to 'the light of day' firm evidence, frequently in the form of photographs of them 'caught in the act'. Photography is a medium whose ability both to see clearly and to occlude has troubled Swift in a previous novel, *Out of This World* (1989), about a war photo-journalist. In *The Light of Day* the photographic images bring the fact of adultery into the open while being unable to tell the full story of the relationships they depict. This in turn becomes a metaphor for George's narrative, which is fragmentary and incomplete in many respects. He acknowledges that there are some things that simply cannot be said or revealed, which cannot be brought to light.

If George puns openly on his forename, stressing that his sordid profession means that he is no 'saint George', it is his surname that transports the active reader into the mythic realms which I am proposing can be brought to bear on this narrative. Web(b)s and weaving carry potent meaning in classical literature, from Homer's *Odyssey*, with Penelope weaving and unweaving her father-in-law's shroud in an effort to fend off suitors during her husband's nineteen-year absence on his epic journey, to Ovid's *Metamorphoses*, where Arachne's tapestry provides the space for several inset stories to be incorporated in a manner akin to Orpheus's song. The webs of connection that Swift's novel encourages carry us as readers across a line from the everyday into the underworlds and recesses of myth. In the same way that the novel imbues commonplace or clichéd phrases with new relevance and resonance – such as 'crossing a line', 'missing persons', 'safe as houses' and 'time to kill' – so the mythic subtexts encourage us to reassess what we are reading, to go beneath the surface, as it were, and bring new things into sight.

For George, the underworld in which his very modern suburban Eurydice is trapped is the British prison system. The focus of his loyal, even obsessive, affection is Sarah, a former client. She, as we only deduce gradually from George's digressive narrative, employed the private detective to ensure that her husband really was ending a relationship with their Croatian-born *au pair*. But Sarah murdered her husband at the very moment when he seemed to have returned to the folds of their married life. This is an act for which a full explanation is never provided and yet about which there is endless speculation in the novel. The narrative is again retrospective; looking back over a period of two years, George's troubled recollections and half-recollections are just one example of many instances of looking back that take place in the narrative. As for Orpheus, this is an action fraught with danger and loss, revealing in the process painful truths as well as suppressions of actuality. This is a text in part about suppression, one in which everything is not brought into the clear light of day; in which motives and actions remain shrouded in darkness, emotions unspoken, issues unresolved. Bob, Sarah's husband, enacts several poignant gestures, real and imagined, of looking back. Leaving the flat in which he had installed his mistress for supposedly the last time, he looks back, as if recalling the previous passionate encounters the space had contained: 'He walked round to his driver's door and before getting in and with an odd quick wrench of the head, looked up, looked round, looked back' (Swift 2003: 126). There is also something furtive, even guilty, about that action, of course, in the eyes of a private detective. Later, driving behind the car in which Bob is transporting his mistress to the airport, George wonders if Bob looks back at his hospital workplace (141). Following the airport lounge separation of the former lovers, Bob returns to their flat one last time. As with Orpheus, this could be interpreted as his fatal mistake. The gesture of looking back – 'That last strange quick lift of his head before he got in the car' (132) – makes him late in returning to the house that he shares with Sarah. This in turn plants in her mind a seed of doubt as to how the future will turn out between them, possibly provoking the fatal stabbing, though the narrative never clarifies any of these points.

What is clear from this reading is that appropriation of Orpheus's story is mediated through at least two characters. Both Bob and George function as Orpheus to a degree; both descend into underworlds; both are engaged in perilous acts of return, of looking back. In a similar vein, Swift's re-creation of the 'underworld' here is present through several of the carefully managed spaces and places of this novel. If the topography of London is all too tangible in Swift's deliberately prosaic narrative, the shadow-world of myth provides an alternative psychic map. It is as if Swift's narrator resides in the same limbo as Bendrix, the first-person narrator of Graham Greene's *The End of the Affair* (1951). Bendrix is another retrospective and digressive narrator suffering from an obsession over a lost love: 'If this book of mine fails to take a straight course, it is because I am lost in a strange region: I have no map' (Greene 2001: 50). Swift's sparing dialogue has often been compared to Greene's, and, intriguingly, in a review of the novel Hermione Lee suggested *The End of the Affair* as a possible intertext for *The Light of Day*. In both texts the female protagonist, obsessed by the first-person narrator, is called Sarah; both are retrospectives of love and loss; and yet it is as if in Swift's novel the focus on Bendrix has been displaced and centre-stage has been accorded to Greene's comic detective Parkis (Swift 2003: 9). Certainly in both novels Sarah herself remains distanced from the reader, an enigma at the heart of the text. The same might be said of Eurydice; often silenced completely in underworld sequences in the myth, she has also been sidelined in many subsequent retellings of the story, placed back into the shadows by an artistic self-interest in the figure of Orpheus. Revisiting the story from a feminist perspective, however, a number of female artists in the twentieth century sought to give her a voice, including H. D. in her eponymous poem of 1917, where the heroine castigates Orpheus's 'arrogance' ('Eurydice', 1. 6, cited in Miles 1999: 159–62) in electing to look back and doom her to the darkness of Hades a second time when, as Virgil so poignantly points out, she was 'on the lip of/ Daylight' (Virgil 1983: 125). This is an example of what Rachel Blau DuPlessis describes as the 'poetics of rupture and critique' that myth is constantly subjected to by women writers (1985: 32).

There are recurring images of darkness in *The Light of Day*; George is constantly positioned in the shadows or in spaces only partially penetrated by light, from his office and car, to various police interview rooms, to the prison waiting room where he visits his Eurydice. The latter encounters provide the rhythm and ritual of his otherwise oddly empty existence. Driving away from the crematorium where he has taken flowers to mark the anniversary of Bob's death, yet another instance of looking back, he describes re-entering the road system as launching himself 'back into the world' (Swift 2003: 135); later, the queue of prison visitors appear to all intents and purposes souls in limbo. The underworld is, then, everywhere and everyday in this novel, remarkable by its being so unremarkable. What the mention of the caves beneath Chislehurst in the closing chapter achieves is to bring into the frame a mythic world of revenants and returns and irreversible actions: 'The echoes, the maze of tunnels, the stories of ghosts. The feeling that you might never get back into the light' (237). The narrative ends with George hoping for the day when Sarah will be released into his arms, into 'the clear light of day'. This can be read optimistically, but any reader alert by now to the Orpheus and Eurydice myth cannot help but fear for the way this story might unfold. The all-too familiar paradigms of myth and the understood terms of encounter between adaptation and the active reader allow Swift to leave much unsaid.

Ovidian metamorphoses and Orphic narratives have serviced a very diverse range of cultural appropriations. In some, though not all, of these reworkings and revisitings that interrelationship is explicit; in others the intertextuality operates in a subterranean mode, occurring beneath the surface narrative. In all instances an awareness of the informing and underpinning myths alters our responses as readers to the adaptive and appropriative texts. Mythic paradigms provide the reader or spectator with a series of familiar reference points or anchors and a set of expectations which the novelist, artist, director, playwright, composer or poet can rely upon as an instructive shorthand, while simultaneously exploiting, twisting and relocating them in newly creative ways, and in newly resonant contexts. Frequently, political commitment informs and influences these acts of re-creation, for, as DuPlessis notes, 'To change a story signals a dissent from social norms as well as narrative forms' (1985: 20). We are entering in this discussion the tricky domain of authorial 'intention', a world which in some respects Barthes's notion of the reader as an active creator of meanings ought to eschew, and yet it seems unavoidable in any genuine study of the motivations behind adaptational art forms (Patterson 1987: 135–46). In works of adaptation and appropriation, political awareness, and even sometimes complicity, is required on the part of the receiver of the re-created text or performance, although there are also important distinctions between responses to adaptations in different generic modes: to film, song or literature, for example. Crucial issues are highlighted here governing the relationship between writer, reader or spectator, and indeed in the digital forum, user-creator, and the genre, medium or mode which the multiple reoccurrences of myth throw into sharp relief. Each moment of reception is individual and discrete, albeit governed by manifold conventions and traditions, and by prior knowledge and indeed previous texts: the old story becomes in this respect a very new one, told – and understood – for the very first time.

5

'OTHER VERSIONS' OF FAIRY TALE AND FOLKLORE

The overlap between the genres of myth, legend, folklore and fairy tale has exercised many scholars (Sale 1978: 23). The well-known story of Robin Hood, for example, moves at various times from exhibiting the conventions of legend to serving as local folklore, while also invoking the witches and fairies from fairy tales (Knight 2003). Fairy tales, with their interest in dysfunctional family structures and personal and civic rites of passage, have much in common with their mythological counterparts. All these forms have also been interpreted from the varying standpoints of anthropology, social history, cultural studies, structuralism, feminism, psychoanalysis and psychology. What they offer are archetypal stories available for re-use and recycling by different ages and cultures. Fairy tale and folklore do, however, possess a very specific set of signifiers and symbolic systems that are worth examining in their own right. Shakespeare, a prime example, as we have already seen, of a cultural repository of archetypal characters and plotlines, dipped into the folk genre of fairy tale as a stimulus for his drama: *King Lear* and *Cymbeline*, for example, both have roots in this form. *Cymbeline* reconstitutes the figure of the wicked stepmother, while *Lear* reworks a folklore storyline of a father and his three daughters, two malign or 'ugly' sisters, and one good and virtuous child.

One of the reasons fairy tale and folklore serve as cultural treasuries to which we endlessly return is that their stories and characters seem to transgress established social, cultural, geographical and temporal boundaries. They are eminently adaptable into new circumstances and contexts, making themselves available for 'other versions' (Atkinson 1997: 348). Writers, artists, performers and directors as diverse as Salman Rushdie, Paula Rego, Angela Carter, Kate Atkinson, the Kneehigh Theatre Company, Walt Disney and Jean Cocteau have all turned to the potent form of the folk story or fairy tale as inspiration for their reimaginings, postmodernist or otherwise. Recent comic, even parodic, versions of the fairy tale include the hugely popular animated *Shrek* films (2001, 2004, 2007) and Stephen Sondheim's 1987 musical *Into the Woods*, directed for the cinema by Rob Marshall in 2014. Both of these examples are an attempt to resist the so-called 'Disneyfication' of the form; so too are the dark, suggestive paintings of Rego which revisit a number of classic Disney films through a Gothic imaginary lens. Disney's animated film versions of *Snow White and the Seven Dwarves*, *Cinderella*, *Sleeping Beauty* and *Beauty and the Beast*, among others, with their explicit stress on happy endings, usually consisting for their female protagonists in marriage and the finding of their personal Prince Charming, have had a profound influence on modern understandings of the form. Nevertheless, these rich repositories of stories have also become a focus for scholarly interrogation; Marina Warner, to cite just one prominent example, is a veritable historian of the form (see, for example, Warner 1994), a fact which has influenced her fictional as well as non-fictional output.

Fairy tales are stories that are essentially variations on particular narrative types. This suggestion brings into the frame the disciplinary concerns of anthropology and the related approaches of structuralist thought and analysis. Structuralism finds much value in analysing the myths and tales of specific cultures but also in identifying the common existence of certain tales, types and paradigmatic structures across cultures. The work of Claude Lévi-Strauss and Tzvetan Todorov, among others, has had considerable impact on those critics who study the presence of mythical and folkloric types in literature ranging from the plays of Shakespeare to magic realism (see Lévi-Strauss 2001 [1978]; Todorov 1990 [1978]). In terms of the ongoing adaptation of fairy tales, the recurrence of particular narrative types and structures in new, culturally embedded contexts generates the same dichotomy between universality and a politicized subject position that Roland Barthes's *Mythologies* was seen to grapple with in the previous chapter's examinations of myth (1993 [1972]). In turn, as we shall see in this chapter, structuralism has been inflected by the findings of psychoanalysis. In Sigmund Freud's theory of *das Unheimliche*, or the 'uncanny', for example, it is possible to identify a version of the compulsion to repetition, the desire to return to or re-create a text, story or paradigm, as both a refusal and rehearsal of loss and as an effort to contain anxiety (Freud 1963 [1919]; Garber 1987). The darker subtexts of many fairy stories, as with myths, raise spectres of incest, familial violence and monstrousness that might elsewhere be seen as the stuff of dreams and nightmares.

If fairy tale and folklore make themselves particularly available for continuous re-creation and rewriting it is partly because of their essentialist abstraction from a specific socio-historical or geopolitical context: 'Although the content of the fairy tale may record the real lives of the anonymous poor with sometimes uncomfortable fidelity ... the form of the fairy tale is not usually constructed so as to invite the audience to share a sense of lived experience' (Carter 1990: xi). The castles, towers, villages, forests, monsters, beasts, ogres and princesses of fairy tale exist seemingly nowhere and yet everywhere in terms of applicability and relevance. But a detectable counter-movement in twentieth-century reworkings of the form can be located in the desire to tie the stories back into a social, even social-historical, context, constituting in some respects an attempt to rationalize their magic. Christopher Wallace's *The Pied Piper's Poison* (1998) revises the familiar children's tale of the Pied Piper of Hamelin. The Pied Piper of the original helped to rid a Northern European village of an infestation of rats which were harbingers of life-threatening plague in the period when the story is believed to have originated, by means of his seductive piped music. When, however, his promised payment is withheld by the town elders the piper returns and entices all the children away, thereby depriving the town of its symbolic future economic security. Deploying the narrative structure of an academic research paper cited within a retirement speech by a doctor, Wallace's novel self-consciously asserts and queries the value and reliability of the Hamelin story. Rejecting the fantasy element of the folktale as handed down through the generations, its author finds a disturbingly material explanation for the events suggested in the story of the Pied Piper. Retrieving the socio-historical context of the Thirty Years War in Europe in the 1630s and 1640s, the essay suggests that Hamelin was not besieged by rats, although in a grain-growing community they were an omnipresent feature of daily life. Instead it speculates – and the speculative and unreliable nature of the historical archive is stressed at various points – that the town was under siege by a band of Spanish soldiers. It is these 'rats' that the Pied Piper offers to rid Hamelin of. The description of the Piper himself extends the mode of social realism that Wallace applies to the tale, as the social causes behind his name are considered:

> 'Pied' could conceivably be a corruption of the French 'a pied', meaning 'on foot', indicating that this man was by nature a traveller. It could also imply the style of clothing he wore, 'pied' meaning mottled or spotted with the kind of bright and bold colour associated with a jester or clown. Finally, the word could be a corruption of his real name, particularly if this was Arabic in origin and therefore difficult for an uneducated German speaker to pronounce.
>
> (Wallace 1998: 160)

The narrative here emulates the discursive style of the rational, scientific age, offering definitions and explanations. The latter explanation gestures towards a cultural awareness of the social and class structures that provide the shaping forces to the supposedly abstract forms of fairy tale, folktale and the related genre of nursery rhyme. The Pied Piper is, in Wallace's estimation, an outsider, possibly an Eastern migrant worker in seventeenth-century Europe. This gestures towards the fact that many fairy tales exhibit a deep-rooted anxiety about the figure of the incomer or the outsider, the person or creature from elsewhere. Marxist interpretations of a tale such as *Rumpelstiltskin*, for example, suggest that it tries to work through a threat to the common means of production – spinning – in many Northern European villages in the Middle Ages. It does not take much of a leap of the imagination to see how this tale could be redeployed in an analysis of the twenty-first-century European paranoia surrounding migrant workers and asylum seekers. Jack Zipes has talked of the 'universal community' implied by fairy tale (1994: 5), but his Marxist analyses of the tales also stress their specific historical and social contexts. For Zipes, *Rumpelstiltskin* is 'about the merchant capitalist intensification of linen manufacture and the appropriation of the means of production through which [the heroine] would normally establish her quality and win her man' (68).

Similarly, Wallace's materialist analysis of the Pied Piper's mythology serves to shed light on a second time-period in the novel, the Second World War, when other forms of social hardship and threat were being faced by European communities akin to those of Hamelin. As well as paralleling the two conflicts via his double time-scheme, Wallace, again via his subject academic Arthur Lee, finds a troubling parallel with the folktale in the twentieth-century wartime practice of torture. In this version of the Pied Piper legend, the children are not seduced into leaving the village by the melodies played by a travelling minstrel but are instead devoured by townsfolk hallucinating in an extreme state of famine. These are people reduced to the condition of rats by starvation. Any metamorphosis in this tale resists fantastic explanation and can instead be tied to very real conditions of hunger and insanity. In turn, the cruelties inflicted upon neighbouring communities during the Second World War are brought into disturbing focus. In the end our need to weave stories around terrible events seems to be remarkably enduring throughout human history; we displace reality in order to survive, and to evade the unbearable truth that the capacity for cruelty rests within us all. Except in our imaginations, there is no Pied Piper to scapegoat.

The language of scapegoating reintroduces the anthropological roots and concerns of structuralist theory into our analysis. In a manner akin to Shakespeare and myth, the impulse towards re-visioning fairy tales can be linked to specific, theoretical movements, but, in addition to charting the rise of anthropology as a discipline in the twentieth century, the fairy tale carries the weight of significance ascribed to it by the emergent modes of psychology and psychoanalysis. A seminal work in this regard is Bruno Bettelheim's *The Uses of Enchantment: The Meaning and Importance of Fairy Tales*, first published in 1975. Influenced by the world of Freud and also Carl Jung, Bettelheim explored the 'psychological significance of the folk fairy tale' (1975: 5). In a manner that shares much of its method with Wallace's rationalization of the Pied Piper story, Bettelheim suggested that many such tales were a means of working through traumatic experiences caused by the social visitation of plague, famine and warfare, or by the sexual and social pressures created by puberty and adolescence. It is notable how many of the protagonists of fairy tales find themselves on a threshold between childhood and adulthood, between innocence and experience in sexual terms: *Snow White, Little Red Riding Hood* and *Sleeping Beauty* all conform to this archetype. As Bettelheim observes: 'fairy tales depict in imaginary and symbolic form the essential steps in growing up and achieving an independent existence' (73). Feminist writers have found a particularly rich source of material in fairy tale for this reason. Kate Atkinson's self-aware narrator in *Human Croquet* instructs her readers early on that it is her birthday, and a significant one at that: 'It's the first day of April and it's my birthday, my sixteenth – the mythic one, the legendary one, the traditional age for spindles to start pricking and suitors to come calling and a host of other symbolic sexual imagery to suddenly manifest itself' (Atkinson 1997: 23). The date of April Fools' Day must give readers pause, in that Isobel, with her postmodern awareness of the available plural readings of fairy tale, is also likely to be an unreliable narrator. Nevertheless, this statement alerts readers to the manifold ways in which Atkinson's text, as already indicated in Chapter 4, will engage in a rich intertextual relationship with Shakespeare, Ovidian mythology and fairy tales ranging from *Sleeping Beauty* through *Cinderella* to *Little Red Riding Hood* and *Hansel and Gretel*.

Atkinson is especially interested in the fairy tale's invocation of the family both as an ideal and as an entity capable of horrific dysfunctionality. She also finds Shakespearean plays a rich source in this respect. The interplay of sibling rivalry and dependency that features in tales such as *Cinderella* and *Hansel and Gretel* figures in Isobel and Charles's relationship in the face of the loss of their mother and the temporary absence of their father. This is also a common motif in fairy tale, one that, while ostensibly about loss, allows the 'orphan' characters a free space for experience. *Human Croquet* is a narrative awash with stepmothers – not all of them archetypally wicked ones – and with parental failures and absences, dysfunctional familial relationships and sexual threat. Although in the early stages of the novel Isobel and Charles appear to nurse the hope that their mother Eliza might still be alive, partly signified by the Cinderella-esque shoe which they hope will one day be filled by the foot of their returned parent, we later realize that they have repressed the brutal fact that they discovered her bloodied corpse in a woodland during an ill-fated family picnic. With the cruellest irony, Eliza was in fact murdered with the missing shoe from the very pair the children hope against hope to restore to unity. Eliza's return is the biggest fairy tale of all.

The deployment of the fairy tale, and indeed quasi-Shakespearean, setting of the forest is another important thread in Atkinson's complex narrative. Isobel and Charles become in this moment the 'babes in the wood' of *Hansel and Gretel*: 'She was so hungry that she would have eaten a gingerbread tile or a piece of striped candy window-frame, even though she knew the consequences' (130–1). The telling point is that Isobel knows the consequences (in *Hansel and Gretel* a life-threatening encounter with a witch and an oven) and as a result the knowing narrative invites us as readers to read between, above, under and through the lines at all times. Fairy tale is the interpretive key to the story Isobel tells us: 'it seems men fall into one of several categories – there are the weak fathers, the ugly brothers, the evil villains, the heroic woodcutters and, of course, the handsome princes – none of which seems entirely satisfactory somehow' (75). The sexual sub-text of many fairy tales, indicated by Bettelheim's contextualization in terms of puberty and sexual adolescence, recurs in *Human Croquet*, finding its most troubling manifestation in the Baxter family, Isobel's neighbours. On the surface theirs is a textbook, albeit antiquated, version of a 'happy family', with a mother constantly baking cakes and attending to her husband's needs, but a postmodernist and post-feminist reader will never be satisfied with this version of events. In fact at the heart of the Baxter family – akin to many fairy tales, with their dark hearts – is domestic violence and incest. This renders all too real the novel's favourite cliché: 'Appearances can be deceptive'. Atkinson has pursued these interests in another novel, *Case Histories* (2004), the first of her Jackson Brodie series, which combines the generic and topographic conventions of contemporary detective fiction with fairy tale tropes and motifs of lost women.

Atkinson's *Human Croquet*, with its parallel worlds and time-travelling motifs, owes much to the genres of fantasy and science fiction as well as to Shakespeare, Ovid and fairy tale. Her narrative technique has, therefore, much in common with the mode of 'magic realism' we have mentioned previously. That genre rose to prominence in the latter decades of the twentieth century, enjoying plural manifestations in the writings of South and Central American authors, in Eastern European art, and in feminist and postcolonial texts; all of which were examples of political resistance to contemporary artistic norms. Chapter 4 discussed the treatment of myth in Salman Rushdie's novels in this context, and a prime influence on Rushdie and on Atkinson's version of magic realism was Angela Carter. It is undoubtedly to the genre of fairy tale that Carter looked for her primary source material for the magic realist impulse in her writing (Bowers 2004: 4):

> It is through her use of fairy-tale components that Carter disrupts the realism that [her writing] otherwise cultivates. Carter recognises the misogyny of the conventional fairy-tale, as well as the amenability of fairy-tales to being rewritten and disseminated in ways which enshrine particular (especially patriarchal) social codes; but it is through this realization that Carter reclaims the fairy-tale as a medium for the feminist writer.

(Head 2002: 92)

Fairy tale was amenable as a narrative form to the cultural work Carter wished it to do. Sarah Gamble suggests that for Carter 'appropriation and adaptation is really what the fairy tale is all about' (1997: 67), citing the author's personal definition of how the genre operates:

> The chances are, the story was put together in the form we have it, more or less from all sorts of bits of other stories long ago and far away, and has been tinkered with, had bits added to it, lost other bits, got mixed up with other stories, until our informant herself has tailored the story personally to suit an audience ... or, simply, to suit herself.
>
> (Carter 1990: x)

This is, of course, also a brilliant summary of the operations of *bricolage* at work in Carter's own *oeuvre*.

Suiting herself and her audience, Carter's re-visionary fairy tales exhibit a deep-seated interest in the sexual undercurrents of the form identified by scholars such as Bettelheim. The collection of ten short stories that make up her 1979 collection *The Bloody Chamber*, and which rewrite *Beauty and the Beast, Puss in Boots, Little Red Riding Hood* and the story of Bluebeard's Castle (in the title story), are awash with descriptions of the human body and the sexual act, as well as female menstruation, which for Carter functions as the epitome of the sexual threshold on which her characters stand in exemplary fairy tale fashion. In 'The Company of Wolves', for example, the unnamed Red Riding Hood's metonymic 'scarlet shawl' not only signifies her traditional literary identity and heritage to the reader but becomes emblematic of the sexual significance of it: it is 'the colour of poppies, the colour of sacrifices, the colour of her menses' (Carter 1995 [1979]: 117). 'The Company of Wolves' also takes place on the calendrical limen of the winter solstice; Carter loved to deploy these 'hinge' moments of the year as a space of possibility in her revisionary writings.

Carter's version of *Little Red Riding Hood* revels in the heroine's wilful sexual coupling with the wolf rather than face the same violent consumption as her grandmother. There is of course here an embedded parable about generations of women liberated by the new equal rights agenda of the 1960s onwards (Teverson 2013: 138). This is also the context for Carol Ann Duffy's dark coming of age poem 'Little Red-Cap' (1999) in her revisionary *The World's Wife* collection, which starts with the placing statement 'At childhood's end' and riffs on Duffy's own relationship with poet Adrian Henri. Duffy's title returns the story to the title first accorded it by the Brothers Grimm. There have also been some intriguing parallel urges in adaptations of the tale aimed more squarely at a youth audience; Marjolaine Leray's exquisite pared-back graphic novel *Little Red Hood*, which uses only red, black and white to tell its unexpected version of the story, is a life-affirming example (Leray 2011). In this particular telling we never actually get to the part of the story that involves the grandmother and the bed; feisty Little Red Hood takes on the wolf in a game of intelligence in which she clearly has the upper hand, even questioning his personal hygiene in the process. This graphic novel has itself been reimagined as dance by the Québécois dance collective Cas Public, in 2014–15, further emphasizing the dynamic and ongoing process of adaptation. Further parallels might be sought in more adult-facing illustrative work such as Paula Rego's *The Little Red Riding Hood Suite* (2003), in which there are very different power relations at play from those of the fairy tale tradition. In this sequence of artworks, Red Riding Hood's mother stabs the wolf (depicted as a predatory male) with a garden fork and then proudly wears his pelt as a stole (Wullschlager 2008). As Andrew Teverson rightly observes, these proliferating examples, impossible to read as a linear sequence of adaptation, invite us to ask 'which' Little Red Riding Hood we are speaking about at any one time (2013: 4); with the advent of digital and game versions also, we are seeing in action what Linda Hutcheon has termed the 'lateral' process of adaptation (2013: xv).

Angela Carter finds in the story of Little Red Riding Hood a troubling potential for sexual coercion and liberation, though she seeks in the process to free her heroine from the restrictive trajectory of her originating tale, whether it be an ending in death or arranged marriage. As Lorna Sage eloquently described it, in Carter's hands 'The monsters and the princesses lose their places in the old script' (1994: 39). But Carter's femino-centric tales do not substitute some naïve version of the female hero for the contained heroines of her sources. In many of the tales the female protagonists prove complicit in their entrapment, travelling, seemingly without question, into the 'unguessable country of marriage' (7). In 'The Bloody Chamber', for example, part of the heroine-narrator's steep learning curve is a recognition that she was seduced by the wealth of her mysterious husband, who the reader swiftly comes to recognize as the murderous Bluebeard from the clues provided by the pornographic literature in his personal library and those all-too significant keys. This story of suppressed violence against women has, of course, a long adaptational history and has haunted much feminist fiction: in the twentieth century, it inspired, for example, Margaret Atwood's *Bluebeard's Egg and Other Short Stories* (1983) and Alice Hoffman's *Blue Diary* (2001), and in the nineteenth century it hovered just beneath the surface of Charlotte Brontë's *Jane Eyre* (1847). In Carter's vivid reimagining, the marquis's gold bathroom taps and the fine fabrics he fills his bride's wardrobe with seem to muffle her ability to question his poor track record in previous marriages. It is in the figure of the indomitable mother who rescues her daughter at the close that Carter allows herself the most dramatic feminist interpolation into the heart of the Bluebeard myth, actively re-gendering Charles Perrault's saviour brothers from the seventeenth-century French telling of the tale.

During her career, Carter edited two collections of fairy tales for the feminist publishing house Virago (1990 and 1992). In 1977 she translated Perrault's influential collection *Histoires ou contes du temps passé* (1697). She was a scholar as well as an adapter of the form: fairy tale was clearly a paradigmatic genre in her work, appearing in various shapes in novels including *The Magic Toyshop* (1967), in which, according to Dominic Head, 'the challenge to the fairy-tale is conducted in an ambivalent spirit. Where the fairy-tales of the brothers Grimm or Perrault suppress their subtext of sexuality, Carter makes the emerging sexuality of her fifteen-year-old protagonist Melanie the narrative's driving force' (Head 2002: 92–3). Post-feminist versions of fairy tales also figure in her short story collections, including *Fireworks* (1988) and the posthumously published *American Ghosts and Old World Wonders* (1994). The latter includes not one but three alternative versions of the Cinderella story. The engaged and intrusive narrator of 'Ashputtle, or The Mother's Ghost, Three Versions of One Story' discusses the possibility of adopting a new perspective on the Cinderella myth: 'you could easily take the story away from Ashputtle and centre it on the mutilated sisters' (Carter 1994: 110). Carter deliberately restores the violence of earlier versions of the story, scenes in which the stepmother of this tale mutilates her own daughters' feet in an effort to force them to fit the prince's found shoe. In context the image is a disturbing one, suggesting the desperation surrounding the marriage potential of women in many societies even today, as evidenced in discussions of so-called 'leftover women' in contemporary Chinese society. Carter drew parallels to other historical and present-day rituals such as foot-binding and female genital mutilation (110). Cornish theatre company Knee-high, who have adapted many fairy and folktales, as well as Angela Carter's novel *Nights at the Circus* (1984; production 2006) for the stage in their inimitable physical style, brought to bear similar observations on the violence of such tales in their vivid performance of *The Red Shoes* based on the Hans Christian Andersen story but also informed by the ground-breaking 1948 Powell and Pressburger film version. This inter-medial production, first staged in 2003 but revived since, was described by one reviewer in these terms: '[it] takes the familiar, and renders it surreal and political, haunting and brave' (Mahoney 2010); this could be a manifesto of sorts for feminist adaptation. Once again we are reminded of the active role of the reader or spectator in these experiences; it is their mobilization of the familiar that sets off a chain reaction which produces new meanings for these versions.

Carter's narrator also ponders the father's failure to act in the face of the violence performed by his second wife on his daughter in the family home in the Cinderella myth, speculating that if you had made all three daughters biological ones that might have altered things: 'But it would also transform the story into something else, because it would provide motivation, and so on; it would mean I'd have to provide a past for all these people, then I would have to equip them with three dimensions' (1994: 110). Carter is being deliberately playful here since it is exactly this provision of pre-history and motivation, the restoration of three dimensions, that we have seen as a central driver for reworkings of Shakespeare, myth and fairy tale in this section and which is certainly key to Carter's own revisionary impulses.

Fairy tale and folklore have a complicated relationship to print history that deserves acknowledgement as part of their story of transmission and transformation. While the names of Perrault, the Brothers Grimm and Hans Christian Andersen have become virtually synonymous with fairy tales, these authors were issuing in print personalized or indeed customized versions of stories that had long circulated as part of an oral, popular culture. As Marina Warner has shown, oral culture was a far more femino-centric community than the early print industry, although both Warner and Carter are aware of one early female print precedent for their modernized fairy tales, Madame d'Aulnoy's *Conte de Fées* (1697–8), which disseminated in print form a number of stories that had been circulating within the context of French salon culture, itself a highly feminized space of intellectual exchange (Zipes 1994: 20; Teverson 2013: 51–60). D'Aulnoy's tales of animal bridegrooms paved the way for the story of *La Belle et la bête*, which is one that has proved of recurring interest to Carter. In *The Bloody Chamber*, in addition to wolf-bridegrooms, there are two specific variations on the Beauty and the Beast tale. 'The Courtship of Mr Lyon' has a self-consciously trite resolution in the marriage of its protagonists, and in the far darker and more sexualized 'The Tiger's Bride', in a typical act of inversion through appropriation, Carter's Beauty does not transform the beast into the normative vision of a prince but, rather, once the tiger-bridegroom has kicked off several layers of her skin, becomes furred herself. In keeping with the cinematic intertextuality of so much of her writing, and much contemporary engagement with fairy tale as a form, Carter's Gothic re-visions of this story are also indebted to Jean Cocteau's memorable film version (1945).

It is striking to note that several of the authors invoked in this analysis of the appropriation of fairy tale plotlines and paradigms also engage actively with Shakespeare: not least Atkinson with the comedies in *Human Croquet* and Carter with the entire canon in her *tour-de-force* late novel *Wise Children* (1992). In a similar vein Marina Warner's novel *Indigo* takes an improvisational approach to *The Tempest* but is also a text steeped in Ovidian mythology and fairy tale, thereby bridging all three chapters in this section. The novel is framed by the storytelling of its quasi-magical character Serafine Killabree, who is linked at various points in the narrative to the offstage Shakespearean witch Sycorax. The first story Serafine tells is of a king, his beautiful daughter, golden-haired as in all the best fairy tales, and an obese suitor who eats oysters. The narrative both invokes the Ovidian metamorphic myth of Midas, who turned objects to gold, and offers a template for understanding the relationship in the novel between the characters of Sir Anthony Everard and his spoiled daughter Xanthe and her future husband, Sy Nebris, who founds an oyster farm on the family's Caribbean landholdings. Xanthe's name means 'gilded one' in Latin and she is also nicknamed 'Goldie' in the novel, evoking several fairy tale paradigms, including the selfish and greedy Goldilocks who consumes the little bear's porridge, as well as endless tales of sibling rivalry between 'good' and 'bad' sisters often marked out by stereotypes of light and dark hair. Xanthe's mixed-race half-sister Miranda is clearly troubled by the narrative implications of such literary traditions. Through her intertextual weaving of the mermaids and sea-changes of Shakespeare's *The Tempest* with those of traditional fairy tales, Warner constructs a distinctly femino-centric narrative. It seems fitting that the novel should close with Serafine still telling and retelling stories in the style of Mother Goose and the ancient spinners of the verbal cloths of fairy tale. Mirroring the postcolonial and feminist concerns of Warner's novel, the myths and tales told by Serafine contain stories of devouring, of death and consumption, sexual or otherwise, but they are being constantly revised, rewritten and retold in new contexts: 'But this savage story isn't seemly for the little English girls, so Serafine has adapted it, as storytellers do' (Warner 1992: 224). This is the self-conscious appropriative art of Warner, Carter, Atkinson and many others. They deliberately break down and deconstruct the convention of fairy tale, viewing things from a new angle. As Jack Zipes reminds us, they do this 'in order to alter our readings of the privileged narratives that have formed a type of canon in

Western culture' (1994: 157). But, as Zipes notes, their 'postmodern revisions ... do not reassemble the fairytales that they break down into fragments into a new whole. Instead, they expose the artifice of the fairytale and make us aware that there are different ways to shape and view the stories' (157). In the end, though, it is the normative happy ending of fairy tale that is most vociferously denied, or at least self-consciously framed, by these revisionary versions. Proving once more that stasis is an unreliable model for the operations of canonical texts across cultures and time, these 'other versions' open up rather than close down possibility, offering 'not recuperation but differentiation, not the establishment of a new norm but the questioning of all norms' (Zipes 1994: 157–8; see also Zipes 1979: 177).

PART III

ALTERNATIVE PERSPECTIVES

6

CONSTRUCTING ALTERNATIVE POINTS OF VIEW

It has become abundantly clear in the discussion of adaptation and appropriation that these processes are frequently, if not inevitably, political acts. While the action of reinterpretation in a new context was viewed by T. S. Eliot in 'Tradition and the Individual Talent' as a necessary, indeed highly valuable, aspect of literary creation, he was ostensibly discussing a form of relationship between intertexts that mirrored his own cultural *bricolage* of quotation and allusion in poems such as 'The Waste Land'. That 1922 poem refers, among copious other texts and influences, to John Webster's *The White Devil*, Shakespeare's *Antony and Cleopatra*, Ovid's *Metamorphoses*, the novels of Henry James and the poetry of Charles Baudelaire.

The relationship between intertexts and the referential process alters in significance when the appropriation extends beyond fragmentary allusion to a more sustained reworking and revision. If readers are to be alert to the comparative and contrastive relationships that Eliot regarded as crucial to the aesthetic process, it goes almost without saying that the texts cited or reworked would need to be well known. They need to serve as part of a shared community of knowledge, both for the interrelationships and interplay to be identifiable and for those in turn to have the required impact on readers or spectators. This is why, as we discussed in the Introduction, adaptation and appropriation have on the whole tended to operate within the parameters of the established canon, serving at times to reinforce that canon by ensuring a continued interest in the original or source text, albeit under revised circumstances, but at the same time ensuring a dynamic revival or 'repair' of the same (Sanders 2011: xii). To repeat Derek Attridge's wise formulation cited in the Introduction: 'The perpetuation of any canon is dependent in part on the references made to its earlier members by its later members ...' (1996: 169). Sometimes this might be about not only reinforcing the canon at any given time but investigating its edges and sometimes reviving and recuperating texts that may actually have fallen out of regular readership in the process. In 2014, for example, Sathnam Sanghera's *Marriage Material*, in the author's own phrase, 'shoplifted' its plot and characters from Arnold Bennett's now little-read 1908 Stoke-on-Trent novel *The Old Wives' Tale* in order to examine a Punjabi-Sikh family in Wolverhampton across three generations. Bennett's draper shop setting becomes (and challenges at every turn) the cliché of the immigrant-run corner shop of 1960s and 1970s Britain. Bennett's confined and constrained sisters Constance and Sophia become Kumajalit and Surinder in Sanghera's 'remix' (again, his phrase). Challenging and comic, and touching in its own right, it might not seem necessary to return to the Bennett at all to appreciate Sanghera's subtle investigation of the multicultural tensions of the provinces in twenty-first century Britain, but a comparative reading alongside *The Old Wives' Tale* enriches the Staffordshire stories of both (Wolverhampton was officially a Staffordshire town prior to being designated a Midlands city), and asks us to read versions of mercantilist cultures across time in ways that are mutually informing for both novels. As Sanghera's narrator Arjan notes: 'not everything can be explained by demographics and generality' (2014: 112). In this example we might go so far as to argue that adaptation ensures survival of a source text that might otherwise have slipped from view.

It is important, however, in the era of dispersed digital cultures to acknowledge that the notion of the canon itself is now increasingly under pressure and that new forms of shared communities of knowledge, ones whose members sit outside or alongside the kind of higher education disciplinary contexts that have been formulated by writers such as Eliot or scholars such as Attridge, are altering the landscape of adaptation studies. Henry Jenkins's work on fan communities and participatory culture has helped us to pay fresh attention to producers of meaning that may be working with texts and intertexts unknown to or unrecognized by conventional educational curricula, where, after all, the canon is in part invoked and strategically maintained (Jenkins 1992: 3; Hutcheon 2013: xx).

Our notion of what is 'shared' or indeed even familiar is rightly challenged by this kind of proliferation of platforms and access that we are currently witnessing in global cultures. *Star Trek* and *Dr Who* or comic book culture fan groups often foster highly esoteric and intimately detailed knowledge of the object of their affection/attention that may not be readily shared by those who stand outside the group, but is that necessarily any different in the twenty-first century to detailed knowledge of Shakespeare among academic associations and societies? Perhaps it is more accurate, then, to talk today of multiple 'canons' and communities for whom the base knowledges may vary. Nevertheless the rules of operation within these alternative user-maker communities are similar to those we might define for canonical adaptations; the new works thrive on the shared knowledge of the base on which they are built and on the circulation of alternatives to a commonly known or understood norm. Jenkins describes these fan subcultures and their 'interpretative practices', which include 'program selection, canon formation, evaluation, interpretation (often gender-specific)' as 'active producers and manipulators of meaning' (1992: 2, 23), and alludes in turn to Michel de Certeau's description of active reading as an act of 'poaching': readers are constructed by de Certeau as travellers, 'nomads poaching their way across fields they did not write' (2013 [1984]: 174). For Jenkins, textual poaching becomes an art form, or, in other words, adaptation as a creative act (see also Sanders 2011).

The rules of operation for adaptation, be they applied in response to the canon(s) or to more idiosyncratic popular cultural phenomena, need not mean, even among fan communities, that the revisionary texts or reworkings merely accept or cite their precursor texts without question or debate. Knowledge begets an ability to query and question, and certainly in an academic context the study of adaptation has been spurred on by the recognized capacity of appropriations to respond to, and to write back to, an informing original from a new and revised perspective. In this set of actions the potential for creativity exists. Adaptations and appropriations, be they prequels, sequels, extensions, amplifications or alternatives, highlight often perplexing gaps, absences and silences within the original. Many appropriations as a result have a deep political and literary investment in giving voice to characters or events which appear to have been oppressed or repressed in the original.

Derek Attridge has usefully drawn our attention to the double bind by which subversive or counter-cultural appropriations end up by reinforcing the status of the very texts they seek to take issue with, but the important point to recall is that as readers or audiences we can never view those novels, poems, plays or films in the same light again: we cannot undo, as it were, the new knowledges acquired via engagement with an appropriation. Charlotte Brontë's 1847 novel *Jane Eyre* cannot be read from a twenty-first-century perspective without acknowledging the informing insights of postcolonialism and feminism; as we will see later in this chapter, a key text in that regard is Susan Gilbert and Sandra Gubar's seminal work of feminist criticism *The Madwoman in the Attic* (1979), which, even through its title, draws attention to Brontë's novel in ways that cannot be reversed or undone. In much the same way readers who have now encountered Jean Rhys's hugely influential appropriation *Wide Sargasso Sea* (1966) can never look on the sidelined or suppressed story of Bertha Rochester in Brontë's novel in quite the same way again. We are, of course, in part, also charting the ways in which mass higher education in the West and now increasingly on the Asian subcontinent is changing what we might regard as shared knowledge and further complicating our understanding of the kinds of communities that might engage in processes of reading and re-reading such texts.

Here we are also beginning to see that as the availability of adaptations grows, not least in multimedia contexts, a reader's or spectator's first point of contact, their point of entry as it were to the story of Jane Eyre or Lewis Carroll's Alice or even Shakespeare's Juliet, might not be through the 'original' or source, and may not even be in the same generic context. This is further complicated by the kinds of lateral adaptations such as fairy tales and myth that previous chapters have explored. Adaptation studies (and indeed its particular pleasures as a field of study) becomes highly subjective to such an extent that what we are beginning to chart is a series of relationships, capturing our first encounter or point of entry and tracing reading or spectating relationships to canonical stories and characters (Bonner and Jacobs 2011: 37–48). If we script our own reading in this way, providing what might be termed diaries of critical encounter, we can begin to see how readings (our readings) and interrogation of the same text change over time and according to the influences of other readings. This seems to me a very genuine and worthy approach to literature and film and digital media as the number of texts, and our modes of access to them, proliferate. This might also be a way of approaching the question of globalization versus localization in understanding what terms like 'shared' or 'familiar' might mean in the context of the world-wide web (Massai 2005) and what the action of 'borrowing' might connote.

A theatrical practice that can be examined from this standpoint of first encounter, and applied in helpful ways to the new global contexts for adaptation and appropriation, is intercultural performance. According to Patrice Pavis: 'In the strictest sense [intercultural theatre] creates hybrid forms drawing upon a more or less conscious and voluntary mixing of performance traditions traceable to distinct cultural areas' (Pavis 1996: 8). This can mean Western performances inflected by the performance techniques and traditions of other cultures, such as British director Peter Brook's Kathakali-influenced version of Indian epic theatre in *The Mahabharata* or French director Ariane Mnouchkine's Japanese Noh- and Kabuki-inspired versions of Shakespeare's history plays

(Kennedy 1993: 279–88); it might also mean Kathakali or Kabuki versions of texts derived from the Western canon. The problem always in cultural encounters of this kind is that the appropriation can seem hostile or simply presumptive depending on the direction from which it stems. Indeed, the question always has to be posed: 'Who is appropriating who and on what terms?' Intercultural performance theorists rightly worry over the politics of the trans-action taking place, since there is always a danger implicit in the appropriation of adopting an imperialist approach; some would, however, strongly defend the practice for its artistic possibilities, as in the case of Marvin Carlson, for example:

> Certain cultural transfers preserve the source culture, the point of view of the other, while it is being absorbed by the receiving culture. Although transformation or re-elaboration of the source material may take place, these are in fact the marks of a truly intercultural repre-sentation. A borrowing from another culture is neither a pure and simple citation nor an absolute duplication.
>
> (Pavis 1996: 12)

Borrowing, poaching even, at least in de Certeau's estimation, are seen in this account as positive acts, more productive of cultural and intercultural dialogue and a genuine transactional encounter between different subject positions rather than mere imitation of one by another. A whole new set of terms to consider when we are studying adaptation and appropriation, not least in an inter-cultural context, are mobilized in the process: preservation, absorption, re-elaboration, duplication and, most importantly perhaps, reception, keeping the audience and readers in view at all times as part of the process.

Gayatri Chakravorty Spivak has argued that postcolonialism is inherently appropriative in its gestures and its political position-taking: 'in postcoloniality, every metropolitan definition is dislodged. The general mode for the postcolonial is citation, re-inscription, re-routing the historical' (1990: 41). Sathnam Sanghera's *Marriage Material* can be understood as a postcolonial novel of sorts even though written by a British subject about contemporary Britain, and his re-routing or remix of Arnold Bennett's novel is a dislodging as much as a quotation. In a parallel move to Spivak's, Sylvie Maurel has suggested that 'feminist discourse is to be found in the margins of any construct, or discursive practice' (1998: 50). Peter Widdowson regards re-visionary writing as 'a crucial component' of the literary, arguing for it as representative of 'a contemporary "counter-culture of the imagination"', which in "writing back" to historical texts, and to the historical conjunctures which shaped them, re-writes Authorised History by way of revising its "master-narratives"' (1999: 166). This chapter, through a case study approach, seeks to examine a cross-section of these 'master-narratives' as they are newly absorbed into, and re-routed by, novels written between the 1960s and 1990s. These 'master-narratives' range from Shakespearean drama to novels authored in the eighteenth and nineteenth centuries and one example of early twentieth-century Modernism. What is of particular interest in these juxtaposed close readings is the way in which these appropriations rewrite their sources from the informing standpoint of the intellectual and social movements of those decades, from feminism to postcolonialism, to queer theory. In the process, though it is important to keep the question of reader-reception and indeed encounter in mind, a case study offers one interpretation often produced from its own critical context and historical subject position. Individual readers will need to consider the questions of point of entry and subject position that we have already discussed. Perhaps the challenge here is also to ask the reader of literary criticism generally, and of this book in particular, to read between the lines and to ask 'How do I read this? What is my response?'

JEAN RHYS'S *WIDE SARGASSO SEA*: 'JUST ANOTHER ADAPTATION'?

During an early period of her life when she is housed and schooled in the Dominican Convent of Saint Innocenzia, the protagonist of Jean Rhys's 1966 novel *Wide Sargasso Sea*, Antoinette Mason, reads the lives of the saints. She notices that Innocenzia herself has no story in these compendious volumes: 'We do not know her story, she is not in the book' (Rhys 1987 [1966]:

45). This phrase could serve as an epigraph to the entire narrative. For what Rhys's novel famously achieves is to provide a marginal character from a canonical work of English literature with a complicated history and a voice. Indeed, Patricia Waugh has suggested that by this action Rhys almost prophetically called into being postmodernism's recurring interest in voicing the silenced or absent characters of the canon: 'prophetically and proleptically she caught what would come to be the dominant literary concerns of the next twenty-five years: the feminist theme of the suppressed "madwoman in the attic"; the structuralist rediscovery of "intertextuality"' (1995: 203). Waugh's own reference here is to Gilbert and Gubar's work of criticism *The Madwoman in the Attic* (2000 [1979]). This text, as Waugh suggests, postdates Rhys's novel but encapsulates and extends her interest in the silenced female character of *Jane Eyre*, Mr Rochester's first wife, Bertha.

The literal (and literary) 'madwoman in the attic' in Rhys's novel is Bertha Antoinette Mason from Jamaica. In Brontë's novel, Bertha is reduced to a mad cackle heard emanating from the upper floors of Thornfield Hall, the sub-Byronic Mr Rochester's family home. Suffering from an hereditary form of insanity, she has been incarcerated by Rochester in an attic room watched over only by the servant Grace Poole and concealed from the world. Bertha is marginalized in the text both socially and spatially: Rochester is even prepared to undergo a bigamous marriage to Jane to conceal the truth. In practice it is during the wedding ceremony that the truth is uncovered in public, with painful results. Rhys's correspondence, in which she describes the composition of *Wide Sargasso Sea*, makes it clear that she was always anxious to address the marginalization of the part-Creole Bertha:

> The Creole in Charlotte Bronte's novel is a lay figure – repulsive, which does not matter, and not once alive, which does. She's necessary to the plot, but always she shrieks, howls and laughs horribly, attacks all and sundry – *off stage*. For me (and for you I hope) she must be right *on stage*.
>
> (Rhys 1985: 156)

Rhys has a personal investment in this approach, being white, West Indian and conscious always of being an outsider in the societies in which she lived. In a movement akin to those we have already explored in re-visions of Shakespearean texts, Rhys transports a marginal character from the periphery to the centre; her onstage, offstage evocations in the quoted letter are highly suggestive in this respect.

In a method comparable to other literary appropriations that seek to voice silenced or oppressed characters, Rhys achieves her aim of recuperating Antoinette in *Wide Sargasso Sea* by means of first-person narration. But instead of according Antoinette the sole perspective in the novel, Rhys interleaves her sections with others articulated by additional voices, in particular that of the novel's 'Rochester' figure, the sanity of whose narrative is ironically unmoored, almost unhinged, by his paranoid response to his situation, both geographical and personal: 'She'll loosen her black hair and laugh and coax and flatter (a mad girl. She'll not care who she's loving)' (Rhys 1987 [1966]: 135–6). In the crucial final section of the novel, when we are finally transported to England, and quite literally enter the terrain of Brontë's text, there is a further unidentified narrative voice which reports an exchange with the servant Grace Poole. The mention of that specific character from Brontë's novel locates the familiar reader for the first time without doubt in the world of *Jane Eyre*, which until this point has been suggested allusively but never explicitly identified.

In *Jane Eyre*, of course, Bertha is accorded no voice, except animalistic, lunatic howls, reinforcing Rhys's theatrical metaphor '*noises off*', and she generates little respect in Rochester's damaging and delimited description, which reduces her effectively to a 'monster' (Brontë 1985 [1847]: 336): 'Bertha Mason is mad; and she came of a mad family; idiots and maniacs through three generations. Her mother, the Creole, was both a madwoman and a drunkard' (320). Her entire life-story is reduced to a single chapter (Chapter 27) in *Jane Eyre*. From this single chapter, Rhys envisions a whole novel. As Nancy Harrison describes it: 'Rhys structures her novel to show us how a muted text can be revealed to dominate a formerly "dominant" text' (1988: 252). What Rhys also reveals in the rich cultural experience and poetic, even musical, voice she accords Antoinette is the latent racism and prejudice of Brontë's novel and culture. The issue of nomenclature is significant; 'Bertha' is a name imposed on Antoinette by the unnamed male figure who stands for Rochester in the novel, Rochester's *supplement* in Jacques Derrida's terminology (Derrida 1976: 141–52). This renaming constitutes an attempt to occlude her genetic links with her mother and, by extension, with the family's supposed hereditary insanity. It also re-enacts what Edward Kamau Brathwaite has described as the process of 'Creolization' in nineteenth-century Jamaica: 'Creolization began with "seasoning" – a period of one to three years, when slaves were branded, given a new name and put under apprenticeship to creolized slaves' (Ashcroft et al. 1995: 203).

Helen Carr has described *Wide Sargasso Sea* as 'a ground breaking analysis of the imperialism at the heart of British culture' (1996: 20). But also, Rhys's motivations are simultaneously driven by ethnic and gender implications. She is giving voice to the suppressed stories of the English literary canon, and in this way her novel has become canonical in its own right, a standard bearer for the revisionary impulse in literature, the counter-discourse or counter-culture that Widdowson regards as central to its practice. *Wide Sargasso Sea* represents a central example of both the feminist and the postcolonial novel. It is intriguing, of course, that Rhys 'writes back' to a canonical text by another woman, revealing in the process that for all the liberatory potential Brontë represents in her identity as a published female author, and one who in certain respects seeks to explore the notion of slavery and bondage from a liberal position in *Jane Eyre*, she remained in her overarching political attitudes a product of an imperial culture (Spivak 1997 [1989]: 148).

It is only in the latter stages of Rhys's novel that *Wide Sargasso Sea* quite literally shares a space with its literary progenitor. It is in the final section of the novel, which opens with the voice of the unnamed narrator, that a distressed and confused Antoinette is trapped in her attic room at Thornfield Hall. It is as if the novel has been moving towards this moment all along, at least in the self-aware reader's imagination; that is to say, the reader who maintains a sense of *Jane Eyre* as an undertow or back-story throughout the reading of *Wide Sargasso Sea*. For it is an inescapable fact that if we read Antoinette's story in the context of Bertha Rochester's we will anticipate her incarceration in the attic, and will also expect her eventual death after attempting to burn down Thornfield Hall. Rhys encourages, nurtures even, this expectation by appropriating Brontë's symbolic use of fire throughout *Jane Eyre*. Early on in *Jane Eyre* the young Jane is unjustly locked in a room as punishment by the family with whom she is living. Dramatically, she falls unconscious in a state of trauma, awaking to a fire in the room, and has to be rescued. By means of this passage, Brontë establishes a number of the central motifs of her novel, not least confinement and fire. Rhys repeats that gesture in *Wide Sargasso Sea* when Antoinette's family house burns down. When in the closing sentences of Rhys's text Antoinette refers to the candle that she is holding, the adaptation-aware reader is already foreseeing the end of Bertha's life in *Jane Eyre*. Bruce Woodcock suggests that Rhys leaves the ending open to alternative readings: 'Rhys's adoption of the present tense and the artistic choice to end the novel by this moment of undefined intent also allow us to imagine Antoinette escaping the pre-determined chain of events into the blank page of the future' (2003: 131). But if the shaping force for interpretation of the majority of Rhys's novel is *Jane Eyre*, then this seems almost too utopian in its hopes. In many readers' minds Antoinette appears doomed to repeat the tragic end Brontë envisioned for her. As Cora Kaplan has noted, *Wide Sargasso Sea* has recast Bertha as a 'tragic heroine' (2007: 154). In the 2006 television adaptation of *Wide Sargasso Sea* (dir. Brendan Maher) this interpretation was further emphasized by this moment acting as a framing device for the whole narrative, beginning as well as ending the adaptation, keeping the tragic ending fully in sight from the start. This intriguingly accords with director Baz Luhrmann's prescription for film adaptations of tragic myths:

> One of the primary ways of telling this kind of story is that the audience must know from the beginning how it is going to end, so that within the first ten minutes you know how it's going to end, but you think, how? ... It's not a revelation of plot, it's how the story is told.
>
> (Andrew 2001)

In a related fashion, when in Rhys's novel 'Rochester' makes a drawing of a house, it becomes in many readers' minds Thornfield Hall, and this already traps Antoinette in that future attic room: 'I drew a house surrounded by trees. A large house. I divided the third floor into rooms and in one room I drew a standing woman' (Rhys 1987 [1966]: 134). Deep in Antoinette's subconscious she too seems to foresee this end: 'For I know that house where I will be cold and not belonging, the bed I shall lie in has red curtains and I have slept there many times before, long ago' (92). This is surely the point of characters, stories and events that are appropriated: their end is predetermined in our imagination via prior knowledge of the precursor text. Antoinette, for all Rhys's investment in according her a voice, agency and history, cannot escape her pre-ascribed plot trajectory: 'Now at last I know why I was brought here and what I have to do' (155–6).

Rhys herself seems to have worried about the extent to which her novelistic creation was dependent on *Jane Eyre*. She genuinely feared that her novel would be regarded as 'just another adaptation' (Rhys 1985: 159) and at one point in her letters she ponders 'unhitching' the novel from its precursor, although she rapidly talks herself out of doing this: 'It might be possible to unhitch the whole thing from Charlotte Bronte's novel, but I don't want to do that. It is that particular Creole I want to write about, not any of the other mad Creoles' (153). Emancipation is a shaping theme in *Wide Sargasso Sea*; the act which promulgated the abolition of slavery in the British colonies is mentioned on the opening page. Yet in linking Antoinette's story so closely to that of Bertha Rochester, Rhys is equally aware that it restricts possibility for her character, preordaining her destiny in the ways we have already described (Maurel 1998: 133–4). She can liberate Bertha from the attic in the sense of according her a voice and a story, but she can never entirely emancipate her from the canonically aware reader's expectation.

Perhaps in the end that is the only fate we can expect for an appropriative text; just as postcolonialism relies on an understanding of colonialism to derive its full force in literary and theoretical terms, so *Wide Sargasso Sea* is eternally tied to the text it seeks to rewrite (Savory 1998: 293). There is, however, some compensation in the fact that the relationship is two-way: *Jane Eyre* can never be read the same way again after an encounter with Rhys's novel. Counter-discourses, in seeking to challenge the values on which a canon is established, cannot help but reinscribe the status of certain texts, but they do so in new and newly critical contexts. If Walter Benjamin's claim is correct in 'On the Concept of History' (2003) (also known as 'Theses on the Philosophy of History') that 'There is no document of culture that is not at the same time a document of barbarism. And just as such a document is never free of barbarism, so barbarism taints the manner in which it was transmitted from one hand to another' (Benjamin 2002: 4.392), then revisionary texts such as *Wide Sargasso Sea* are able to demonstrate what *Jane Eyre* and, by extension, nineteenth-century society suppressed. As Michel Foucault's study of the repressive Victorian discourse on sexuality indicated, the process of revisiting can prove liberating and not merely recursive (1984 [1978]: 92–102). This is certainly true of the novel we will now discuss, J. M. Coetzee's *Foe*, which, like Rhys's novel, has become canonical in its own right, an exemplar of the counter-discursive strategy of cultural appropriation.

J. M. COETZEE'S *FOE* AND THE MASTER-TEXT

The origins of parody are ancient. It is a form of imitation, usually undertaken for satirical effect or purpose (Dentith 2000). Pastiche is often regarded as a related literary form since, as with parody, it involves imitation, often at the level of style. In its strictest usage, however, in the domain of fine art and music, a 'pastiche' refers more specifically to a medley of references to different styles, texts or authors. This in turn relates to the previously explored term *bricolage*, and pastiche would seem to constitute its natural mode of discourse. The question raised by any act of imitation is whether the impersonation is carried out in a mode of celebration or critique; in many cases, however, the truth is a rather more complex hybrid of both.

The recourse to the literary canon in the making of adaptations and appropriations in order to mobilize a reader's or audience's sense of similarity and difference has been a recurrent theme in this study. It is perhaps no surprise, then, that the prose narrative often regarded as the foundational text for the English novel, Daniel Defoe's 1719 *Robinson Crusoe*, has been a focus of a number of reworkings. As well as flattering parallel texts about castaways on desert islands, such as *The Swiss Family Robinson*, a number of these retellings offer a conscious critique of the ideologies and politics of the original. In 1921 Jean Giraudoux published his *Suzanne et le Pacifique*, which, with its female desert island protagonist, immediately took to task the patriarchal and imperialist values of *Robinson Crusoe*. Genette describes this text as a 'refutation' rather than a reworking of Defoe's novel (1997 [1982]: 303). Giraudoux's concern was to expose, in a parallel move to Rhys's treatment of *Jane Eyre* in *Wide Sargasso Sea*, the problematic politics of the original. His novel celebrates the natural fecundity of the island in opposition to the mechanistic impositions of imperial ambition. There are, of course, debates to be had with Giraudoux's seemingly unproblematic identification of the female with the natural, and the privileging of the island's naturalness above all else, but it is an approach that was repeated in Michel Tournier's 1967 novel *Vendredi ou Les Limbes de Pacifique*, which was translated into English in 1984 as *Friday; or, The Other Island* (the subtitle is a reference to the novel's French epigraph: '*il y a toujours une autre île*'). As well as indicating the primal instincts that life on the island brings out in Crusoe: 'he returned to the swamp where he had come so near to losing his reason, and stripping off his clothes, let his body sink into the tepid slime' (1984 [1967]: 4), Tournier's sub-Freudian reworking of the novel addresses the sexual needs of his protagonist, which were almost entirely absent from Defoe's text. The island becomes Crusoe's sexual partner, the product of this union being mandrake-like growths across the island that serve as Tournier's symbol for the transformative effect and impact of colonial activity. This is a third-person narrative but one concerned with Crusoe's appropriation of Friday's mind and person in support of his subjection of the island and its flora and fauna to his mastery. Friday's point of view is a driving concern in many twentieth-century post-colonial reworkings of Defoe's text, and it is worth noting that Tournier's text, inflected at all turns as it is by psychoanalysis, is another example of a revisionary work shaped by the theoretical interests that defined its moment of composition.

Genette's concept of the hypertext, which this study has invoked on several occasions, might appear to wrest the term away from its more contemporary usage in the idiom of computer science, where it refers to interconnected texts and graphics on a screen that enable the reader to read (or scroll) across and to cross refer between documents. That idea of connection and cross-referral between texts and between texts and images, of hypertextuality, remains a potent one in the context of adaptation studies. One common pattern that emerges from many of the texts discussed in this study is that hypertexts often become 'hyper-hyper-texts', allusive not only to some founding original source but also to other known reworkings of that text. Both Giraudoux and Tournier's texts are relevant to one particular *Crusoe*-influenced narrative which has become canonical in its own right, J. M. Coetzee's 1986 novel *Foe* (Attridge 1996: 169). *Foe*, like *Suzanne et le Pacifique*, is a feminization of Defoe's novel; indeed, its central character, and for much of the narrative its first-person narrator, is called Susan. The intertextual resonance of this is further extended when we realize that Susan Barton is the central character in another Defoe novel, *Roxana* (1724), about an eighteenth-century courtesan. These layers of fictional citation are deliberate strategies in this novel, which has usefully been described as a 'textual decolonization' by Dominic Head (1997: 14). H. Porter Abbot uses the term 'master-texts' to describe those 'stories that we tell over and over in myriad forms' (2002: 42). A large number of the hypertexts under consideration here are definitive examples of 'master-texts' according to this definition, especially *Robinson Crusoe*, which, by being crowned the founding father (and I use the phrase advisedly) of the English novel, has both erased an earlier tradition of women's prose fiction with a romance strain, including the work of Aphra Behn, and enshrined at the head of the English novel tradition a narrative that completely suppresses any role for women.

Coetzee's aim is clearly to undermine the master-text of *Robinson Crusoe* through the mechanism of his metafictional novel. The author of that eighteenth-century text is known in the novel simply as 'Foe', not only playing on the sense of an enemy or antagonist but also drawing our attention as readers to the real-life Defoe's adoption of a writing pseudonym to obscure the class realities of his position: this is a novel concerned at every turn with forgery, fakery, counterfeit and appropriation in the fictional process. In addition there may be an embedded reference to gender issues in that in early modern literature women were often referred to as 'foeminine' (see, for example, Edmund Spenser's sixteenth-century epic poem *The Faerie Queene*). Since gender is essential to Coetzee's 're-visioning' of Defoe's text this seems highly feasible. This is a novel that constantly offers alternative viewpoints, outcomes and interpretations; and the plural possibilities of its title are no exception (Head 2009: 61–5).

In all kinds of ways, literary 'truth' and authenticity are challenged by Coetzee's text. The novel opens with a first-person perspective that the reader immersed in readings of *Robinson Crusoe* might expect to be that of Crusoe himself: 'At last I could row no further' (Coetzee 1987: 5). The narrative voice turns out, however, to belong to Susan Barton, who has been shipwrecked on the hot sands of this particular desert island. The crucial signifier is the 'petticoat', which is all she has escaped with (5). This is, then, a narrative conscious from the start of readerly expectation: 'For readers reared on travellers' tales, the words *desert isle* may conjure up a place of soft sands and shady trees where brooks run to quench the castaway's thirst ... But the island on which I was cast away was quite another place' (7). That all-signifying 'But' signals the narrative's decisive turn away from its source text.

We do encounter 'Cruso' in Coetzee's text, although his name is spelt differently on the page (that all important slipped 'e'), and he proves somewhat different compared to the figure in Defoe's text; here he is an old man with a rambling mind and a contradictory memory. Cruso's unreliability as a source of truth is not entirely incompatible with Defoe's text, which is famously full of inconsistencies such as ink running out and Crusoe continuing his journal writing only moments later. Coetzee's Cruso, however, writes no journal; that act of creation belongs to Susan Barton, in another crucial reimagining of the original. And it is a journal that she keeps once she has escaped the island and returned to London. In the course of re-creating this journal and the (often unsent) letters that Susan addresses to Foe when she believes he has departed London for Bristol, Coetzee indulges in a virtuoso literary performance, a conscious pastiche or ventriloquism of many of the dominant prose styles of eighteenth-century literature, ranging from the pseudo-authentic journals and 'autobiographies' of Defoe himself to the epistolary ventures of Samuel Richardson. Henry Fielding's fondness for the picaresque road-novel in texts such as *Tom Jones* (1749) and *Joseph Andrews* (1742) is also evoked in that section of the novel where Susan sets out for Bristol to find Foe, selling his books en route as a very pertinent proof of the material value of literature.

What Coetzee eruditely problematizes here is the vexed question of copyright, the ownership of stories. In any feminist argument it would be reasonable to claim that the island story is Susan's, given up to Foe purely to write and publish; yet in that act of onward creativity and publication there is surely also a relinquishing of intellectual property rights that cannot be ignored. Was it ever even Susan's story to own? The island story is after all a shared one, and one which she herself suggests is Cruso's and which she is merely telling in his absence (in this version Cruso dies on the ship journey homeward). The additional question of Friday's rights, to both story and island, is one we will return to since it obviously brings the issue of First Nation rights into the heart of the narrative. Susan clearly feels a loyalty to the dead Cruso, with whom she had a relationship on the island, but if it is Susan's story or even Cruso's, it is not one she is equipped to tell in the masculine context of eighteenth-century literature and publishing: for that she relies on Foe's established reputation and voice. There is, then, a sense in which handing over her story results in a concurrent loss of identity on Susan's part; with no tangible record of her time on the island, she becomes a 'being without substance, a ghost' (Coetzee 1987: 51) unless Foe tells her tale. The authenticating and authorizing processes of literature are clearly being evoked, but so too is the suggestion of (De)Foe as a thief of other people's stories, a plagiarist by any other name. His main profession as a journalist further complicates our understanding of his relationship to the source material for his 'fiction'. In this subtle and complex way Coetzee reanimates a centuries-old debate about legal copyright and the ownership of intellectual material. He does so even in the careful punctuation of his novel in printed form: Susan's narratorial statements are encased throughout in quotation marks. This fact emphasizes that the words 'belong' to her, but also problematizes them, rendering the reader painfully aware at all times of the words' retrospective, literary and therefore constructed nature. The quotation marks are simultaneously a claim to originality and yet a recognition of artifice. On the page Coetzee's technique replicates the typography of eighteenth-century printing and therefore in the very movement towards supposed ownership or originating authority we see Susan's words being handed over to the literary space of the page as well. Writing about the legal operations of quotation marks, Margreta de Grazia observes that 'Quotation marks punctuate a page with sanctions – enclosing private materials from public use' (1994: 290), yet whose use are we witnessing in operation here? Susan's intention throughout appears to be to make public her experiences on the island, but in order to achieve this outcome the handover of the raw materials to Foe and therefore, to the printed page, seems inevitable.

This reading of Susan's claim to her 'history' ('herstory'?) as a property or commodity in the public domain is further complicated by the layers of internal intertextual reference in Coetzee's text. For, as already mentioned, Susan Barton is herself a fictional construct, a character from another Defoe novel. One possible implication, then, is that Foe steals Susan's life-story from her to form the base material of another profitable 'original work of fiction', *Roxana*. Another is that he steals from that fictional narrative to give her a false understanding of her own history. Susan seems unable to distinguish truth from fiction by the end and maybe as readers we are in a comparable position. She assumes that the young woman who claims to be her daughter is a fictional creation of Foe's, which of course she is, if we as readers choose to invoke the specific intertext of *Roxana*. In that novel Susan Barton's long-lost daughter returns only to be murdered in a hideously misjudged act of loyalty by Amy the maidservant. But this reading in turn reduces the Susan of *Foe* to purely fictional status. Coetzee's novel appears to toy further with these deconstructive possibilities when, at the close, Susan's first-person narration having been replaced by that of an unidentified narrator, thereby destabilizing the narrative further in both temporal and fictional terms, the opening action of slipping overboard is repeated. Narrator and reader travel to the island a second time only to discover, in the ultimate example of narrative slippage, that Susan's corpse is still lying on the ship. This suggests that the narrative we have just been following was entirely fictitious and without any foundation in tangible fact.

Amid all these concerns with Susan Barton's rights to the narrative of the island experience, there is another character who shared that experience whose voice is entirely silenced: Friday. As a South African writing in the late twentieth century, Coetzee was all too aware when composing his version of the castaways' story that history is often an imperial narrative in which the voices of the oppressed or the vanquished are silenced: 'In every story there is a silence, some sight concealed, some words unspoken ...' (1987: 141). As Attridge has observed: 'In so far as the oppressed *are* heard [in canonical literature], it is as a marginalised dialect within the dominant language' (1996: 184). The silencing of Friday in this narrative is literal as well as psychological: his tongue has been cut out, possibly, the text intuits, by slavers, possibly by the colonizing Cruso himself. In a reverse move to Jean Rhys's desire to give Bertha Rochester a voice in Antoinette's narrative in *Wide Sargasso Sea*, Coetzee maintains Friday's silence until the close of his novel. As Dominic Head notes, this is both 'a resistance to, yet also the product of, the dominant discourse' (1997: 121). Friday becomes, albeit in a sideways move, a cipher for the prevalent silences of apartheid in Coetzee's native South Africa; sideways references in the novel point us to this contemporary context for understanding the politics of this historical fiction. In the strange and unsettling end section of *Foe*, the previously mentioned unnamed and unidentified narrator enters a London property and finds Susan and Foe, presumably dead, in a bed, and Friday, in a chilling variation on the trope of the madwoman in the attic, bricked up alive in an alcove. Pressing his ear close to the door, the narrator hears an inexplicable set of noises emanating from behind it: 'From his mouth, without a breath, issue the sounds of the island' (Coetzee 1987: 154). Friday, still literally silent in vocal terms, becomes or is rendered in his silence a semantic signifier of the island and all that was suppressed, oppressed or repressed in Defoe's 'master text' and, by extension, in all stories authored from the colonial point of view.

CARYL PHILLIPS'S *THE NATURE OF BLOOD*: INTERWOVEN NARRATIVES AND CIRCULATORY SYSTEMS

We witnessed in Chapter 3 the numerous ways in which adaptations and appropriations of Shakespeare have demonstrated an interest and investment in giving motivation to, voicing or 'bringing onstage' the victimized, marginalized or silenced characters from his plays, from Gertrude in *Hamlet* to Sycorax in *The Tempest*. In turn, novels such as Jane Smiley's *A Thousand Acres* have chosen to accord complex psychological motivation to what in large part amount to cardboard cut-out villains such as Goneril and Regan in *King Lear*, in the process transporting Shakespeare's play to the 1970s American Mid West. Caryl Phillips's novel *The Nature of Blood* (1997) does something rather different in that it gives voice to an already central Shakespearean character, Othello, but subjects his narrative and tragic trajectory to re-examination. This is achieved by means of the multi-perspectival context of juxtaposed first- and third-person narratives in the novel, and within the shaping context of analogous stories of diaspora and exile. The novel is structured around the experiences of a sequence of social outsiders, interweaving, and therefore connecting, their tales of persecution on the grounds of ethnicity and religion.

Othello's story is just one of several interleaved narratives in the novel which ranges across historical and geographical boundaries and frames. Indeed, although the appropriation of Shakespeare's 1604 play can be seen as a guiding creative force in Phillips's text, what we come to recognize as Othello's story does not appear until some one hundred pages in, and the majority of the events in his life that are dealt with occur either prior to or during the opening act of Shakespeare's play. Tellingly, in this name-obsessed novel, Othello is never directly named, even though, ironically, the last words of those passages in his narrative voice are 'my name' (Phillips 1997: 174). If many appropriations actively give voice to certain characters, Phillips seems equally compelled to silence the character usually charged with defining and manipulating Othello in the play: Iago, the Ancient, who is mentioned only once in *The Nature of Blood*, and then only as 'the Ancient' entrusted with the care of the African general's Venetian wife during the sea-journey to Cyprus. The reader is, of course, invited to participate by filling in the gaps with the known names and details, and in the process to apply a sense of tragic inevitability to the events being described. As with Antoinette Mason's fate in Thornfield Hall in *Wide Sargasso Sea*, we know all too well the future story of this Cypriot encampment and that it will realize something far from the 'happy conclusions' this Othello foresees (174).

What we as readers also recognize in this narrative are lexical signifiers of non-Shakespearean but equally tragic content, the story of the twentieth-century Holocaust, here synecdochally signalled by mentions of trains, camps, showers and gas. In his careful interleaving of early modern Venetian elements with scenes situated in twentieth-century concentration camps, Phillips is primarily concerned with a need to revisit Othello's narrative through the lens of the life-stories of other migrants, outsiders and refugees. He juxtaposes Othello's plotline and other aspects of the story with those of twentieth-century Jewish experience, in particular through literary strategies of echo and parallel. Stephan Stern, for example, who begins the novel in a mid-twentieth-century refugee camp in Cyprus just prior to the formation of the modern state of Israel, has, like Othello, deserted his wife and child to make life in a new homeland. Eva Stern's suffering in the Nazi concentration camps is directly paralleled with the execution of Jews in fifteenth-century Venice: the fire and ashes of execution and genocide provide haunting continuities across the centuries.

The Nature of Blood, then, is a veritable echo-chamber of a text; its full emotional and poetic impact is achieved by means of parallels and analogues found between its variant constituent parts and historical timeframes. We move, in a deliberately unguided if not unstructured way, between fifteenth-century Venice, where members of the Jewish community are wrongly burned at the stake for the supposed murder of a Christian child, the late sixteenth-century Venice which Othello inhabits, and in which we see him visiting the Jewish ghetto of Canareggio by night, the internment camps of Nazi Europe and the post-war refugee camps in Cyprus and Israel. In the midst of all these movements Shakespeare's *Othello* is not the sole informing intertext. The Venetian episodes of the novel suggest and echo the bard's *other* Venetian play about ethnic prejudice, *The Merchant of Venice*. The traumatized first-person narrative of Eva (Stephan's niece) recalls in turn Anne Frank's *Diary*, a canonical text of Holocaust literature. Phillips is offering a troubling version of that old adage that 'History repeats'. One of the most unsettling aspects of this novel is that, having evoked empathy with the persecuted Jews of previous centuries, the narrative closes with a rumination on the inverse prejudice of modern-day Israel in the disenfranchised figure of the Ethiopian Jew Malka who, as Phillips has noted elsewhere, would not be allowed to give blood in her new homeland for fear of polluting 'pure bloodlines' (Ledent 2002: 138).

The Nature of Blood is intricately structured via a series of repeating images and phrases: blood, fire, smoke, ashes, rivers, food. These words and ideas serve as leitmotifs, refrains in the text, and the 'musicality' of this technique has been noted by Bénédicte Ledent (2002: 160). Interestingly, the most obvious sources of echo or musical refrain – the lines of Shakespeare's tragic drama – are held at bay for the majority of the novel. Although the events of the 'Othello' passages have obvious connection to those described at the start of Shakespeare's play – 'Her father loved me, oft invited me ....' (1.3.127), 'These things to hear / Would Desdemona seriously incline ...' (1.3.144–5), only some of Othello's sentences actively recall famous lines from Phillips's source: 'I possessed only a rudimentary grasp of the language that was being spoken all about me ...' (1997: 108), for example, clearly suggests Othello's claim at 1.3.81, 'Rude am I in my speech', although these words are not directly used until page 181 of the novel and only then in the mouth of a very different character:

And so you shadow her every move, attend her every whim, like the black Uncle Tom that you are. Fighting the white man's war for him / Wide receiver in the Venetian army / The republic's grinning Satchmo hoisting his sword like a trumpet / You tuck your black skin away beneath their epauletted uniform, appropriate their words (*Rude am I in speech*).

(Phillips 1997: 181)

This is one of several moments in the narrative when voices and discourses other than those of the central protagonists are heard. The signifiers here clearly indicate a late twentieth-century voice deriving from the USA, as in the phrases 'wide receiver', 'Satchmo'. The 'Satchmo' reference recalls (negatively) jazz great Louis Armstrong, and the verse layout recalls both jazz lyrics and the dramatic verse of Shakespeare's play, as well as evoking the rhythms of contemporary rap, all inherently appropriative and referential forms, as we have noted. That the term 'appropriate' appears in this passage draws attention to Phillips's fictional methods, as does his inclusion elsewhere of encyclopaedic and dictionary references to a number of his key themes and foci: Venice, ghetto, suicide. These include an entry on *Othello* which emphasizes Shakespeare's own reworking of an Italian source, a short story by Cinthio, when manufacturing his remarkable play.

In *The Nature of Blood*, an individual's narrative often commences at a supposed endpoint or terminus (Eva's liberation from the camp, for example), only to move backwards in time. The interlocking and circular movements of the novel leave the question open as to whether the ultimate vision is hopeful or despairing. Malka's story would seem to imply that history simply repeats a series of mistakes, tragedies and cruelties; the novel closes, after all, with the image of an impossible embrace. But these movements also exist as the end-stop or terminal point, so perhaps the real answer lies in the image or idea of circularity. There can be no easy answers or closure on such complicated themes. In this subtle examination of memory and forgetting the reader cannot shut out knowledge of certain facts. Just as Eva's story cannot, and does not, end at the point of liberation from the camps – readers are forced to witness her painful efforts to survive after the war, her failed trip to England and her eventual suicide – so we know that Othello's story does not cease at that moment of happy arrival on the shores of Cyprus. Phillips's allusive frames force us to read on further, beyond these pages even, and the tragic impetus of the novel proves inescapable as a result.

MICHAEL CUNNINGHAM'S *THE HOURS*: RIFFING ON *MRS DALLOWAY*

Michael Cunningham has described his 1998 novel *The Hours*, a novel told via a triptych of female voices stretching from early twentieth-century England through 1940s Los Angeles to 1990s New York, as a 'riff' on Virginia Woolf's *Mrs Dalloway* (Young 2003: 31). Woolf's 1925 novel tells the story of a group of Londoners on a single day in June 1923. Cunningham never directly retells or rewrites these events, and yet their diffused and dispersed presence can be felt everywhere in *The Hours*. Indeed, 'The Hours' was Woolf's working title for her efforts to develop and extend her short story 'Mrs Dalloway in Bond Street' into novel-length form, and her diary entry on this for 30 August 1923 is used as an epigraph to *The Hours* (Woolf 1981: 263). At various stages in Cunningham's narrative we witness Virginia Woolf thinking her experimental novel into being; we also see a 1949 housewife, Laura Brown, escaping from the quotidian *ennui* of her life by reading the novel; and in the 1990s sections, the implicit connection between Clarissa Vaughan and her novelistic counterpart is made explicit: Richard, Clarissa's friend and a writer, jokingly calls her 'Mrs Dalloway', forcing her to reflect: 'There was the matter of her existing first name, a sign too obvious to ignore' (Cunningham 1998: 10–11). Cunningham enjoys the postmodern joke here; his intertextual pastiche is redolent with signs and signifiers of a literary precursor 'too obvious to ignore'. Other names in this novel prove equally telling: Laura Brown's deliberately invokes the character in Woolf's highly influential essay 'Mr Bennett and Mrs Brown', which constituted, in part, a manifesto for a new approach to fiction and which differentiated her own writing from that of contemporaries such as Arnold Bennett, H. G. Wells and John Galsworthy (Woolf 1988 [1923]).

Cunningham's musical analogy of the 'riff' is insightful. As Tory Young notes: 'In its suggestion of a known melody reverberating throughout a new score, this musical definition is more compelling than some of the literary terms such as "imitation", or "homage" that critics have used to describe it' (2003: 33). The specific analogy of 'riff' with the approaches to adaptation adopted by jazz music practitioners – 'riff' in the *Oxford English Dictionary* definition is a 'short repeated phrase in jazz' – is worth pausing to reflect upon. Throughout his career the literary critic Terence Hawkes has drawn suggestive parallels between persistent inter-pretations and reinterpretations of Shakespeare in Western culture and the improvisational tactics of jazz (see, for example, Hawkes 1992). Here, Cunningham does not riff exclusively on a single source text, although *Mrs Dalloway* is clearly the central intertext for his novel, but rather creates a work that exists in symbiotic interplay with Woolf's fiction and non-fiction (letters, essays, diaries), and her personal biography. Something similar has been achieved in dance more recently when choreographer Wayne McGregor produced his experimental ballet *Woolf Works* (2015), based on a triptych of novels, *Mrs Dalloway, Orlando* and *The Waves*, but also interleaved with Woolf's life-story. In a haunting moment in the ballet an actor reads Woolf's suicide note as an older dancer performs her death by drowning on stage. Cunningham has frequently acknowledged his creative debt to Hermione Lee's magisterial 1996 Woolf biography, and in his narrative the symbiotic interplay occurs at the level of form as well as plot. The prose style of *The Hours* consciously imitates Woolf's stream-of-consciousness technique, echoing resonant words and phrases from *Mrs Dalloway* such as 'plunge' (Woolf 1992 [1925]: 3; Cunningham 1998: 9). These echoes are not restricted to *Mrs Dalloway* but extend to other works in Woolf's *oeuvre* as Cunningham produces loving pastiches of her writing style.

Events in *The Hours* are, however, persistently shaded and shadowed by those of *Mrs Dalloway.* Septimus Smith's suicide – achieved by leaping down from his residence on to the railings outside his London home as he is pursued by doctors whom he regards as unsympathetic to the post-traumatic stress disorder he is suffering following first-hand experience in the trenches of the Great War – is reworked as Richard's own suicidal leap from his New York apartment. Richard chooses to end his life because he is dying of AIDS. Cunningham's personal sexual politics, as well

as his obvious feminist sympathies, inform this particular appropriation. This *Mrs Dalloway* is shaped as much by late twentieth-
century queer politics as it is by feminism and postmodernism.
Cunningham's particular 'movement of proximation' (Genette
1997 [1982]: 304) finds a millennial equivalent in virulent pan-
demics such as AIDS and the horrors of warfare that shaped the
early part of the twentieth century. *The Hours* is not, however,
wholly tragic in tone or approach; there is liberating treatment of
gay rights at the heart of the novel that lends it an optimism as
well. Cunningham achieves for his ensemble of characters a freedom of relationships that exists beyond heterosexual norms,
something well beyond the reach even of Woolf's own highly
experimental Bloomsbury community. In Cunningham's version
of the story Clarissa does not marry Richard, who is openly gay,
but is instead in a rich and rewarding lesbian relationship of her
own with Sally Seton; this realizes a possibility that was only
hinted at on a subterranean level by the 1925 novel, even though
in turn it reworked the real-life relationship between Woolf and
Vita Sackville-West.

   The triple timeline of Cunningham's novel helps the reader to
register the seismic social shifts that have taken place since Woolf
created her novel: the tense and contained same-sex kiss between
Laura Brown and her neighbour Kitty serves as an indication of
the containment of female sexuality for a large part of the twentieth
century, and certainly the social restrictions constraining the
possibility of lesbian relationships in America in 1949. But in the
1990s sections of the novel the full potential for diverse relationships and friendships is realized as Cunningham brings Woolf's
story up to date in successive movements through his triptych of
characters and through the juxtaposed spaces, places and times of
the narrative. London in the 1920s is superseded by Los Angeles in
1949 and then 1990s New York. *Mrs Dalloway*'s spatial location in
Westminster is now substituted by New York's West Village, itself
a site of political fame as the heartland of the 1969 Stonewall
Riots, which are linked to a dawning of gay rights consciousness
in the wider metropolitan community in the 1960s. This is a novel
that builds into its music and movements, its narrative choreo-
graphy, the translocations and transpositions that are a recurring

feature of appropriative literature. In this movement of succession, no one place or story fully replaces the other; each element in the triptych contains within it links and connections to the others. This is perhaps made most obvious in the closing moments of the novel when, following Richard's suicide, his estranged mother arrives at Clarissa's apartment. Belatedly readers realize that this Toronto librarian, whose absence from his life obsessed and troubled Richard but whose love of books and reading clearly coloured his development as a writer, is in fact Laura Brown from the LA segments of the novel. Similarly, a novel that commences with Woolf's 1940 suicide by drowning, comes full circle with Richard's death, but we are also reminded of Laura's own dreams of death and escape while reading *Mrs Dalloway* at key moments earlier in the narrative.

Circular and repeating movements are a vital aspect of this novel's composition, but this is, of course, a mode that we have already seen in operation in Rhys's repetition-soaked *Wide Sargasso Sea*, in the repeating events, albeit in revised circumstances, of Philips's *The Nature of Blood*, and in the narrative slippages and returns of Coetzee's *Foe*. As well as these web-like connections between the three voices and settings of *The Hours*, there are numerous repetitions of lines and symbols which are themselves circular or spherical and which form a verbal leitmotif: a narrative of cups, bowls, and cakes, ordinary and everyday household items related to women's lives in the twentieth century. In director Stephen Daldry's 2002 film version of Cunningham's novel this imagery was played out a second time in a visual context, but the truly connective tissue was provided by Philip Glass's remarkable river-like, undulating, piano-based soundtrack.

Part of the distinct music of *The Hours* is temporal as well as spatial; linear sequence is deliberately repulsed and we begin with Woolf's ending, as it were, her riverine suicide, but then revert to a time before that and before *Mrs Dalloway* has even been written. These movements backwards as well as forwards in time are crucial to the anti-linear structure of other appropriative novels that this chapter has considered, such as Phillips's history-driven *The Nature of Blood*. It has perhaps become something of a commonplace to associate circular or anti-linear style with women's writing (Sanders 2001: 142), but perhaps it would be more accurate to associate it more generally with a disruptive or non-normative stance. Phillips's novel engages with issues of ethnic identity and marginalization, Cunningham's with gay rights. All of these writers are reclaiming (as Woolf herself did) the right to describe certain territories and agendas. Once again, these are political and ideological strategies performed via a series of highly personal and localized positions and stylistic effects. The repetitions and circular sweeps of *The Hours* are perhaps inevitable in a novel that looks back on a canonical source and which embeds within its own pages the textual traces of Woolf's own highly circular and musical creation. As Clarissa Vaughan observes, stepping out into the streetscape of 1990s New York on her own urban walking experience, one that re-creates the activity of a British fictional namesake at seventy years remove, and one which repeats the very action or intended action of the 1920s novel: 'There are still the flowers to buy' (Cunningham 1998: 9).

7

'WE "OTHER VICTORIANS"'
OR, RETHINKING THE NINETEENTH CENTURY

What becomes evident from any historicized consideration of appropriation is that interest invariably clusters around certain authors and texts: Shakespeare, mythology and fairy tale have all been advanced in this volume (see Part II) as repositories of archetypal narratives, ripe for appropriation and re-vision and in increasingly global and multimedia contexts. The interest in specific texts, such as Defoe's *Robinson Crusoe* or Charlotte Brontë's *Jane Eyre*, has also in part been explained in terms of the canon: what these texts have come to represent and the high levels of access to them as a result. As Chantal Zabus eloquently observes: 'Each century has its own interpellative dream-text: *The Tempest* for the seventeenth century; *Robinson Crusoe* for the eighteenth century; *Jane Eyre* for the nineteenth century; *Heart of Darkness* for the turn of the twentieth century. Such texts serve as pre-texts to others and underwrite them' (2002: 1). Defoe's novel carries the specific burden of signification as an early experiment in the form; *Jane Eyre* is a signifying text for feminism, as well as an intriguing dalliance with popular genres such as the Gothic romance. Canonicity, alongside a strong presence in the popular cultural imagination, might almost be viewed as a required feature of the raw material for adaptation and appropriation. The pleasure of assessing the similarities and differences between texts, and of judging the levels of conformity and dissent in their approaches, requires prior knowledge of the work(s) being assimilated, absorbed, reworked and refashioned.

What, however, also emerges from any historical exploration of appropriation is that it is not only specific texts or even authors who elicit the kind of ongoing, evolving and kinetic interest that stimulates the adaptive process, but specific genres, or, perhaps even more specifically, genres, and indeed epochs, as they become culturally visible at particular temporal moments, which become the focus of a shared (re)creative impulse. One particular and sustained example of this is undoubtedly the Victorian era (1837–1901). As this chapter will indicate, appropriations return again and again to the scene of the mid-nineteenth century to plunder characters, plotlines and generic conventions, as well as narrative idiom and style. What we will now examine are the motivations behind this compulsion.

It is fair to say that the Victorian era had its own investment in adaptation as a practice. Adrian Poole has written of the pre-dominance of Shakespeare in the artistic productions of the period, from plays to poetry to painting to fiction (Poole 2004). George Eliot, Thomas Hardy, Charles Dickens and the Pre-Raphaelites all alluded to the Bard. And it was not only the writers of previous eras who were subject to these re-creative impulses: Dickens's novels and characters, and those of Sir Walter Scott, enjoyed a vivid afterlife on the public stages of the day. Dickens even satirized this fact in *Nicholas Nickleby* (1838–9), when Nicholas encounters a 'literary gentleman' who 'had dramatised in his time two-hundred-and-forty-seven novels as fast as they had come out – and some of them faster than they had come out' (cited in Cox 2000: 136). John Fowles makes similar comic capital in his own postmodern re-creation of the Victorian novel, *The French Lieutenant's Woman*, when the servant Sam Farrow is compared to Sam Weller in *Pickwick Papers*, a character we learn that he knows *not* from Dickens's novel but rather from a populist stage adaptation

(Fowles 1996 [1969]: 46). Dickens's objections to the quality of at least some of the dramatic adaptations of his work are a further indication of a marked distinction between the productions of so-called 'high' and 'low' culture in the period. High art was invested with the values of authorship and originality; popular culture was imbued with the belatedness of adaptation. In the twentieth century, with the advent of the newly inaugurated discipline of Cultural Studies, scholars such as Stuart Hall and Raymond Williams saw rather more cause for celebrating the adaptive tendencies of popular cultural forms (Hall 1972: 96). It is worth emphasizing that the Victorian era appealed as a subject to that revisionary moment of scholarship partly because of the lively interaction and cross-fertilization between the so-called high and low arts in this period.

The genre which most obviously bridged the threshold between high and low, elite and popular, in the nineteenth century was the novel (see Wheeler 1994). Many novels were published in instalments, encouraging readerly addiction to plotlines and characters, and honing the authorial skills of creating suspense by means of the 'cliff-hanger' ending, designed to hook the reader into staying loyal and buying the next instalment. That practice still influences the contemporary soap opera genre on radio, television and streaming sites. The nineteenth century witnessed a proliferation of sub-genres within the novel form: there were early experiments with suspense fiction, encouraged by the tendency to publish in instalments; sensational literature, which found its own provenance in a contemporary predilection for scandalous legal trials and which had a markedly feminocentric character, reached its peak in the 1860s; detective fiction began to emerge as a genuine sub-genre in its own right, related as it was to a wider interest in crime, criminology and forensic science in the Victorian novel; and there were developments such as the industrial and the provincial novel, as pioneered by Elizabeth Gaskell, Thomas Hardy and George Eliot, among others.

In the late twentieth century, then, as the postmodernist movement developed its own interest in metafiction and writing which acknowledges its sources in a more explicit and deconstructive mode than previously, the Victorian era offered a diverse range of genres and methodologies to examine and appropriate. Dominic Head identifies this impulse in Graham Swift's *Waterland*, for example: 'Part of Swift's self-consciousness is to make use of a number of fictional genres identified with English fiction in the nineteenth century: the dynastic saga, the gothic novel, the detective story and, most important, the provincial novel in which character is closely linked with environment' (Head 2002: 295). Head stresses that Swift's reworkings are not parody but rather a process of reinvigoration achieved via modern and postmodern inflection (205). Subjects are fleshed out by modern psychological and scientific knowledge, and descriptions are filled in as a result of the more permissive approach to sexuality and identity. The impulse is towards quotation and re-creation, but with amplification and alteration within the new context enabling new findings or insight in shared material.

Many of the best-known modern 're-creations' of the Victorian novel self-consciously position themselves in relation to populist sub-genres of the nineteenth century but engage in a critical re-evaluation of those forms rather than simplistic mimicry. Fowles's *The French Lieutenant's Woman* is a romance that carries within its core traces of the mystery novel and the scientific tract; A. S. Byatt's *Possession* is a self-conscious reworking of the act of literary criticism itself as a form of detective fiction: 'Literary critics make natural detectives' (1991: 237). We have purposely moved away here from a one-to-one relationship that underpins more traditional forms of adaptation studies or much maligned forms of fidelity-based criticism. Instead what we have are writers who are conscious of the fact that they are refashioning an entire period as a means of speaking about their own, through a form of what Graham Allen has termed 'transtextuality': 'Novels may signpost their architextual relation to certain genres, sub-genres or conventions by including a subtitle, as in Ann Radcliffe's Gothic novel *The Mystery of Udolpho: A Romance*' (Allen 2000: 102). Byatt's *Possession: A Romance* repeats this pattern and may be a direct allusion to Radcliffe as well as signalling the link of her narrative to the romance genre. Both Fowles's and Byatt's texts are laid out on the printed page in a manner reminiscent of much nineteenth-century fiction, not least the novels of Eliot and

Hardy, with copious literary and, in the case of Fowles, historio-graphical quotations providing shaping epigraphs to individual chapters. In this respect they materially as well as aesthetically re-create the mode of the Victorian novel, with all its paratextual material.

In the case of *The French Lieutenant's Woman*, these quotations derive from actual and identified nineteenth-century sources, but also from 'historical' re-creations such as the work of Asa Briggs and G. M. Young. There is an interesting recognition implicit in this of the textuality of history and of history's status as text or narrative. In *Metahistory*, Hayden White famously argued that any work of history was as much a piece of rhetorical construction as any work of fiction, and that the play of rhetorical surfaces across historical narratives influences the reader as much as the events or 'facts' being recounted (1973: 3). History, in this account, is a matter of perspective; it is influenced and shaped by the ideology and the subject-position of the historian. Several of the adaptations we are considering here that revisit the nineteenth century, or seek to voice marginalized or repressed groups, suggest something similar in their search to reveal 'hidden histories', the stories between the lines of the published works of fact and fiction. Metafiction and meta-history collide in interesting and provocative ways in the course of this self-consciousness about the constructed nature of texts.

In Byatt's *Possession* the chapter epigraphs she provides stand at one stage further removed from the period she is appropriating since they are authorial creations that merely resemble 'real' litera-ture from the nineteenth century. In (re)creating the verse of her Victorian poets Randolph Ash and Christabel LaMotte – the subjects of the academic research of her modern counterpart characters Roland Michell and Maud Bailey – Byatt alludes to the work of actual nineteenth-century poets such as Robert Browning, Christina Rossetti and Emily Dickinson. Ash's work offers a parti-cular parallel with Browning, who was admired for a kind of poetic ventriloquism in his work, notably his ability to create and re-create individual voices, real and fictional, in his dramatic monologues. Indeed, the biography of Ash written by one of the novel's main characters, Mortimer Cropper, is entitled *The Great Ventriloquist*, as if to draw attention to this mode within Byatt's own writing (Hulbert 1993: 56), which in the course of this novel pastiches letters, journals and poetry from the Victorian era, as well as the tone and idiom of feminist and postmodern literary criticism.

'AT THE TIME OF MY STORY'

'Re-creational' fictions are never pure ventriloquism. They rely on their readers' awareness that they are reading from the vantage point of a different era. Byatt ensures this deliberate disjuncture in *Possession* by interweaving dual storylines and parallel romances in the nineteenth and twentieth centuries. Fowles goes even further by building into his postmodern narrative a metafictional awareness of the modern idiom and understanding, determining his, and our, responses to his historical characters and themes. Phrases in *The French Lieutenant's Woman* such as 'We meet here, once again, this bone of contention between the two centuries' (1996 [1969]: 52) draw attention to the encounter between the mind-sets of the two periods, as does the encounter between the author and his character in a railway carriage in one notorious chapter of the novel. Fowles's method is one that resists wholesale ventriloquism of Victorian narrative style, depending instead on the juxtaposition, comparison and contrast which we have already identified as a driving force in the appropriative mode. He asserts, for example, that he is not the omniscient narrator so memorable from much of nineteenth-century fiction: 'If I have pretended until now to know my characters' minds and innermost thoughts, it is because I am writing in (just as I have assumed some of the vocabulary and "voice" of) a convention universally accepted at the time of my story: that the novelist stands next to God' (97). His is, by contrast, the era of the 1960s, sexual liberation and post-structuralism: 'I live in the age of Alain Robbe-Grillet and Roland Barthes' (97). Indeed, in Chapter 13 of *The French Lieutenant's Woman* Fowles's God proves to be an existentialist creation. This represents not so much a deconstruction of authorship as an overt rejection of it, and as such offers an intriguing echo of Barthes's arguments for the 'freedom' of the reader in his theoretical writings, although in Fowles that freedom is reimagined primarily as the freedom of the novelistic character which the author claims that he is forced to respect. There is an intriguing link here with the contemporary novels of Jasper Fforde, where novelistic characters from canonical texts are wilfully cut free from their source and allowed complete independence. In *The Eyre Affair* (2005), for example, literary detective Thursday Next finds herself solving a mystery involving aspects of Charlotte Brontë's *Jane Eyre*, and in later novels in the series intertexts from Jane Austen's *Pride and Prejudice* to the Just William novels of Richmal Crompton play their part.

James Wilson's *The Dark Clue*, while less explicit about the metafictional aspect of its appropriation of Victorian fiction, achieves something similar to Fowles's and Byatt's novels by pastiching the style of nineteenth-century sensation fiction, a mode which reached its peak in the 1860s (Pykett 1994: 1). Wilson re-creates sensation fiction's meticulous reconstruction of quasi-legalistic eye-witness statements in its first-person narrative, while also alluding to a specific canonical text: Wilkie Collins's 1860 novel *The Woman in White*. That novel is famous not only as the progenitor of this particular mode of sensation fiction but also as the precursor of crime fiction as a genre, and the specific mode of the detective novel, which Collins would realize in a fuller incarnation in a later text, *The Moonstone* (1868). Again, Wilson signals his interest in the revisiting of the Victorian sub-genres of the mystery and the crime novel in his subtitle to *The Dark Clue*: 'A novel of suspense', and in his expert pastiching of Collins's own predilection for a narrative constructed via a combination of letters, journal entries and legal testimonies. Lyn Pykett has indicated just how much Collins's novels owed to the popular stage melodrama of his day (1994: 4), and Wilson appears to acknowledge this via his inclusion of a pastiche of a play at one stage in the narrative.

Such was *The Woman in White*'s significance in its own era that there were multiple stage adaptations and even tie-in merchandise (Collins 1999 [1860]: vii); this cultural potency continues into the present day when it is the subject of musical and television adaptations, once again acknowledging the novel's creative proximity to melodrama. Wilson's novel meanwhile reanimates and re-voices two protagonists of *The Woman in White*: Walter Hartright the painter and his sister-in-law Marian Halcombe. Between them this incongruous pair solved the original mystery of Collins's story, which was concerned with the feigned demise of Marian's sister Laura, who has in truth been placed in an asylum under a false identity by her villainous husband, Sir Percival Glyde. In *The Dark Clue* Walter and Marion serve once again as amateur sleuths. This time, however, their assigned task is to research the life of the late painter J. M. W. Turner, about whom Hartright has been commissioned to write a biography. In a parallel mode to the 're-creations' of Byatt and Fowles, Wilson here merges fictional and real figures from the period. What he is also able to do, in the process, is to make explicit many of the sexual tensions which are only implicit in Collins's text but which have certainly been brought to light by generations of critics and scholars of the novel subsequently. John Sutherland, for example, has located the sexual undercurrent of *The Woman in White* in the face-off between Marian and Count Fosco, the melodramatic Italian villain of the piece, but there is surely also sexual chemistry between Marian and Walter despite the latter's marriage to her more conventionally beautiful half-sister. Wilson seems almost to satisfy readerly expectation in this respect when a troubled sexual encounter takes place between his protagonists late in the novel.

This sexually aggressive element of the text of *The Dark Clue* is part of the novel's wider investment in exploring the sexual undercurrents and repression of the Victorian era. This constitutes much of the hidden mysteries of Turner's life which Walter uncovers in the course of his research (intriguingly this theme is also picked up in a more recent biographical movie, *Mr Turner*, directed by Mike Leigh in 2014). In a manner parallel to that of Byatt's *Possession*, the art of the biographer is compared to that of the detective or forensic scientist. Walter has, in turn, to confront darker aspects of his own personality in the process, which further complicates this depiction of Collins's rather too-perfect hero. One of the aspects of Turner's painterly technique that begins to fascinate Hartright is his deployment of *chiaroscuro*, which the *Oxford English Dictionary* defines in multiple ways. First, in fine arts terminology, it is 'the treatment of light and shade in drawing and painting'. This is a recognizable element of Turner's style and one that Hartright seeks to emulate: the novel encourages a strong awareness of Turner's paintings throughout as a means of decoding how and why events unfold in the way they do. But *chiaroscuro* can also mean 'the use of contrast in literature', which might serve as a working description of the appeal of adaptation. Finally, it refers, via its Italian etymology, to the 'half-revealed' (*chiaro* = clear, *oscuro* = dark/obscured); Wilson's title is a transliteration of this idea but it also highlights the investment of detective fiction in bringing things to light that we witnessed earlier in Graham Swift's knowing venture into the form in *The Light of Day* (see Chapter 4). These attentions to hidden or dark things also invite us to consider the darker side of Victorian culture as revealed in the novel, such as the worlds of prostitution and pornography with which Turner's life intersected and which drag Walter quite literally into their back alleys. This same dark undercurrent to Victorian society troubles Fowles in *The French Lieutenant's Woman*, where the dual perspective instructs us as readers to recognize the discrepancies and contradictions inherent in Victorian society: 'What are we faced with in the nineteenth century? An age where woman was sacred; and where you could buy a thirteen-year-old girl for a few pounds ....Where more churches were built than in the whole previous history of the country, and where one in sixty London houses was a brothel' (1996 [1969]: 258). The reader is acting as a detective of sorts when encountering this kind of layered fiction, deciphering clues and recognizing the parallels, but also registering the significant differences between the rendition of the nineteenth century achieved in the novels and the current context of the interpretation. This is one of the particular literacies encouraged by adaptation, and comprises the process of what Thomas Leitch calls 'rereading through adaptation' (2007: 303).

The Victorian era, with its impressive surface achievements, but equally its active underworlds and subcultures, offers a very specific example of the cultural contradictions that adaptational work can seek to highlight, and this may in part explain the ongoing fascination with 'Neo-Victorianism', as it has sometimes been called (Kaplan 2007; Heilmann and Llewellyn 2010; Boehm-Schnitker and Gruss 2014). There are also obvious connections with the science fiction sub-genres of Steampunk, which blends industrial era and futuristic technologies in its artistic engagements. Thinking with and through the Victorian era certainly enables reflections on global urbanization, from London to Shanghai, and throws into relief in the process questions of class and hierarchy as well as empire and imperialism. As Gayatri Chakravorty Spivak has noted, 'It should not be possible to read nineteenth-century British literature without remembering that imperialism, understood as England's social mission, was a crucial part of the cultural representation of England to the English' (1997 [1989]: 148). All of these are strong explanations for the ongoing interest in reworking and rearticulating the concerns of Victorian fiction in the modern era, through fiction, film and other media. But it is worth investigating even further the motivations for this interest.

As well as the Victorian era in its totality, a particular interest in the decade of the 1860s has emerged. This was the decade, as already noted, of sensation fiction and the emergence of fictional genres such as the detective novel and the murder mystery. All of the strategies we have focussed on so far in this chapter find their roots in that decade. Charles Dickens's *Great Expectations*, though its action was set some years earlier, was published in the 1860s and bears the traces of the contemporary interest in crime as well as the vogue for new models of writing to reflect that interest. Wemmick's private library packed with studies of criminology and convict literature is just one obvious signifier of this relationship in the novel. But, as that novel's acknowledged and highly developed interest in theories of nature and nurture suggests (Dickens 1994 [1861]: xiv), the 1860s represent a decisive turn in terms of postmodern reimagining of the Victorian novel and its roots in the deeper context of Victorian social and cultural values. This was the era that witnessed one of the greatest ever challenges to religious understandings of the world and identity, in the shape of Darwin's theory of evolution. The impact of *The Origin of Species*, published in 1859 and its own narrative of environmental adaptation, has already been registered in a novel we discussed in Chapter 3, Graham Swift's *Ever After*, but it also furnishes many of the epigraphs for Fowles's *The French Lieutenant's Woman* (another of Swift's intertexts for his novel), whose central character is a geologist open to the scientific challenges posed by Darwin to the conventional Victorian way of looking at and understanding the world. That the first volume of Karl Marx's *Das Kapital* was published in 1867 lends credence to the notion of the 1860s as an epoch-changing decade.

Great Expectations was first published in instalment form in the periodical *All the Year Round* between December 1860 and August 1861. In 1860 this periodical had also published two significant extrapolations in essay form of Darwin's theory of adaptation, variation and survival: 'Species', published in June, and 'Natural Selection', published in July. The influence of this on Dickens's novel, which argues, via the plot trajectories of both Pip and Estella, that biological origins are only ever one part of our complex social and environmental make-up, should not be underestimated. In *Darwin's Plots*, Gillian Beer has argued that Darwin's prose was informed by his reading across several disciplines and that he found the literary figure of the analogy particularly instructive when articulating his scientific discoveries (1983: 80). It seems equally apposite that novels engaged in the process of literary adaptation, in creating analogues and variants of their own according to their cultural, geographical and historical context, should be drawn to Darwinian theories.

So the Victorian era proves ripe for appropriation because it highlights many of the overriding concerns of the postmodern era: questions of identity; of environmental and genetic conditioning; of repressed and oppressed modes of sexuality; of criminality and violence; of an interest in urbanism and the potentials and possibilities of new technology; of law and authority; of science and religion; and of the postcolonial legacies of empire. In the rewriting of the omniscient narrator prevalent in nineteenth-century fiction, often substituting for him/her the unreliable narrator we have recognized as a type in appropriative fiction, postmodern authors find a useful metafictional method to reflect on their own creative and authorial impulses. As previously, while close reading and case studies can never be the only methodology of adaptation studies, they remain valid means for effecting comparative readings alert to the functions of analogue and to the potential of the new multimodal literacies or readers and audiences in the modern era that critics such as Thomas Leitch have alerted us to (2007: 3).

This chapter will therefore now turn to a close reading of one particular contemporary novel which embodies many of the impulses outlined above in its knowing appropriation of Charles Dickens's *Great Expectations*, Australian novelist Peter Carey's *Jack Maggs* (1997), and then close with a consideration of the rich afterlives and remediations of Sir Arthur Conan Doyle's archetypal detective Sherlock Holmes.

COMING OUT OF THE SHADOWS: PETER CAREY'S *JACK MAGGS*

Like so many of the writers and creative adaptations and appropriations invoked in these pages, Peter Carey's interest in appropriation is not limited to a single work in his *oeuvre*. In a manner akin to J. M. Coetzee or John Fowles, he has long been recognized as deeply intertextual, though also as someone interested in the politics of his own moment. Novels such as *Illywhacker* (1985) and *Oscar and Lucinda* (1988) have been linked to nineteenth-century writing, in particular the work of Charles Dickens, to South American texts of magic realism and to the films of Werner Herzog, to name just a few (Woodcock 2003: 82). The arresting opening sequence of *Oscar and Lucinda*, which depicts Oscar's upbringing among the Plymouth Brethren, and its episode of the forbidden plum pudding owe much to Edmund Gosse's work of retrospective Victorian autobiography *Father and Son* (1907). Possibly in an act of deliberate disingenuousness, Carey denied at the time of *Oscar and Lucinda* that he was well read in Dickens (Woodcock 2003: 58), but there could be no doubt of his immersion in the works of the Victorian novelist by the time of his 1997 novel *Jack Maggs*, which is a direct appropriation of *Great Expectations*. The 'Jack Maggs' of Carey's title is his postcolonial reworking of Dickens's convict Abel Magwitch, the man whose New South Wales fortune is deployed in fashioning Pip Pirrip as a gentleman of 'great expectations' in that novel. If Dickens's text is, as Kate Flint has suggested, one imbued with the motif of return or, at least, of trying to return (Dickens 1994 [1861]: vii), then Carey's fiction is doubly so. He returns to the story of Magwitch and the return of the convict to London to meet with his

'adopted son', Pip, here transfixed into the rather more reprehensible figure of Henry Phipps; in the process, Carey imposes a
distinctly postcolonial set of political values and concerns on the
story. As with Jean Rhys's exposure of the imperialism implicit in
Jane Eyre throughout *Wide Sargasso Sea*, Bruce Woodcock suggests that Carey exposes the prejudices at the root of Dickens's
creation and Victorian culture:

> *Jack Maggs* juxtaposes the hidden and the visible to reveal a terrible
> social violence beneath the surface of the imperial ideal ... [It] is Peter
> Carey's *Wide Sargasso Sea:* an act of postcolonial retaliation against a
> parent culture. Like Jean Rhys's novel, it rewrites elements of a canonical
> text from the heart of the English literary tradition to reveal the
> hidden alternative history that cultural hegemony has effaced or
> suppressed.
>
> (Woodcock 2003: 120)

If Dickens's novel views Abel Magwitch almost entirely through
Pip's eyes and partial first-person narration, Carey inverts that
perspective so that we see events from Maggs's point of view. The
novel begins at the point of Maggs's return from the penal colony of
New South Wales. Carey quite literally effects for him a conditional
pardon within the context of the novel. As well as the obvious
Dickensian hypotext, Carey reworks the genre of Australian convict
literature, the prime example of which is Marcus Clarke's *His
Natural Life* (1885). Thomas Keneally's *The Playmaker*, discussed
in Chapter 2, works within a similar textual framework. Both
Carey and Keneally write from a self-consciously postcolonial
vantage point, 'writing back' to the central narrative of convict
transportation and the creation of the British penal settlement in
Australia. For Keneally this has the further resonance of the
damage it wrought in the indigenous aboriginal communities.

Influential on Carey's response to questions of empire in
Australian culture was historian Robert Hughes's *The Fatal Shore*,
published in 1988, which directly discusses *Great Expectations* in a
postcolonial context. In turn, and in a passage that cites Carey as
a postcolonial author, Edward Said picked up on this study in the
introduction to *Culture and Imperialism* (1993: xvi–xvii), further

evidence, were it needed, of the direct influence of theory and criticism on literary and cinematic appropriations. Said suggested that in *Great Expectations* the transported convict Magwitch serves as a metaphor for the relationship between England and its colonial offspring: 'The prohibition placed on Magwitch's return is not only penal but imperial: subjects can be taken to places like Australia, but they cannot be allowed a "return" to metropolitan space, which as all Dickens's fiction testifies, is meticulously charted, spoken for' (xvii). Carey allows Magwitch that return in the context of a novel, which, like so many of the adaptations of nineteenth-century fiction discussed in this chapter, evinces a deep fascination with the metropolitan space of London.

In *Jack Maggs*, Carey rewrites the conventional convict's ending as well as Magwitch's specific fate in Dickens's novel, where he dies in Pip's arms. Carey permits Maggs an additional 'return' to his Australian 'home' and family. This proves a more complex rewriting than first appearances might suggest, since throughout the narrative Maggs persistently denies his Australian identity, rejecting his family there in favour of an obsessive interest with the aborted child in his criminal past and the 'adopted' Phipps. Máire ní Fhlathúin indicates the ways in which the novel, imitating the generic conventions of 1860s sensation fiction, repeats tropes of failed parentage, not least via the figure of the dying King William IV. The novel opens in 1837 with an ailing monarch and the accession of Queen Victoria imminent. Ní Fhlathúin argues that Carey does not entirely escape the paradigms he seeks to expose since he merely substitutes an idealized Australian patriarchy for the imperial version that the novel critiques. The final image that readers are given of Magwitch on his return to New South Wales is one of imperial re-creation both within his family set-up and in the loaded space of the local cricket club (ní Fhlathúin 1999: 90); the limits to Carey's postcolonial perspective are, perhaps, revealed in this, as well as by the absence of the aboriginal voice from the text. However, just as the novel's extended debate about property and ownership is an oblique engagement with the legal discourse of land rights in his con-temporary Australia, so Carey's approach to Maggs's 'happy ending' deserves further analysis. Many critics at the time of the novel's publication declared themselves dissatisfied with the novel's impositional and quasi-imperial act of closure, but they were perhaps reading the narrative too superficially.

Like Fowles before him, Carey is deeply self-conscious about the symbolism of endings. In *The French Lieutenant's Woman* Fowles offered some three alternative endings to the reader, while acknowledging that 'the conventions of Victorian fiction allow, allowed, no place for the open, the inconclusive ending' (1996 [1969]: 38). That masterful slip into the past tense – 'allow, allowed' – highlights the fact that Fowles can, and will, break free of past literary conventions and write out of his own context. I would suggest that *Jack Maggs* retains the possibility of alternative endings right up to its notional end. Interestingly, *Great Expectations* is invariably now published in modern editions with alternative endings: the first was a quasi-happy conventional ending imposed on Dickens by his editor Bulwer Lytton, in which a strong hint is given that Pip and Estella might live happily ever after as a couple; the second is the much darker ending, one where the emphasis is placed on severance and separation, and was initially preferred by the author. There is then a distinctly Dickensian precedent for the false consciousness which surrounds Carey's recounting of the 'happy ending' for Maggs, one in which he and Merry Larkin made a new life back in Australia (Porter 1997: 16; cited in ní Fhlathúin 1999: 91). As Woodcock observes, there is a 'fairy tale, deliberately unreal' air to this section (2003: 137), with its idyllic depiction of happy families and provincial neighbourhood contentment; none of what precedes this in the novel appeared to have been leading to this kind of outcome. This atmosphere of unreality, of conscious inauthenticity even, is further compounded by the overall ending which refers to Mercy's collection of first editions of the Tobias Oates novel about Maggs (there has been at the heart of Carey's fiction a novel within the novel, as it were, one which itself has gone through multiple iterations, and Oates is an adapted version of Dickens himself). In an act of narrative circularity, this connects back to the first time we see Mercy in the novel, where she is handling books in Percy Buckle's personal library. There is a consciously artful, fictional and literary aspect to this ending, one that asks the informed reader to bring additional meaning to bear, to read between the lines, as it were, in a mode parallel to the act of reading adaptations more generally. Even the fulsome printed dedication to Buckle in *The Death of Maggs* appears false in view of what we have read previously. Texts can lie and mislead, and Carey's fiction toys with this possibility throughout its narrative and retains its sceptical awareness of unstable textuality right to its close.

Carey's appropriation of *Great Expectations* not only rewrites events in Dickens's canonical novel, but goes one step further by bringing a version of the author himself into the heart of the fiction. Oates, a journalist in the early stages of a career in novel writing, anxious for patronage and success, is a thinly veiled variation on aspects of Dickens's biography. Kate Flint has noted that Dickens wrote *Great Expectations* during a particularly vexed period in his personal life. On 11 March 1861, he wrote to a friend, W. H. Wills, that he felt 'quite weighed down and loaded and chained in life' (cited in Dickens 1994: x; Dickens 1938: 212). He had separated from his wife in 1858 and he became the subject of considerable popular scandal surrounding his rumoured relationship with the actress Ellen (Nelly) Ternan (Kaplan 1988: 416–17). That relationship, and the questionable light it throws on Dickens's moral character and reputation as a family man, has since been depicted in a film entitled *The Invisible Woman* (dir. Ralph Fiennes, 2013; based on Tomalin 1990), including a memorable sequence where 'Nelly' praises Dickens for the ending to *Great Expectations* that holds Pip and Estella apart. More generally, the importance of Darwin's evolutionary theory on Dickens's novel has already been noted, and the year 1861 was also an unsettled time on the world stage, witnessing as it did the outbreak of the American Civil War. Carey's fiction is then interested in Dickens's troubled family life, though less with the relationship with Ternan than with hints earlier in the author's career of an affection verging on an obsession with his wife's sister, Mary Hogarth. Mary died a tragic early death aged seventeen, and although Dickens was distraught at her death the vanity of his account of it is chilling: 'Thank God she died in my arms ... and the very last words she whispered were of me' (Ackroyd 2003 [1990]: 226).

In *Jack Maggs*, Tobias Oates proves a vain, fairly reprehensible character, one who not only exploits those around him as fodder for his fiction, with little sense of ethical responsibility, but whose personal life renders his wife Mary (the slippage of Mary Hogarth's name into that of Oates's wife is surely deliberate on Carey's part) and her sister Lizzie Warrinder the victims of his egotism. Carey's fictional re-creation of Dickens appears to owe much to the vain, if brilliant, individual depicted by Peter Ackroyd's monumental biography of the writer (2003 [1990]). As well as these obvious parallels between Oates's life and what is known of Dickens, *Jack Maggs* is structured around a series of parallels and echoes, both external and internal. There are several textual affinities with *Great Expectations*, but also internal echoes of the wider Dickens canon; the thieving community in which Maggs finds himself placed as a child is a version of Fagin's factory of child-thieves in *Oliver Twist*, for example. And Oates, we learn, uses the figure of Maggs in several of *his* future novels: 'Finally they slept, and Tobias Oates crept out. This scene, or rather the specifics of its setting, reappears not only in *The Death of Maggs* and *Michael Adams*, but in almost everything Tobias ever wrote' (Carey 1997: 197).

Great Expectations is a narrative founded on the connections between things and people. Pip tries increasingly to keep the constituent parts of his life and biography separate, embarrassed as he is when blacksmith Joe Gargery visits him in London, feeling that the world of the Kent marshes compromises his new existence as a city gentleman. What Pip fails to realize, however, is how intimately his new life is connected to his experiences in 'th' meshes' (Dickens 1994 [1861]: 222), enabled as it is by Magwitch's wealth and benefaction. Other threads eventually connect in the novel when we learn that Magwitch's arch-rival Compeyson is the same bridegroom who deserted Miss Havisham on their wedding day and that Estella is really Magwitch's child. The connectivities of Carey's novel are achieved both through the relationships between hypotext and hypertext and the parallels identified with Dickens's life-story, but there are also numerous links within the narrative itself, echoing *Great Expectations* at a stylistic level. Oates becomes Maggs's shadow and counterpart, perhaps Carey's deployment of another popular figure of nineteenth-century fiction, the *Doppelgänger* or double. Events in the two men's lives mirror and mesh with disturbing frequency. The harrowing abortion of Maggs's child with Sophia in Ma Britten's house, told in flashback within the narrative, itself a textual echo of the narrative structure and form of Dickens's novel, is mirrored by the abortion induced by drugs administered to Lizzie, without each other's knowledge, by both Tobias and Mary, with devastating effects. In turn, the manuscript of Oates's projected novel based loosely on Maggs's life-story which burns at Maggs's behest prefigures the burning of Lizzie's bedsheets, following her painful death; thereby also destroying the aborted foetus and evidence of her relationship with Oates, and drawing a dark parallel between the novelist's various ill-fated creative offspring.

Oates is rendered a criminal by the narrative as much as the convicted Maggs; labels such as 'thief', 'convict' and 'writer' become treacherously entangled in the course of the novel such that they can apply to either Maggs or to Oates at different times. Several of the inset narratives in the text are products of the eponymous protagonist's compulsion to write down his story for Phipps's consumption, and in a related slippage of textual certainty Maggs actively eschews the label of 'Australian' that Oates, and in some sense Carey, has imposed upon him (Carey 1997: 312–13). Instead of the hallmarked silver that Maggs is trained as a child to steal, Oates ransacks 'real' lives for his fiction; Maggs describes his sensation of having been 'burgled' after the first episode of somnambulism during which Oates makes careful transcripts of the returned convict's outbursts about his life in the penal colony: 'He was burgled, plundered, and he would not tolerate it' (32). That there are also connections here to suppressed experiences of rape, male and female, in the novel is deliberately unsettling.

In a further direct parallel with his Dickensian precursor Oates is fascinated with the workings of the criminal mind and is a proponent of the nineteenth-century pseudo-science of mesmerism (Ackroyd 2003 [1990]: 448–51). Mesmerism is often viewed as a forerunner of modern psychology as a discipline, and in this way Carey parallels not only his modern method of psychologizing Dickens's characters but also the acts of theft and appropriation inherent in imperialist ideology:

> The metafictional strategies of the novel are integral to the exposure of colonial delusions. They call attention to the process of fictional invention ... as appropriation, theft. Just as England stole Maggs's birthright by making him a thief, so Tobias Oates colonises Maggs for his own imaginative purposes, stealing Maggs's life for his fiction.
>
> (Woodcock 2003: 129)

There is an overriding anxiety for the reader of *Jack Maggs*, as there is for the reader of *Wide Sargasso Sea*, that the protagonists may prove unable to escape the plot trajectories determined for them by their names and literary counterparts; indeed we already know the ending. The sense that Pip has in *Great Expectations* that Magwitch cannot escape his initial identification as a convict has obvious implications for his own attempts to escape his life with Joe at the forge:

> The more I dressed him and the better I dressed him, the more he looked like the slouching fugitive on the marshes. This effect on my anxious fancy was partly referable, no doubt, to his old face and manner growing more familiar to me; but I believed too that he dragged one of his legs as if there were still a weight of iron on it, and that from head to foot there was Convict in the very grain of the man.
>
> (Dickens 1994 [1861]: 333)

Rather than considering narrative destination in the original novel as a metaphorical leg-chain, Carey seems to enjoy considering his character's ability to rewrite his destiny. In one central encounter in a moving horse-drawn carriage – a scene which knowingly recalls Fowles's seminal moment of postmodern literary encounter between author and protagonist in a train compartment in *The French Lieutenant's Woman* – Carey has Maggs confront Oates over the novel he is writing. The returnee challenges the vindictive end the author has in mind for the character based on his life-story. As we have already seen, Carey also rewrites Magwitch's end; Maggs's Australian deathbed scene in old age acting as a self-aware counterpart to that in *Great Expectations* and the fictional death by fire envisaged for him by Oates. That death by fire is both a reworking into fiction of an earlier real-life journalistic experience by Oates and by Carey of Miss Havisham's demise in the Dickensian source. The fantasy element of Maggs's ending already discussed, its overt textuality, leaves us still in some doubt, however, of the convict's ability to entirely cast off his textual shackles.

What Carey does achieve for this character is to place him centre-stage in this novel in a way he could never be in *Great Expectations*, where the narrative is decisively voiced from the perspective of Pip. Carey's novel is deliberately named for his protagonist, and an image that Carey deploys in the text itself on regular occasions to metaphorically represent his approach is that of bringing Maggs out of the shadows. As in much nineteenth-century fiction and many of the 'Neo-Victorian' appropriations we have been considering, the city of London is a vibrant but double-sided entity in *Jack Maggs*: a metropolis of gas-lights and side-streets (the former representing the newest technology when Maggs returns to London in 1837 at the start of the novel and therefore a symbol of change), a place of fine houses but also alleyways and back-passages where more threatening events unfold, of the lit and the unlit, and of the visible and the unseen. It is in the unlit spaces that Maggs is all-too frequently depicted skulking, but Carey quite literally brings his character and his marginalized experiences out of the shadows and into the light in his appropriation. Elsewhere, of course, this is also a novel concerned with subtexts and subterranean truths, many of them of a sexually violent kind: Mercy has been rescued by Buckle from an horrific instance of child prostitution but there remains something deeply unsavoury in the power dynamics of their relationship; Pip's dark counterpart or *Doppelgänger* in *Jack Maggs*, Henry Phipps, is guilty of violently sodomizing the footman Edward Constable, an act that contributes to the suicide of Constable's partner. In other ways, Oates violates Maggs's life and thoughts in a Gothic representation of the novelist's vampiric art. Carey in this way makes explicit what can only exist in an implied sense in Victorian fiction 'at the time of his story', as it were, be this colonialism, sexual repression or violence. In this way, Carey's narrative brilliantly 'vents' the world of the Victorian novel and the Dickensian idiom, but the light he brings to bear on his subject is inescapably modern.

WATCHING THE DETECTIVE: THE AFTERLIVES OF SHERLOCK HOLMES

Numerous examples in this study of Genette's 'movement of proximation' have indicated the ways in which adaptations frequently seek to bring a modern perspective to bear on older material by updating events to new and frequently contemporaneous contexts. The media of film and television seem peculiarly attuned to this mode of working, relocating 'classic' or well-known stories in new geographical and sociological settings, often in order to appeal to, or target, new audiences through greater accessibility or familiarity, but also to ask questions from this modernized vantage point which challenge the original. Modern-dress stage productions of canonical plays are a common variant on this theme. The 1998 film version of *Great Expectations* (dir. Alfonso Cuarón), which relocates the story to a combination of the Floridian Coast (standing for the Kent marshes) and artistic communities in Manhattan (for London) in the immediate present, and a similar move in the 2012 *What Maisie Knew* (dir. Scott McGehee and David Siegel), which reconfigures Henry James's 1897 novel of divorce and family dysfunctionality as another variant on the New York present, are examples of this particular tendency. Both continue the interest in nineteenth-century fiction as a foundation for these kinds of modernized reworkings. But the major global cultural phenomenon of this kind in the early part of the twenty-first century has been the BBC television series *Sherlock*, the first episode of which aired in the UK in 2009.

Sherlock sees Sir Arthur Conan Doyle's fictional detective series – he wrote fifty-six Sherlock Holmes stories – updated to a modern context where ubiquitous computing facilitates the solving of crime. Sherlock (played by Benedict Cumberbatch as a brilliant, charismatic but also somewhat autistic individual) and his sidekick John Watson deploy mobile technologies, smartphones, GPS and blogging, and these engagements are wittily represented through novel visuals on the screen, text messages replacing the telegrams of Conan Doyle's narratives, where Holmes was equally keen to deeply the latest technology, and overlaying the filmed action in various signifying fonts. We might also note in passing that the first Holmes novel was also the first crime fiction to deploy the magnifying glass as a tool for detection. The London of the television series is an equally fascinating hybrid of the late nineteenth-century capital of fogs, restaurant rendezvous and dark alleyways and a more recognizably presentist space (cf. O'Rourke 2010). Similarly, Holmes wears a deerstalker in a pastiche moment of attempting to avoid the paparazzi door-stepping 221B Baker Street, but his Victorian pipe has been replaced by nicotine patches in an effort to cure his smoking habit: one crime is described as a 'three-patch problem' in a knowing echo of Holmes's 'three pipe problem' from *The Red Headed League* (1891). This series is highly self-aware, arch even, about its relationship both to the Conan Doyle 'originals' and to the long afterlife of adaptation that the Sherlock Holmes stories have enjoyed. As early as 1900 the novels were being adapted into short silent film versions, and the Basil Rathbone fourteen-film series made in the 1930s and 1940s set the trend for modernization, staging the stories as they did in the inter-war years. Since then there have been adaptations on radio and in song, puppetry, graphic novel, manga comics, board games, computer games and novel forms. Notable among these include *The Mandala of Sherlock Holmes: The Missing Years* (2000) by Tibetan author Jamyang Norbu, which incorporates a re-evaluation of Sherlock's 'lost years' following his supposed suicidal leap from the Reichenbach Falls in Switzerland, alongside characters and subject matter from Rudyard Kipling's *Kim* to produce a subtle form of 'writing back' to the British imperial moment. Norbu's novel, drawing on biographical theory, purports to be an 'authentic' manuscript that the narrator has discovered. By accounting for Holmes's so-called lost years, the narrative renders his life 'real' rather than fictional and encourages intriguing parallels with scholarly speculation on the 'lost years' of William Shakespeare. These modernizing and relocating impulses with regard to the Sherlock Holmes cultural legacy come right up to date with the US television series *Elementary*, which sets the storyline in contemporary New York City and features Holmes as a recovering drug addict and a female Dr Joan Watson played by Lucy Liu.

The first episode of the BBC series, 'A Study in Pink', offers us in microcosm an insight into the ways in which this modernized

Holmes enables the interactive viewer to oscillate between the nineteenth century and the present. Martin Freeman's John Watson suffers from post-traumatic stress disorder following a period of service as a military doctor in Afghanistan; we first witness him attending psychotherapy and it later becomes evident that the blog by means of which he engages with the general public on Sherlock becomes a form of therapy, of writing out his story. In a neat trick the BBC actually had the actor online communicating in character with fans on the corporation's website after the episode's first screening, collapsing the lines between fiction and reality in ways that Conan Doyle would have enjoyed. There is a strong line of connectivity to the hypotext in this regard since at the beginning of *A Study in Scarlet* (1887) Watson has been invalided out from the Second Anglo-Afghan War (1878–80). That novel begins with a text-within-a-text, Watson's reminiscences of the first encounter with Holmes and their first case: 'Being a reprint from the reminiscences of John H. Watson MD, late of the Army Medical Department' (Conan Doyle 2011 [1887]: 1). There are all kinds of examples of these conscious moments of cross-reference to the original novels in the series; for example, in later episodes the Reichenbach Falls episode mentioned earlier, when Conan Doyle scandalously appeared to have killed off his most successful literary creation, is translated to St Bartholomew's Hospital (commonly known as Barts) in London, but even that relocation is linked to Watson's workplace at the start of *A Study in Scarlet*; analytical dissections that Holmes undertakes of new media, such as John's mobile phone, relate back to his similar deconstruction of Watson's pocket watch in *The Sign of Four* (1890).

In these deliberate collisions, we witness the real sites and artefacts of contemporary London shading into the world and geography of the novels, collapsing and enfolding as they do so the similarities and differences between 1880s London and that of the twenty-first century in ways that engage the knowledgeable Holmes fan while also enabling entirely new points of entry for those who do not know the novels in any detail but who are now stimulated to trace the connections back from the television experience. This is a perfect working example of the new forms of sequencing enabled by a mature adaptations industry that scholars including Christine Geraghty, Linda Hutcheon and Thomas Leitch have rightly suggested might change our ways of thinking and writing about the adaptation process (Geraghty 2008; Hutcheon 2006, 2013; Leitch 2007). As Jim Collins notes, we need to take account of 'the multiple determinations that shape adaptations and the multiple pleasures they provide, even for those who may be unfamiliar with the source text' (2010: 130).

These different routes and entry levels into the Sherlock Holmes tradition also connect in important ways to film scholar Thomas Leitch's work on 'Entry Level Dickens' (2007: 66), where he makes the provocative case for the significance of adapted children's versions of canonical works as first encounters that enable access, and a foundational platform on which a relationship to key texts and corpuses might develop; his example was *The Muppet Christmas Carol* (dir. Brian Henson, 1992) and its joyous reimagining of Dickens's 1843 novella *A Christmas Carol* through the medium of singing frogs, rats, pigs and vegetables. The *Sherlock* instance is a particularly instructive one in that it provides an example of proliferating global fan communities who are extremely proactive, not only in developing relationships with Conan Doyle's texts through a series of lateral and non-hierarchical artistic and popular cultural engagements, but also in actively remaking the object of their affection through online networked relationships with fellow aficionados (on networked cultures, see Bruhn *et al.* 2013). Nowhere is this more evident than in modern China, where the BBC series has been a huge hit, finding its way into diplomatic contexts involving, for example, a visit from the UK Prime Minister in 2014 when an online discussion with Chinese people on popular social media site Sina Weibo in the presence of Chinese President Xi Jinping produced more questions about the popular television series than any other subject. But more importantly perhaps, and with an underground and online fan base, 'Curly Fu and Peanut', as Holmes and Watson are affectionately known (the nicknames relate to their titles in Mandarin Chinese), are creatively appropriated in order to speak to contemporary issues of diversity and identity (Jones 2015). Many decades on from Theodor Adorno and Max Horkheimer's exposition of their theory of a 'culture industry' (1944), we are seeing played out in these instances the impact of mass media and capitalism on the canon they were seeking to describe. As the editors of a volume on the fan community phenomenon surrounding the Sherlock novels have observed: 'The injunction in the new age of fan fiction, social media, and e-commerce is not simply to consume passively but instead to be a creative participant' (Ue and Cranfield 2014: 6). The Holmes industry plays this idea out on a global stage and ensures that the nineteenth century continues to be relevant in ways those who lived through it could barely have imagined.

8

STRETCHING HISTORY
OR, APPROPRIATING THE FACTS

'The author willingly admits to having once or twice stretched history to suit his own fictional ends.'

Peter Carey's 'Author's Note' to *Jack Maggs*

Up until this point we have discussed adaptation and appropriation primarily within the intertextual framework of texts adopting and adapting other texts. In the next two chapters, following Kristeva's lead in her writing on intertextuality in *Desire in Language* (1980), we will expand the parameters of the debate to include the companion art forms of painting and music. But there is a further parallel mode of appropriation that uses as its raw material not artistic matter but the 'real' matter of facts, of both historical events and personalities. What happens, then, to the appropriation process when what is being 'taken over' for fictional purposes really exists or existed?

The kinds of literature we are examining under this heading are often grouped together by categories such as 'historical fiction' or 'real-life drama', or, in the film studies context, 'true stories' or the sub-genre of 'biopics' (Bingham 2010; Brown and Vidal 2013).

These are wide umbrella terms which can cover novels, plays or films which choose to locate themselves in the 'past', known or otherwise, providing contextual details of that past as an authenticating strategy: in these instances we 'believe in' or subscribe to the events of the novels or the dramas partly because the background is so accurately drawn or imagined. There have, of course, been separate studies made of the larger impulses behind the writing of historical fiction and drama (see, for example, De Groot 2009, 2015), but of more pressing concern to this study are those texts where the author or playwright or filmmaker is consciously appropriating the known facts of a particular event or of a particular life in order to shape their fiction or work of art. Their motives for doing so can vary hugely.

In some instances, the familiar operations of analogy are at play. A historical event is depicted and deployed both for its own rich literary and imaginative content and for the parallels it evokes with more contemporaneous or topical concerns for the author. One of the best-known examples from the theatrical canon is Arthur Miller's 1953 play *The Crucible*. That play depicts the events surrounding the witch-hunts conducted in 1692 amongst the New England Puritan colony in Salem, Massachusetts. It is an empathetic study of the personal rivalries and psychological disorders which contributed to rampant accusations of witchcraft against several women, and eventually also against men, from that community and which resulted in a series of gruesome public executions. But Miller's purpose in selecting this particular moment in history as the focus of his drama was twofold. While he was clearly interested in the group hysteria and religious ardour that contributed to the Salem executions, he also sought to establish a direct comparison with the contemporary 'witch-hunts' being conducted in his native USA in the 1950s against allegedly 'communist' sympathizers by Senator Joe McCarthy and his government committee. Via the mechanism of the House of Representatives' House Un-American Activities Committee (HUAC), this group was hell-bent on exposing left-wing political elements in US society. Those in the performing arts, actors, directors and playwrights among them, were a particular focus of surveillance and accusation, culminating in a number of public show trials in which individuals were encouraged and coerced to inform on their colleagues. Miller was himself sentenced to prison in 1957 for his failure to act as an informant for HUAC, although the sentence was later quashed (Bigsby 1997: 3). Nowhere in the play-script does *The Crucible* ever make this modern analogue explicit: Miller trusts his audiences to draw their own conclusions. Of course, audiences today most likely come to the play in performance with prior knowledge of both the historical and political allusions, but *The Crucible* remains a powerful example of how the historical past can be evoked in a literary context as a means of critiquing, albeit obliquely, the present political regime.

What Miller was doing was in many respects nothing new; the early modern playwrights William Shakespeare and Ben Jonson achieved something remarkably similar in the seventeenth century when, in plays such as *Coriolanus* (Shakespeare 1605–8) or *Sejanus* (Jonson 1603) they deployed the settings and stories of Ancient Rome as a means of evading the censor while at the same time critiquing present government policies and failings. Ronan Bennett has also evoked seventeenth-century society and its atmosphere of religious fervour and fundamentalism in his novel *Havoc in Its Third Year* (2004). Set in Northern England in the 1630s, the decade immediately preceding the outbreak of civil war, in the novel Bennett depicts a town where the restrictive Puritan leadership has fostered a world of paranoia and surveillance where neighbour is pitted against neighbour, with often fatal consequences. The parallels between the world depicted in the novel and the rise of religious fundamentalism taking place in the early twenty-first century, not least in the aftermath of 9/11, proved inescapable for readers and reviewers alike. There were also very personal resonances for Bennett as an author with religious roots in the Irish Troubles of the late twentieth century, leading to political events in which he had played a role and even been imprisoned on two occasions.

History can often be evoked, then, for the purposes of comparison and contrast, but, as Peter Widdowson has stressed, 'there are many ways in which "the literary" uses history, and many ends to which it is put' (1999: 154). Hilary Mantel's *Wolf Hall* (2009) and its sequel *Bring Up the Bodies* (2012) are rarely categorized as formal appropriations but they adapt (not without scholarly controversy) the known facts of Thomas Cromwell's life for the purposes of historical fiction. Writing about the sixteenth century, and using a striking version of the 'historical present', Mantel puts us quite literally in Cromwell's shoes while also allowing for resonances with the here and now. Witness the opening sentences of *Wolf Hall*:

> Felled, dazed, silent, he has fallen; knocked full length on the cobbles. He turns his head sideways; his eyes are turned toward the gate, as if someone might arrive to help him out. One blow, properly placed, could kill him now. Blood from the gash on his head – which was his father's first effort – is trickling across his face.
>
> (Mantel 2009: 1)

At various points in this study, we have considered postmodernism's questioning of the past and the status of so-called historical 'facts'. Jean Rhys appropriated Charlotte Brontë's *Jane Eyre* in *Wide Sargasso Sea* in order to reveal the embedded racism of the British imperial age and its literature; Peter Carey rewrites Dickens's *Great Expectations* in *Jack Maggs* in order to highlight gaps and absences in Dickens, but also by extension those neglected or mistreated by the Victorian regime, not least those transported to the penal colony of Australia. History, literary or otherwise, is redeployed in these instances to indicate those communities whose histories have not been told before, the marginalized and the disenfranchised as represented by Rhys's Antoinette or Carey's Maggs, or indeed Coetzee's doubly silenced Friday in *Foe*. Don DeLillo achieves a related effect in his novel *Libra* (1988) by viewing an iconic historical event, the assassination of President John F. Kennedy in Dallas in 1963, not just from the perspective of the identified assassin Lee Harvey Oswald, but via the interior voices and mind-sets of others in Oswald's life. What is revealed in the process is a world of deep poverty and social injustice, often entirely absent from conspiracy-led historical accounts of the shooting.

The retrieval of lost voices or lost histories is a motif we have identified as common to many of the appropriations considered thus far. In prose fiction re-visions of Shakespearean plays, such as *The Tempest* in Marina Warner's *Indigo* or *King Lear* in Jane Smiley's *A Thousand Acres*, both of which deploy first-person narration, a conscious effort is made to give voice, and by extension motivation, to marginalized or excluded characters. A shared purpose can be identified in much postmodern historical fiction – or historiographical metafiction, as it is sometimes called – that utilizes the technique of first-person narration. Peter Carey's *True History of the Kelly Gang* (2000), for example, has been praised as a remarkable achievement in ventriloquism. Certainly, Carey vividly re-creates the idiom, slang and idiosyncratic punctuation that persuade us that we are receiving Ned Kelly's voice unmediated. The novel is structured as a series of letters written by Kelly to his daughter in order to ensure that she hears his life-story directly from him as well as from others who might write from a biased perspective. For this reason, 'parcels' of letters substitute for chapters in this self-aware novel. Carey confidently plays with the methods of recording archival detail in the framing authorial introduction to each 'parcel': '59 octavo pages all of high woodpulp content and turning brown. Folds, foxing, staining and minor tears' (2000: 73). This framing material achieves two conflicting ends within the narrative. It serves as an authenticating presence; as readers we are trained to trust the historical evidence of archival material catalogued in this way. Yet these frames also serve as a reminder of historical interpreters other than Kelly himself; we are, by this method, reminded that postmodernism's favoured strategy of unreliable narration may be relevant in Ned's case. As much as he is mythologized in Australian history books as that nation's version of the Robin Hood legend, a poor man of Irish provenance who suffered intense racism and who took on the authorities in several daring raids and sieges, Kelly may also be rewriting his own history, censoring certain 'truths' or embellishing others in view of the intended audience of his own daughter.

The title of Carey's novel performs a similar sleight of hand. *True History of the Kelly Gang* would seem at first sight to emphasize the veracity of this version of the story, told as it is from the gang's point of view. Yet Carey has self-consciously avoided the use of a definite article here – it is not *the* true history or story. This identifiable absence suggests that we as readers need to question such phrases. An alert reader may even suspect a deliberate oxymoronic quality to the term 'true history' since, as much late twentieth-century scholarship was at pains to point out, history itself is often one historian's interpretation of events, an assessment made from the available or extant documents and evidential traces, and therefore necessarily partial. What happens to those traces, such as Ned Kelly's immediate family, for example, whose illiteracy reduced or deprived them of the capacity to leave behind accounts of their existence? How does history speak for, or about, them? Carey, as in his earlier *Jack Maggs*, is concerned with articulating those lost voices; as Bruce Woodcock notes, his fictions 'are inhabited by hybrid characters living in in-between spaces or on the margins' (2003: 1); he adds that 'They retell the stories of marginalized characters, outsiders, and outlaws … in reinvented voices' (138). Woodcock has memorably described this technique as less outright ventriloquism than a 'performative act of habitation, an occupation' (138). By appropriating Kelly's life-story, Carey enacts appropriation's semantic meaning by carrying out an 'occupation', or a 'takeover', but not as a hostile act; he is anxious to give voice to the poor whose lives he feels have been marginalized in and by the historical record. His model for this is undoubtedly the American author William Faulkner, who provides the epigram for this novel: 'The past is not dead. It is not even past.'

It is important to understand that Carey is retelling but also reinventing history. The phrase 'true history' connects his project not only to historical research as an academic discipline but also to the art of fiction. In the seventeenth century, many prose novellas and romances declared themselves to be 'true histories' in this manner, while simultaneously availing themselves of the conventions of romantic fiction (cf. Woodcock 2003: 142): Aphra Behn's *Oroonoko, or The Royal Slave* (1688) and *The Unfortunate Happy Lady: A True History* (1698) are facilitating examples. Behn plays on the etymological link between the word 'history' and the French term for a 'story' or fiction, *histoire*, in a manner that prefigures and pre-empts much of postmodernism's playful encounters with the discipline. By devising a novel constructed from letters, Carey simultaneously evokes historical modes of life-writing and fiction. His inspiration for the novel came from witnessing first hand a genuine Kelly-authored document, which in turn evokes the parallel genre of biography, which we have seen inform several appropriations already; the engagement with the text invariably becomes an engagement with the writer behind that text, from Cunningham's *The Hours* to *Shakespeare in Love*. A. S. Byatt's *The Biographer's Tale* (2001) is a novel that captures the complexity of such attempts to recover and authenticate a person's life with its focus on a postgraduate student who seeks to capture the life-story of an obscure biographer in ways that in turn engage with research on real-life historical figures such as Carl Linnaeus and Henrik Ibsen. Of course, the example of *Shakespeare in Love* (dir. John Madden, 1998) is equally multi-layered. Tom Stoppard's screenplay was based not upon a standard biography but upon another novel, *No Bed for Bacon* (1941) by Caryl Brahms and S. J. Simon, and in the process became in part about his own engagement as a playwright with Shakespeare's texts and influence.

A veritable sub-genre of fiction about writers of fiction has dominated Western booklists in recent decades: to name just a few, Colm Tóibín's *The Master* (2004) is a rumination on Henry James at the time of his own failed venture on to the London stage with *Guy Domville*; Patricia Duncker's *Sophie and the Sibyl: A Victorian Romance* (2015) engages with the life and works (in particular *Daniel Deronda*) of George Eliot through an exercise in Neo-Victorian pastiche; Peter Ackroyd speculated on Oscar Wilde's last days in Paris in *The Last Testament of Oscar Wilde* (1983); and Carey's own tussle with Charles Dickens through the medium of *Jack Maggs* was examined in Chapter 7. Carey's Kelly is not a canonical author in the strict sense but his documentary presence in Australian accounts of national history renders him of comparable significance in that country's cultural imaginary. As well as biography and memoir, though, Carey's informing literary models here are clearly those of the eighteenth-century epistolary and picaresque novel. History is not being undone by these self-consciously literary applications but the stability of history is effectively challenged. As Linda Hutcheon observes: 'Postmodernism does not deny [history] ... it merely questions how we can know past real events, today, except through their traces, their texts, the facts we construct and to which we grant meaning' (1988: 225). Carey seems acutely aware of these traces and constructions and of the complex and questioning way that we must handle them.

This all has interesting connections with Thomas Leitch's reflections on the particular tendency in 1980s and 1990s films to attach the epithet 'Based on a true story'. Citing the output of Oliver Stone (e.g. *Salvador* [1986]; *JFK* [1991]; *World Trade Center* [2006]) alongside that of Martin Scorsese and Stephen Spielberg, Leitch suggests that: 'The phrase ... appeals to the authority of a master text that has all the authority of a precursor novel or play or story with none of the drawbacks' (2007: 289). The 'drawbacks' would be an available 'source' to check the consistency or accuracy of the historical revisionism being presented on the big screen, especially since in Stone's case these are often films made with the express intent of 'setting the record straight' (289). There are common tropes, however, by which such films signal their relationship to available documentary evidence at the same time as 'stretching history' through the process of adaptation and fictionalization; witness, for example, the 'montage of television images that opens *JFK*' (294), which draws viewers into accepting Stone's customized narrative of events as trustworthy. This requires once again a very active awareness and critical stance on the part of audiences. One experimental contemporary director who is also testing the limits of the biopic in this regard is Steve McQueen, who has reworked the events of the Northern Irish prison hunger strikes in Belfast's Maze Prison in 1981 in his 2008 'historical drama' *Hunger*, and who has also adapted the story of Solomon Northup, a free man kidnapped and sold into slavery in the 1840s in *Twelve Years a Slave* (2013). In McQueen's work, we can recognize a kinship to other novel adaptations we have considered in this volume which look to retrieve lost voices or suppressed histories in their precursor texts: 'to tell stories that haven't been heard', to use the director-artist's own words from a video interview with the *Guardian* newspaper in January 2014.

Engagements with past events and past lives at whatever scale of historical distance or proximity can function as a means to think through current affairs via the process of textualization, through dramatic or filmic adaptation. When those events are very recent this can sometimes have an unsettling effect on the audience, prompting the question of how the characters or events on stage are to be read against the living inspirations. Where do departures from the known facts, and entry into the realm of speculation, become unethical or morally dubious, or do we enact the concept of artistic licence at all times and simply demand of the audience an awareness that what they are watching is, to all intents and purposes, an adaptation? In 2015, the playwright Steve Waters created a play, *Temple*, which is based on events that took place in London in October 2011 when the proximity of the Occupy movement's protest camp caused St Paul's Cathedral to close its doors to worshippers and to the general public, and when subsequent attempts to legally evict the protestors led to high-profile resignations in the Church. The play does not use real names and it is 'based on' the events of 2011 rather than claiming to be a verbatim retelling; as the author himself stresses, 'This is a fiction: a fiction informed by factual circumstances'. Nevertheless, the references to real people as well as places are almost inevitable and deliberately invited by the play in order to provoke a broader consideration of the Church, of the current state of British politics and, as Waters puts it, 'how we keep alive in our work' (Waters 2015). The ethics of adapting events in this way are much debated, but the practice is in reality far from new. This is in a sense exactly the same compulsion that drove the genre of the Shakespearean history play in the 1590s. Play-texts such as *All Is True, or Henry VIII* (c. 1613), co-written with John Fletcher, told the very recent family history of the reigning monarch at the time, Elizabeth I, and even in some productions staged scenes such as the divorce hearings of her father Henry and his first wife Katherine of Aragon at Blackfriars, the very site where those legal hearings had taken place (Dillon 2012: 77–9). In all of these instances we might wish to register how authors and directors are stretching history to ask important ethical questions about the everyday and about the here and now, as well as about our individual and collective engagements with the past(s). In this way our attention is drawn to the 'institutional practices of rewriting' that Leitch has urged us to see as the focal point of adaptation studies in the future (Leitch 2007: 303).

It is through the framing device of the third-person narration of events following Ned Kelly's execution and the voicing of the reaction of the man entrusted with responsibility for Kelly's manuscripts that Peter Carey seems to hint at one of his personal motives for appropriating history and 'the facts' in the way he does for *True History of the Kelly Gang*. Curnow asks enviously: 'What is it about we Australians, eh? ... What is wrong with us? Do we not have a Jefferson? A Disraeli? Might we not find someone better to admire than a horse-thief and a murderer? Must we always make such an embarrassing spectacle of ourselves?' (Carey 2000: 419). Kelly's iconic fame in Australia, in large part deriving from the mode and manner of his death, and countless cultural reproductions of that moment, from the thought-provoking artwork of Sidney Nolan to films (from the 1906 *The Story of the Kelly Gang* [dir. Charles Tait] to the 2003 adaptation of another novelistic retelling of Kelly's life by Robert Drewe [*Our Sunshine*, 1991, dir. Gregor Jordan]), would appear to confirm Jean Baudrillard's suggestion that in the modern era history has transmuted into myth and that early death in particular accrues a particular kind of mythic dimension (Innes, 2008). Baudrillard cites in support of this theory the examples of Marilyn Monroe, James Dean and JFK (1981: 24). He declares: 'History is our lost referential, that is to say our myth' (43). We might again register overlaps here with the directorial *oeuvre* of Oliver Stone, who has spent his career responding to and in many respects rewriting (at least from a personalized perspective) quasi-mythic events in US public history from the Vietnam War, to the assassination of John F. Kennedy, to the collapse of the Twin Towers in New York in the 9/11 attacks.

Carey certainly questions the mythologizing tendency of the modern era through the mechanism of his novel, but he is not exactly on the side of the cynical Curnow in this. In the same way that his postcolonial revision of *Great Expectations* found considerable empathy for the convict community of New South Wales, so here he seeks motive, reason and understanding from the reader for Kelly's life and actions. Just as the appropriation of a canonical novel relies upon the foreknowledge of the precursor text for the fullest appreciation of its stance, and its revisionary achieve-ment, so the retelling of Kelly's life in *True History of the Kelly Gang* relies upon a reader's awareness, albeit in outline, of his life and the mythology surrounding it. Carey uses this to foster a sense of predestination and predetermination in the novel which is very much akin to the awareness of plot trajectory and denouement in a canonical work of literature; in a sense, both we as readers and Carey's Kelly writing his personal history know how it will end. Carey ensures this is the case even for the unini-tiated by opening the novel with the infamous shoot-out that led to Kelly's arrest and eventual execution. The iconic signifier of his hand-crafted armour, and his assumed persona of the 'Monitor' (the name derives from the goanna, or monitor lizard, an inhabitant of Australia's rainforests and outback), immediately locates the reader in terms of the historical record. Like Rhys's Antoinette, Ned's life is shaped by our awareness of his end; as Woodcock observes, 'Ned is dogged by a sense of fatalism and destiny. Unlike Jack Maggs, Carey's Ned Kelly seems trapped by the script history has written for him, and despite his hope that he will be able to read his account in the future with his daughter in America, he is all too aware of his coming doom' (2003: 150).

Another novel that both appropriates a historical life and a mythology and indeed begins with the tragic demise of its protago-nist is Joyce Carol Oates's *Blonde*, her 'fantasy biography' (the phrase is Hilary Mantel's, quoted in the paperback edition of the novel). *Blonde* relates the life of cinema icon Norma Jeane Baker, better known by her stage name Marilyn Monroe. Monroe's life (and untimely death), as mentioned above, are singled out for mythical status by Baudrillard in his *Simulacra and Simulation* (1981) and Oates clearly relies on her readership's shared perception of this iconographic status in the construction of both her novel and its resultant effects. In her authorial preface, Oates asserts that '*Blonde* is a radically distilled "life" in the form of fiction, and ... synecdoche is the principle of appropriation' (2000: ix). The cover of the first paperback edition of the novel in the UK appeared to emphasize Oates's point: it depicted a fragment of a much-reproduced photograph of Monroe, one actually described in detail in one chapter, a still taken as a publicity shot for the film *Bus Stop* (dir. Joshua Logan, 1956). The chapter in question is entitled "'The American Goddess of Love on the Subway Grating". New York City 1954':

> A lush-bodied girl in the prime of her physical beauty. In an ivory georgette crepe sundress with a halter top that gathers her breasts up in soft undulating folds of the fabric. She's standing with bare legs apart on a New York subway grating. Her blond hair is thrown rapturously back as an updraft lifts her full flaring skirt.
>
> (Oates 2000: 201)

The fragment of this image we are given on the cover as con-sumers of the novel is just a glimpse of Monroe's platinum blonde hair. The 'blonde' of the title, it seems, is sufficient to connote the whole story of Marilyn, that dress, that image, the myth. Of course there is added irony in the fact that her blonde hair was itself an act of fakery and simulation, a self-fashioning in the context of Hollywood's creation and manipulation of her image. Oates captures in this process a crucial point about appropriation: synecdoche *is* the principle of the form in the respect that appro-priation relies on simple or distilled signifiers to tell far larger stories: a wisp of peroxide blonde is enough to suggest the myth and the iconicity of Monroe as well as the attendant tragedies of her life in the same way that, for Carey, Ned Kelly's homemade 'Monitor' armour conjures a life-story. In Rhys's *Wide Sargasso Sea*, as we saw in Chapter 6, an English stately home and a lit candle are enough to suggest the fire at Thornfield Hall and all that ensues in *Jane Eyre*. In *Blonde* Oates's self-conscious nomen-clature (or strategic lack of it) relies on the readers' knowledge of the 'facts' of Monroe's life and their ability to fill in the gaps in the narrative; we are introduced to several unnamed but nevertheless recognizable agents in her life-story: the 'Ex-Athlete' stands for celebrated baseball player Joe Di Maggio; the sexually tyrannical 'President' is John F. Kennedy (although intriguingly there were also topical resonances with the Bill Clinton–Monica Lewinsky affair of the late 1990s); 'O' is Laurence Olivier; the 'Playwright' is Arthur Miller. The postmodern reader is alert to the workings of these signifiers, to the semantic interplay between the informing source that is conjured into view and the supplementation or amplification that surrounds the fragmentary evocations of real-life precursors.

Like Carey's *True History*, Oates's *Blonde* starts at the end, with Monroe's death, an event around which conspiracy theories have swirled for decades. Once again the reader's foreknowledge and the functioning of expectation prove a crucial element in the construction of the narrative dynamic and teleology. We become participants in the action of appropriation, reading between the lines in a very active fashion. A parallel effect was achieved by another Oates novel which responded to an actual historical event, one once again connected to the Kennedy dynasty in the US. *Black Water* (1993) has as its factual hypotext the so-called Chappaquiddick tragedy, a storyline involving Senator Edward Kennedy. In the actual event, which occurred in 1969, Mary-Jo Kopechne drowned in a car driven by Kennedy. He was later found guilty of having left the scene of an accident, though many questions remain to this day as to exactly how Kopechne died. What is clear is that Kennedy's hopes of securing his party's presidential nomination, which had seemed to be running high until this incident, also drowned in the Cape Cod marshes that July night. In Oates's novel events are transposed to the state of Maine in the 1990s. This historical setting is carefully signalled via discussions of Michael Dukakis's failed presidential campaign against George Bush Senior in 1988. Nevertheless, the narrative's account of the power-hungry 'Senator', the accidental drowning of Kelly Kelleher and the subsequent cover-up to protect the senator's presidential hopes unmistakeably call to mind the events in Chappaquiddick. As with Miller's *The Crucible*, Oates relies on the readers' recognition of the real-life counterparts. The cover of the paperback edition again emphasizes this relationship with its reference to 'a shocking story that has become an American myth' without ever specifically alluding to Chappaquiddick: synecdoche in operation, we might say.

The narrative of *Black Water* is brilliantly structured, and its tension exacerbated, by means of an interior monologue taking place inside Kelly's head during the minutes – or is it hours?, since time is deliberately ambiguous in this novel – in which she drowns. We know that Kelly has found an air-pocket in the submerged vehicle, but there remains the possibility that she is seeing her life flash before her eyes in the seconds before she dies. The sections of the narrative which occur in a rush of words with minimal or no punctuation underline this terrifying possibility. The verbal refrains further serve to emphasize that, for all the rewritings and alternative possibilities of Oates's project, the end is inescapable: 'Just before the car flew off the road'; 'As the black water filled her lungs and she died'.

This project can be compared to Carey's *True History of the Kelly Gang* in the sense that Oates appropriates the story of the Chappaquiddick incident, transforming history into fiction, in an effort to give back a voice and history to the silenced Mary-Jo Kopechne. There is a conscious effort to retrieve a lost history and to see her life on its own terms, and with its own intrinsic value, rather than simply as an adjunct or footnote to the Kennedy family story. In the course of the narrative, Kelly even reflects on the fact you never doubt that you will be able to tell your own story, while realizing that this right is being taken from her in the moment of dying. Oates allows the novel to speak for Kelly/Mary-Jo in a way that the historical record does not. The discipline of history is, as we have seen on countless occasions in this study, and this chapter, in truth a history of textualities, of stories told by particular tellers according to particular ideologies and viewpoints (see White 1987). In this sense, history proves a ripe source for fiction, and for *histoire*, to adapt. In turn, the facts are adapted and appropriated, and they become a matter of interpretation.

9

CUSTOMIZED NARRATIVES
COPYRIGHT AND THE WORK OF ART IN THE AGE OF TECHNOLOGICAL REPRODUCABILITY

Literature has found endless inspiration in canonical works of art as well as literature. Tracy Chevalier's *Girl with a Pearl Earring* (1999) creates a history for the enigmatic woman represented in Johannes Vermeer's remarkable painting of the same name from 1665, and that same author has carried out a similar exercise in fiction with the famous medieval tapestries of the Musée National du Moyen Âge (Cluny Museum) in *The Lady and the Unicorn* (2003). Julian Barnes uses as his inspirational spring-board in *A History of the World in 10 ½ Chapters* (1989) Gericault's 'The Raft of the Medusa', alongside the biblical parable of Noah's ark and the Great Flood. In the novel *The Dark Clue* (2001, discussed in Chapter 7), James Wilson embeds references to specific works by Turner within the action. All of this is an extension of the impulse to read between the lines and fill in the gaps that we have seen in practice in much adaptational writing. In each instance the author relies on the reader's knowledge of the work of art being alluded to for the purposes of releasing the narrative's full range of meanings.

Michael Frayn's *Headlong* (1999) achieves something similar, if even more embedded, with its deployment of Pieter Breughel's remarkable painting of the 'Fall of Icarus', a mythological adaptation in itself in which Icarus's demise is famously off-centre, marginalized by the artist to the corner of the frame. Combining a researcher's knowledge of Breughel with the conventions of detective fiction, Frayn has his art-dealer protagonist (wrongly) believe he has discovered a lost painting that will secure his fortune. En route, Frayn has tremendous fun invoking the proverbial axiom that pride comes before a fall to identify this overweening narrator with the fate of Icarus. This is, of course, far from the first time that this particular artwork has been 'remade' in an alternative literary genre or medium, since W. H. Auden's 1938 poem 'Musée des Beaux Arts' captured beautifully the painting's decentring of the archetypal myth of over-reaching ambition in its account of the work's depiction of the everyday events on land carrying on regardless of Icarus's demise at sea.

Appropriation clearly extends far beyond the adaptation of other texts into new literary creations, assimilating, as we saw in Chapter 8, both historical lives and events and companion art forms, such as painting, into the process. What distinguishes appropriation from straightforward adaptation at this point is the specific intent behind the act of reinterpretation. Painting, portraiture, photography, film and musical composition all become part of the rich treasury of 'texts' available to the adapter. This is nothing new as such; it is a process that has been underway for centuries and which persists across cultural boundaries. Nevertheless, it has gained a particular imaginative purchase in the wake of late twentieth-century postmodernist theory, which has made us intensely aware of the processes of intervention and interpretation involved in any engagement with existent art forms. Postmodernism has certainly agonized over the replacement of the 'real' by the reproduction. With our ever more skilful capacity to clone and reproduce objects, art forms and now even human tissue, a world further complicated by the advent of 3D printing and additive manufacturing capabilities, imitations in the age of mass production acquire a 'hyper-real' quality. As already noted, Baudrillard offers one of the most expansive theoretical meditations on this theme in his account of simulacra and simulation in the modern age (Baudrillard 1981), but perhaps the seminal account remains Walter Benjamin's influential essay 'The Work of Art in the Age of Its Technological Reproducibility' (Benjamin 2002 [1935]: 4.252). This essay, perhaps better known by the title 'The Work of Art in the Age of Mechanical Reproduction', suggested that there had been a loss of 'aura' of the original work of art in the modern age of reproduction and cloning. Benjamin did not necessarily regard this as a negative outcome; indeed, in a formulation relevant for our accounts here of the adaptive process, he suggested that the attendant deconstruction of 'aura' in many respects freed these objects from the stranglehold of originality (Eagleton 1994 [1981]: 40; Ferris 2004: 47). His productive resolution of the dichotomous relationship between originality and repetition, which has troubled literary critics from T. S. Eliot to Harold Bloom, and also legal theorists and copyright specialists alike (see Gaines 1991: 64), is important for the discussions that both precede and follow in this study.

Returning in the light of Benjamin's theory to Eliot's notion of tradition and the individual talent, we need, perhaps, to enact a paradigm shift away from the idea of authorial originality as a definer of value to a more collaborative and societal understanding of the production of art and meaning. In the digital era of networked communities and open sourcing this need becomes even more pronounced. Richard Powers suggests as much in his response to new technology in the wake of Benjamin's theories in his 1985 novel *Three Farmers on Their Way to a Dance*. Dissecting both photography and film's abilities to provide access to a communal and democratized form of history, by according the masses the power to select and record the moment, Powers observes with proleptic skill in that novel what have effectively become the quotidian working practices of the Web 2.0 world:

> a new technology, already on us, extends this ability well beyond still photography. Every home is about to be transformed into an editing studio, with books, prints, films, and tapes serving the new-age viewer

as little more than rough cuts to be assembled and expanded into customized narratives. Reproduction will make the creation and appreciation of works truly interactive.

(Powers 2001 [1985]: 260)

What Powers brilliantly foresees here is the current moment in the early twenty-first century of content curation and assemblage which is facilitated by the online space and new media technologies: the world of 'apps' and specific platforms for uploading creative and personalized content such as YouTube, YouKu, Vimeo and others (on 'popular curatorship', see Collins 2010: 29, 35). These are what the digital era and its new delivery systems have to offer, what Jim Collins has evocatively called the 'literacy of infinite personalization' (2010: 9), but they have a particular cultural currency in relation to adaptation and appropriation.

It is certainly the interactive quality of appropriative art that emerges with most force from all of the analyses conducted in this volume, and this serves, in turn, to question any bland account of meaning having been evacuated from postmodern art simply by dint of its imitative or recursive qualities. Andy Warhol's artistic output has often served as a crucial touchstone in debates about the evacuation of meaning effected by derivative artworks. His 'multiples', repeated, screen-printed images of twentieth-century icons ranging from Elvis Presley and Mao Zedong to Marilyn Monroe, are an interesting case study. What the reproductive, adaptive element in Warhol's artworks achieves is to underscore the iconicity, and therefore the duplicability, of such images ('global brands') in the age of mechanical reproduction, but that does not automatically mean that his work is simply emptied of meaning in the process. The 'multiples' comment on the power and glamour of celebrity and fame in the modern era but also the manipulated nature of that fame; by extension, they subject something like Monroe's image to the same kind of synecdochal appropriation explored in detail by Joyce Carol Oates in *Blonde* and discussed in Chapter 8. Particular works such as the 'Campbell's Soup Cans', produced in 1962, are a powerful statement about branding and commodification, which when set beside screenshots of Marilyn Monroe also subject her 'life' and image to a similar line of questioning.

Monroe's image is an interesting case since it raises concomitant issues of copyright and ownership that have provided a backdrop to many of the discussions of adaptation in recent years. Legal theorist Rosemary Coombe has examined attempts made by the pop singer Madonna to copyright her image in the law courts. The difficulty comes with the allusive and referential quality of Madonna's own image, which has invoked Monroe's film career and physical appearance on numerous occasions: in the accompanying video for her song 'Material Girl', for example, Madonna consciously imitates Monroe's performance of the song 'Diamonds are a Girl's Best Friend' in *Gentlemen Prefer Blondes* (dir. Howard Hawks, 1953). If Madonna trademarks her appearance in this way, effectively closing down any future possibilities for adaptation, what are the legal implications? Coombe contests that

> If the Madonna image appropriates the likenesses of earlier screen goddesses, religious symbolism, feminist rhetoric, and sadomasochistic fantasy to speak to contemporary sexual aspirations and anxieties then the value of the image derives as much, perhaps, from the collective cultural heritage on which she draws as from her individual efforts. But if we grant Madonna exclusive property rights in her image, we simultaneously make it difficult for others to appropriate those same resources for new ends, and we freeze the Madonna constellation itself.
>
> (Coombe 1994: 107–8)

From the standpoint of contract law, Coombe argues for greater flexibility in our approach to artistic form, proposing a strategy whereby we would move away from the assignment of specific individual copyright towards acceptance of the fact that a fundamental part of the artistic and indeed intellectual and scientific process is adaptation, appropriation and (re)interpretation, improvement and iteration. Jane Gaines advances a comparable argument about 'iconic similarity' in her book *Contested Images* (1991: xvi). Such thoughts also lie behind the move towards open access publishing in the digital creative space and the idea of the 'creative commons'. Without this flexibility, it is argued, access within the public domain would become choked by the need for consent, and the outright monetization of creativity and experiment will, in the end, stifle discovery and intellectual advancement (Lessig, 2008).

Chapter 3 considered the particular cultural potency of Shakespeare as a source for adaptive and appropriative responses, but there are practical economic motivations behind this phenomenon that deserve acknowledgement. As an 'out of copyright' author, Shakespeare's work becomes a form of open access content available to the global community for glorious reinvention. Where the work is 'owned' by a living author or performer, the ramifications of reworkings are more complex, though comic pastiche can provide a legal get-out clause for some works of adaptation. The artist Cindy Sherman has deliberately provoked debates about originality, authenticity and intellectual property by means of her photographic reworkings of iconic Renaissance paintings (Cruz et al. 1997). There is both fidelity and infidelity simultaneously at work in her photographs of herself in the position of a Caravaggio subject, such as, for example, her restaging of the picture 'Boy Bitten by a Lizard'. She has in this work shifted genre, from fine art to photography, and in all kinds of ways signals that this is a conscious restaging, therefore this cannot be deemed plagiarism; and even if it is understood to fall within the realm of 'copying', she raises through her modern versions, which are not, straightforward reproductions of the original, issues of gender and representation by means of inserting herself as the visual alternative to Caravaggio's boy model. The work is 'hers' in so far as it raises questions and encourages applications that depend entirely on her artistic intervention in the original piece; but in the respect that this is also a site upon which further meaning will be overlaid both by the gazes of those viewing this work and through their own recollection of the original artwork, and by new cultural conditions and contexts, then this cannot in any simple sense be copyrighted as belonging exclusively to Sherman.

A similar doubleness adheres to the work of Tom Hunter, whose photographs are 'carefully staged to include references to the past, be they citations of Old Master paintings or abandoned warehouses, evoking London as a durable, living palimpsest' (Rhodes 2012: 214). In *The Way Home* (2000), part of a larger series of works entitled *Life and Death in Hackney*, the 'visual quotation' (215) is to the Pre-Raphaelite painter John Everett Millais's 1851–2 depiction of the drowned Ophelia, itself a re-creation of an off-stage scene from Shakespeare's *Hamlet*. The event is now clearly in modern dress (patched blue jeans are visible through the water) and the episode, narrated in Shakespeare's play, is relocated to a contemporary Hackney waterway, sharing in the process the London psycho-geographical space of contemporary authors such as Iain Sinclair. The image practises both 'adherence to and departure from' (215) the original in ways that challenge simplistic ideas of imitation versus originality. In an earlier sequence, 'Persons Unknown' (1997), Hunter restaged a number of famous paintings by Johannes Vermeer to depict the challenges of very modern-day lives of the poor; 'Woman Reading a Letter' (1663–4) becomes 'Woman Reading a Possession Order' as the world of the everyday and officialdom are brought into stark juxtaposition with a canonical work of art. Hunter's is obviously a very political and politicized act of appropriation, a form of recycling with commitment, but one which challenges any neat legal definition of intellectual property rights in the process.

There is, in some sense, an historical 'return' taking place in this kind of activity, in the world of the creative commons as it were, that takes us back to the kinds of freedom exercised in the world of imitation, borrowing, assimilation, and *bricolage* witnessed in the works of Shakespeare and his contemporaries. By means of developments such as the creative commons licences (first developed in 2002) enabling texts or ideas to be used for educational and/or non-commercial purposes, we have the opportunity to move away from purely legal definitions of plagiarism and copyright infringement, which still dominate the courtrooms of the Western, and now increasingly the Asian, world. In China, for example, there is much current interest in the opportunities posed by so-called 'Shanzai culture' (a particularly vibrant and dynamic form of copycat manufacturing) to abandon a previous reputation for piracy and illegal copying for one of creative innovation and re-creation, or one that recognizes the 'intimate connection between creativity and copying' (Pang 2012: 26). This idea of rejecting the ethos of intellectual property rights in favour of a world of open access is, of course, a controversial and contested one, but one which certainly raises central ideas about creative freedom that the global society would do well to ponder.

Discussing the function of the author, Michel Foucault suggested that the value placed on 'authorship' in the creative process tended to end up by denying or prohibiting intertextuality (1979: 20). What is sought in any argument mounted against 'individual rights' in, or ownership of, a particular image, concept or pose requires a more collaborative and societal understanding of both production and reproduction: 'The very concept of authorship overrides the generic and conventional indebtedness that would mark works as the product not so much of individuals as societies' (Gaines 1991: 77). There are kinships here with traditional folk music, where the song is not owned by any one person or group, but individual arrangements might be respected as having ownership or recognition of a sort. It is this collaborative production of cultural meaning, not least in the practice of history, that Richard Powers interrogates in *Three Farmers on Their Way to a Dance*. That novel commences with, not one, but two suggestive artworks in view: Diego Rivera's Henry Ford-commissioned murals in Detroit, both an homage to and a terrifying portrayal of the age of the machine as Powers reads them, and August Sander's evocative and yet enigmatic photograph of three young farmers perhaps on their way to a village dance, taken in 1914 when Europe stood poised on the brink of change in the face of the terrible collective trauma of the First World War. Powers's novel and narrator are anxious to imagine a history and back-story for these three unnamed men who would most likely have been conscripted into the Prussian army within months of the photograph being taken. In a creative move akin to those authors we have looked at previously who have sought to retrieve 'lost' voices, Powers is writing a story into the historical gaps and *lacunae* offered up by the few known facts about the photographic image. By including a third narrative strand that tells of a US IT worker who discovers a personal connection to this photograph (thereby also introducing computer science as a discipline into the novel), Powers reflects on its reception and the meanings read into it by members of the general public as well as academics. In doing so he makes a powerful case for the collaborative production of meaning, stressing 'the impossibility of knowing where knowledge leaves off and involvement begins' (2001 [1985]: 206). Reflecting that 'describing and altering are two inseparable parts of the same process' (206), Powers asserts that 'there can be no interpretation without participating' (207). It is this crucial notion of participation, social, cultural and ethical, that I wish to suggest underpins adaptation and appropriation as concepts and processes.

It would be erroneous to imply that the line of influence between art and literature is mono-directional; painting and photography have long enjoyed an allusive intertextual relationship with literary texts. The paintings of the Pre-Raphaelites in the nineteenth century endlessly reworked scenes and images from Shakespearean drama, frequently realizing in visual terms events that in the plays themselves occurred offstage, such as Ophelia's flower-bedecked drowning as described by Gertrude at 4.7.138–55 of *Hamlet*. This moment, as already discussed earlier in this chapter, is exquisitely realized by Millais's influential painting 'Ophelia', and Angela Carter's revisiting of Ophelia's death in a number of novels and short stories has been attributed as much to the impact of this painting as to the Shakespearean dramatic verse itself (Sage 1994: 33). Jonathan Bate has also commented on actor-director Laurence Olivier's conscious referencing of the painting in his Freudian cinematic interpretation of the play filmed in black and white in 1948 (Bate 1997: 266). Pre-Raphaelite art in turn influenced the theatricalized photographic tableaux of Julia Margaret Cameron, whose work also influenced the forays into fiction of Virginia Woolf, in particular her 1941 novel *Between the Acts*, which sees a group of actors producing historical tableaux on a provincial village stage. Of course, in a wonderful extra twist to the story, the same Pre-Raphaelite images, not least Millais's 'Ophelia', are now actively working their way back into cinematic and Shakespearean forms by means of dozens of YouTube and YouKu directors, professional and amateur alike, who reference this painting, along with others (often far more explicitly than the play), in their own film-work and video format creations, which on the surface are promoted as Shakespearean adaptations (see Peterson and Williams 2012: 3–4). As connections and interconnections of this kind proliferate in our argument and in the new digital environment, we need to think less in terms of lines of influence in the older Bloomian model than in terms of webs and networks of allusion; these models are distinctly less hierarchical in structure and allow for great mutuality in terms of impact and creativity.

Music, too, has found a significant reference point in well-known works of literature. Opera, ballet and musical, as mentioned in Chapter 1, have looked to the Shakespearean canon and to fairy tale and mythology, among many other sources, for the plotlines and raw material for their own creative outputs. Musicology has had a longstanding interest in the practice of adaptation and appropriation, and much of the terminology that we have deployed when discussing literary adaptation resurfaces in this context: version, interpretation, replication, imitation, variation. But there are some subtle differences in the semantics that deserve mention. In the musical context, words that might in a strictly literary sphere be taken to suggest direct copying without alteration undergo a shift of register, implying instead the kind of simultaneous acts of interpretation that Richard Powers suggests are the true mode of the reader's, spectator's or listener's response to art. In musicology, for example, replication refers not to a simple cloning of a precursor tune or tonal pattern, but to a repetition played at one or more octaves above or below the precursor tone; a musical 'version' is a recognized 'variant' on a previously existent form, musical or otherwise; and 'imitation' means not unproblematic or unquestioning imitation, as it is often assumed to mean in a literary context, but the repetition of a musical phrase in a different pitch. I have argued strongly elsewhere in this volume for the value in deploying terms from musicology when discussing adaptational processes, and once again these kinetic definitions of phrases which in literary criticism have become more stultified or overly static in their applications are hugely helpful.

Music has fed into the pages of fiction in an equally rich and informative way. E. M. Forster's evocation of Beethoven's Fifth Symphony at the heart of his novel *Howard's End* is a case in point. The music is literally experienced in the narrative in the form of a concert jointly attended by the Schlegel sisters and the impoverished clerk Leonard Bast, but it also serves as a central metaphor and shaping movement throughout Forster's text.

Helen Schlegel warns us early on both as readers and interpreters of the symphony to 'look out for the part where you think you have done with the goblins and they come back' (Forster 1985 [1910]: 46), and Forster makes determined space for the 'goblin footfalls' of the musical composition within his own narrative. In Chapter 4 we explored the relationship of Richard Powers's novel *Orfeo* to the Orpheus and Eurydice myth and its particular afterlife in opera, but the novel as a whole is worked around, and through, specific musical compositions and productions, many of which involve the protagonist Peter Els, a composer, and which, perhaps even more significantly, involve descriptions of the *experience* of music by listeners and audiences as well as players. The participatory aspect of the creative process once again comes to the fore. In his early novel *The Gold Bug Variations*, Powers made comparable use of Bach's *Goldberg Variations*, a musical sequence evoked elsewhere in this volume as a supreme example of the process of adaptation made into an art form. Intriguingly one of the best-known modern interpretations of the Bach by pianist Glenn Gould exists in two distinct versions, separated by historical and playing time (1955 and 1981); there are, it seems, always different versions available.

Powers's novel does not appropriate the music of Bach alone; the title puns on the popular name for Bach's composition but also Edgar Allan Poe's 1843 short story 'The Gold Bug'. That tale has at its heart a cracked cipher or decoded mystery, and this connects in turn with Powers's scientific concerns in the novel. *The Gold Bug Variations* looks at the race to crack the genetic code of DNA in the earlier part of the twentieth century. His novel takes variation, then, as the central theme. On the surface an inter-weaving of two love stories, the narrative structure deliberately imitates the intertwined patterns of the double-helix structure of DNA. Powers's writing persistently interweaves and connects scientific and artistic paradigms in the process. The actual cracking of the cipher, the solving of the mystery, by Francis Crick and James Watson, and its publication in essay form, is described with great poetic beauty in the novel: 'The piece breaks his heart with poignancy. It is a beautiful late-twentieth-century pilgrim's narrative – exegesis pressing outwards' (Powers 1991: 481).

The theory of DNA is all about correspondences and consonances, but, perhaps even more importantly, Powers finds links between the patterns of variation in Bach's compositions for Goldberg and the patterns of genetic adaptation that are in many respects the story told by the double helix. In Chapter 7 the Darwinian model of environmental adaptation was advanced as one important analogue to the literary practice of adaptation, but in the double helix Powers finds a twentieth-century scientific equivalent. By doing so, he argues for an enlarged understanding of a term like 'translation' and by extension our understanding of adaptation: 'The aim is not to extend the source but to widen the target, to embrace more than was possible before ... variation grows rich in a new tongue' (491). Translation studies is an important cognate area to adaptation studies for this reason, and, as Susan Basnett has indicated, as it is recognized that 'The twenty-first century is the great age of translation', an era of migrations, movements, displacements and of new global and international space facilitated by the rise of electronic and digital media (Basnett 2014: 1), so the older idea of translation as simply the movement of a text from source to target language is under pressure. Translation too is a form of rewriting, a transformative act of adaptation and variation in which the notion of what constitutes the 'original' is increasingly unclear and that now requires new kinds of literacies (Basnett 2014: 177).

In Powers's account, art, for all its inherent intertextuality, like science, proves to be less about echoes, repetitions and re-phrasings, less about reproduction *per se*, however fundamental this might feel in practice, than about the identification of shared codes and possibilities. Baz Luhrmann, a film director we have had cause to invoke on a number of occasions in this study, has articulated the importance of 'encoding' both as internal navigation and as creative act in its own right. Describing his self-conscious referencing of codes and genres from spaghetti westerns to the music of Kurt Cobain via the films of Franco Zeffirelli in his ground-breaking Shakespeare adaptation *William Shakespeare's Romeo + Juliet* (1996), he stresses: 'The coding and referencing are to help the audience understand where they are as well as making a new work in itself' (Andrew 2001). The discovery of codes, then, offers the satisfying placement that comes with familiarity and recognition but also enables acts of endless (re)creativity in new contexts. Scientific discovery and the act of reading come together in a beautiful ballet or a double helix of their own in this moment of realization.

Part of the original journey of this book was to find a means of discussing and interpreting adaptation and appropriation as literary and artistic processes in ways that would transcend the rather static or immobilizing discussion of source and influence that had previously dominated studies in this domain. That kind of nuanced work is now happily well underway as adaptation studies has gained credence as a form of academic research, and as contemporary audiences for film and related media and online communities on sites and platforms such as YouTube, YouKu and Vimeo are all proving highly adept at both understanding and adopting such processes. Quotation, allusion, homage, parody, re-vision and pastiche are dominant modes in many popular cultural contexts, from television programmes such as *The Simpsons, South Park* or *The Big Bang Theory*, through computer games and graphic novels, to the proliferating work of online fanfiction communities: 'The injunction in the new age of fan-fiction, social media, and e-commerce is not simply to consume passively but instead to be a creative participant' (Ue and Cranfield 2014: 6). It could be argued of course that adaptation (and perhaps literature and film in general) has always assumed active audiences in this way, but with readerships now skilled in the art of searching online (and off) for wider referential frameworks and contexts for almost any type of material they are receiving, we need, in turn, to develop an ever more agile theoretical and critical vocabulary to describe, understand and indeed mobilize these processes of response.

In searching for more kinetic models and terminology to provide the 'new critical idiom' for studying adaptive forms in the so-called 'post-literary era' (see, for example, Leitch 2007: 257–8; Collins 2010: 2), musicology has proved one particularly helpful discipline offering us templates as diverse and suggestive as baroque variation on themes, the riffs of improvisational jazz and contemporary digital sampling techniques. Science, too, in particular the theories of adaptation expounded by Mendel, Darwin and those who have deployed the theories of Crick and Watson, has proven to be an equally potent reference point. It seems fitting therefore that we move towards a conclusion with the recurring yet innovative patterns of Bach's *Goldberg Variations* and the double helix of DNA uppermost in our minds.

AFTERWORD
DIFFERENT VERSIONS

'A classic is great because it does something for someone.'
Jim Collins, *Bring on the Books for Everybody*

In Lloyd Jones's novel *Mister Pip* (2006), Charles Dickens's *Great Expectations* has a talismanic presence in the narrative. First-person narrator Matilda unfolds her dramatic story of life on a remote Pacific island, a story told, like Pip's early narrative, from a young person's perspective, which is one of petty brutalities, educational inspiration and migrations of various kinds. Overall, a relationship with the Dickens novel in particular and with reading in general begins to define her life-story. She is first introduced to the text by a maverick schoolteacher on the island, Mr Watts, and like many of the children in her class she is enraptured by this story of a young boy, life on the Kent marshes and convict Magwitch, all occupying a world palpably different from her own:

> By the time Mr Watts reached the end of chapter one I felt like I had been spoken to by this boy Pip. This boy who I couldn't see to touch but knew by ear. I had found a new friend.

(Jones 2006: 20)

As the class group explores the story in instalments, re-creating in very different circumstances the publishing history of Dickens's 1860 novel, so too the children carry the story home in their heads and retell it to their parents. In numerous ways, different versions of Dickens's story start to emerge, in a manner that describes the powerful collective and individual nature of reading but also the power of analogue, comparison and the personalized response. Matilda filters her responses to the novel through the world and landscape she knows well, through a concept of 'home':

> By now I understood the importance of the forge in the book. The forge was home: it embraced all these things that give life its shape. For me, it meant the bush tracks, the mountains that stood over us, the sea that sometimes ran away from us.
>
> (Jones 2006: 46)

Matilda is of course becoming literate, learning to love finding patterns in what she reads and ultimately to become a writer herself; in a circular movement familiar to us from novels like *Foe* in discussions elsewhere in this study, we find Matilda writing the first line of the novel we ourselves have been reading later in the text. But she is also learning about the adaptation process. After an encounter with the random cruelties of rebel soldiers occupying the village, the single copy of *Great Expectations* available on the island is burned and Mr Watts, in a remarkable act of emotional resilience, encourages the class to collaborate in remembering the text he had read to them, and to re-create the story from their memories: 'We would retrieve *Great Expectations*' (108). The teacher affords them considerable licence in their remaking process:

> Mr Watts instructed us to dream freely. We did not have to remember the story in any order or even as it really happened ... When we have gathered all the fragments we will put together the story. It will be as good as new.
>
> (Jones 2006: 108–9)

The novel becomes, then, an extended philosophical exploration of the afterlife of texts, the power of personalized reading experiences, and the existence of 'different versions' of canonical texts, of history and of lives lived. Matilda later discovers that the version of Dickens's novel that Mr Watts read to the class (and the version which was therefore the focus of their reconstructive efforts) was not a verbatim version of the 1861 edition; omitting more complex storylines such as Compeyson's, and abridging the language to suit his young audience: 'Mr Watts had rewritten Mr Dickens's masterwork' (193). As a result she initially feels betrayed, but she comes to celebrate and honour this 'Pacific version of *Great Expectations*' (149). Her own life-story becomes itself a story of returns and connections, enacting some of the central tropes of Dickens's narrative, and in the process we as readers are given a point of entry to the excitement of reading and revisiting texts in different versions and in different contexts. There is in an embedded sense a one-to-one relationship being played out here between *Mister Pip* and a canonical literary text, *Great Expectations*, but, more important perhaps than the adaptation of specific characters or plotlines to an understanding of Lloyd Jones's novel, is what Thomas Leitch has suggested is 'textualizing ... the processes by which some intertexts become sanctified as texts while others do not' (2007: 302). That sanctification may happen for a combination of cultural, economic or indeed highly personal reasons, but we are, therefore, reading or seeing and encountering afresh a 're-reading through adaptation', as Leitch puts it (293).

This exploration of literary adaptation and appropriation has inevitably had recourse to many companion media and art forms, from film and music, to the scientific domain, especially with nineteenth-century theories of genetic inheritance and environmental adaptation, whose tendrils reach well into the twenty-first century with ongoing debates around genetic engineering and modification (Tudge 2002). Contemporary science talks about the modern synthesis of Mendel's theories of inheritance and Darwin's notions of diversity and variation in neo-Darwinianism, and this synthesis of ideas has had very genuine outcomes in the fields of molecular biology and research into DNA. While readily acknowledging that a volume on the literary and textual processes of adaptation and appropriation can only ever deploy such complex thinking at the level of metaphor and suggestion, it remains true to say that the Mendel–Darwin synthesis offers a useful way of thinking about the happy combination of influence and creativity, of tradition and the individual talent, and of parental influence and offspring, in explicitly appropriative literature, and perhaps in all literature. In his autobiography, Darwin reflected on the 'endless beautiful adaptations that we everyday meet with' (cited in Beer 1983: 39), and it can only be hoped that the aesthetic picture painted here has been one of comparable beauty, richness and potential.

This is an afterword, then, that is deeply conscious that it does not aim towards neat closure or summation but gestures instead towards future possibilities and ongoing textualizing processes. By choosing the title 'Afterword' I am equally aware of how many appropriations have positioned themselves in relation to precursors via this notion of coming 'after', behind, in the shadows, footprints or in the wake of others. John Gross edited an anthology of Shakespearean appropriations entitled *After Shakespeare* (2002); Patrick Marber's English relocation of August Strindberg's 1888 naturalist tragedy *Miss Julie*, which elected for a 1945 setting in the wake of the British Labour Party's landslide election victory following the war, thereby enabling a powerful variation on the class-driven sexual politics of the original play, was entitled *After Miss Julie* (1996); Polly Teale's play for the Shared Experience company, which explored the life of novelist Jean Rhys, alluded to her seminal work of appropriation *Wide Sargasso Sea* and its re-vision of *Jane Eyre* (discussed in detail in Chapter 6) in its title, *After Mrs Rochester* (2003). Teale had herself previously adapted *Jane Eyre* for the stage and so there was a multi-layered textual engagement taking place even in these 'afterwords'. 'After' can, then, simply signal a chronological relationship across time and need not endorse an attitude of belatedness, but it might also signal new forms of creativity. To 'go after' something could suggest an active mode of pursuing an original for a purpose. Certainly, the drive of many of the appropriations studied here is to 'go after' certain canonical or high profile works and to question their basis or foundation in earlier patriarchal or imperial cultural contexts, and this is an important act of questioning that moves us well beyond an act of simple imitation.

Yet in some postmodernist accounts of the late twentieth and early twenty-first centuries all artistic endeavours are seen as coming 'afterwards' because nothing entirely new or original is possible in our belated condition. In this version we come too late to the stage to achieve anything completely fresh or original, and 'after' as a concept in this context becomes a signifier of reduced or debased value. Those who attack the referential qualities of hip-hop music or digital sampling, or who bemoan the popularity of cover versions in popular music, or suggest that no film adaptation could ever be 'better' than the book are all expounding this somewhat stifling interpretation of postmodernism. Those who attacked Graham Swift's novel *Last Orders* and suggested that it did not deserve to win literary prizes because it was 'after Faulkner' (and indeed 'after Chaucer', 'after T. S. Eliot', and 'after Powell and Pressburger'; see the fuller discussion in Chapter 2) were indulging in a similar line of argument. The ease of copying in the digital era can in these versions mean that creativity has reached a dead-end and is simply endlessly recycling the same things in slightly different formats.

But, as the visceral excitements of reading and re-reading and re-creation as described by Matilda in *Mister Pip* make clear, 'after' need not mean belated in a purely negative sense. Coming after can mean benefiting from accrued wisdom or experience; it can mean finding new angles and new points of entry into the supposedly familiar. We are increasingly finding ways as scholars to discuss adaptational and appropriated literature in ways that register influence but do not assume that sources are either strangleholds or the only filters through which an adapted or appropriated text or experience might be approached. This invites us to look for the possibilities enabled by, rather than the prescriptiveness of, what comes before. The arts of adaptation and appropriation are now acknowledged as having a potential, both as influences and as shaping effects in their own right.

Charlie Kaufman's meta-fictional, meta-cinematic screenplay for *Adaptation* (dir. Spike Jonze, 2002) wrestles very openly with the processes and pitfalls of adaptation as he explores, with grim irony, his repeated failure to render on film in any satisfying way a popular work of non-fiction called *The Orchid Thief* (by Susan

Orlean, 2000). Kaufman's plot actively explores the issues of interpolation, alteration and imagining that form an inevitable part of any process of adaptation. But it is equally important to note that the impact does not only occur in one direction. No appropriation can be achieved without altering in some way the text which inspired that adaptation. This is Matilda's realization when she is able to celebrate Mr Watts's adaptation of *Great Expectations* in their Pacific island context and to see that he is 'her' Dickens. Few readers who know Jean Rhys's *Wide Sargasso Sea* can now approach *Jane Eyre* without the filter of feminism and post-colonialism and without actively seeking out 'the madwoman in the attic' in that text. As Michael Worton and Judith Still note, 'every literary imitation is a *supplement* which seeks to complete and supplant the original and which functions at times for later readers as the pre-text of the "original"' (1990: 7). If 'supplement' here operates in the sub-Derridean sense of a virtual substitute or replacement for the original (Derrida 1976: 141–57), then the filtering and mediation of many of the appropriations studied here through other works of adaptation are further proof of this web of intertextuality which resists easy linear structures and straightforward one-to-one and one-way readings of 'influence'.

A limited or foreclosed sense of 'the belatedness' of adaptive literature would restrict the capacity of the appropriation to function actively as a textual force in its own right. A more positive approach is signalled by J. Hillis Miller in his study of multiple versions of the Pygmalion myth; acknowledging the 'perpetual belatedness' of these versions, Miller nevertheless stresses that they are 'affirmative, productive, inaugural ... they enter the cultural and historical world to change it and keep it going forward' (1990: 243). A potent example of this affirmative movement forward is Philip Pullman's collection of novels for young readers *His Dark Materials* (1995–2000). This trilogy acknowledges its indebtedness to John Milton's seventeenth-century epic poem *Paradise Lost* in its title, which is a direct quotation from the Miltonic precursor. Pullman's secularizing narratives of parallel worlds, *daemons* and Dust owe much to Milton's eighteenth-century commentator and adapter, the poet-illustrator William Blake, who in *The Marriage of Heaven and Hell* declared that Milton was unknowingly of

Satan's party (Squires 2002). Few would wish to ascribe either to Blake or to Pullman the condition of belatedness, yet it is clear that both come willingly and deliberately 'after Milton' in this way.

Another work that has come 'after Milton' but which enacts numerous filtering and associative effects of its own is Geoffrey Hill's remarkable poetic sequence *Scenes from Comus* (2005). Ostensibly a contemporary meditation on Milton's 1634 occasional masque for the installation of the Earl of Bridgewater as Lord President of the Council of the Marches ('I've not pieced out the story', Hill stresses [21]), the poem is also a deep reflection on masquing, music, ephemera and ageing: 'So let there be nothing where it stood, / Ludlow's brief mirage' (62). Dedicated to the composer Hugh Wood on his seventieth birthday, the poem, both in its title and dedication, calls into focus Wood's own allusive symphony *Scenes from Comus*, first performed in 1965, which was also based on Milton's masque. Once again the process of adaptation proves multi-layered and endlessly plural in its gestures and effects, a version, dare we suggest, of Louis MacNeice's sense in his poem 'Snow' (1935) of the 'drunkenness of things being various'.

A similar restrictive argument about lack of imagination and creativity often surrounds the culture of remakes in a cinematic context. Gus Van Sant's 1998 shot by shot 'remake' of Alfred Hitchcock's seminal *Psycho* (1960) re-created Hitchcock's editing and camera angles and raised many eyebrows as people questioned what was new or purposeful in an example of adaptation that involved neither shift of genre, language nor aesthetic but only a movement of proximation to the present day. Thomas Leitch has argued for a need to consider this remake as a 'twin' to the Hitchcock precursor, which brings yet another concept into the language of adaptation: twinning (Leitch 2013: 73). It is interesting to note that Hitchcock was himself adapting a 1959 novel of the same name by Robert Bloch and that Bloch had based his narrative 'on a true story', so there are archaeologies of interpretation at play here also.

There was equal critical resistance to Spike Lee's 2003 remake or 'twin' of Park Chan Wook's South Korean thriller *Old Boy*, which perhaps made the highly acclaimed film (itself an adaptation of a manga precursor) more accessible for a target audience resistant to subtitling on non-Anglophone films. Certainly recent decades have seen several conscious relocations of non-English-language films and television series, including *The Killing*, relocated from Copenhagen to Seattle, and perhaps these are not adaptations in the enmeshed manner of many of the texts we have been discussing in this volume, but they do point to a rather more intriguing direction of travel, of the increased cinematic and textual migration of texts. In the context of the newly globalized film industry, and with the importance of translation as a transformative and creative act now firmly established in scholarly terms, the remake too is clearly becoming an increasingly nuanced category for consideration. In the era of ubiquitous computing, where points of entry into adaptational processes are becoming increasingly diverse, diffuse and dispersed, we would do well to pay heed to Jim Collins's statement which forms the epigraph to this afterword: that classics are not defined by an executive board sitting in a corporate office but by the work they do in the world, and by the pleasure they give. Any text or event is rendered significant because it does something for someone, because it *means* for that individual.

We need, then, to restore to adaptation and appropriation a genuinely celebratory comprehension of their capacity for creativity, commentary and critique. The pleasurable aspects of recognizing patterns, as evinced by Matilda in her auditing of *Great Expectations* in *Mister Pip*, of identifying intertextual relationships between adaptations, appropriations and their various informing sources, is in the end an important part of the process. The discipline of English Literature, while it cannot and should not be easily reduced to a detective-like mode of cracking codes and ciphers, nevertheless thrives and is enabled by endless and ongoing practices of 'reading alongside', of comparison and contrast, and of identifying intertexts and analogies, often from a highly personalized context and experience, that are central to the studies undertaken here.

Adaptation studies as a sub-discipline has certainly emerged from the shadows since the first edition of this study was published. Many volumes, focusing on a range of genres, now study adaptation as a process and there are scholarly journals devoted to the topic, while in the public domain the popularity of films, comics, games, songs, novels, poems and plays that adapt and appropriate seems undiminished. My earlier clarion call for adaptations to be valued as creative works in their own right has therefore undergone its own rewriting in this version. We are much better positioned now to understand that these are not belated and unoriginal practices but rather vitally creative ones, ones that provide new cultural content in an increasingly diverse range of contexts and communities. Adaptations and appropriations deserve to be seen as influential and agenda-setting in their own right, and in the process they acknowledge something fundamental about literature and art: that their impulse is to spark thoughts, associations, relationships, and stimulate emotional response.

To return to a quotation from Derrida cited earlier: 'Perhaps the desire to write is the desire to launch things that come back to you as much as possible in as many forms as possible' (1985: 157–8). Derrida seems here to respond to observations made on the natural world by Darwin a century before: 'But the environment is not monolithic and stable: it is a matrix of possibilities, the outcome of multiple interactions between organisms and within matter' (cited in Beer 1983: 23). Adaptation and appropriation, we might add – supplementing, complementing, coming after Derrida and Darwin, as it were – are all about multiple interactions and a matrix of possibilities, about different versions of things. They are, endlessly and wonderfully, about seeing things come back to us in as many forms as possible.

Glossary

affordances   phrase first coined by perceptual psychologist James J. Gibson (2014 [1986]) to refer to those relationships between an object and the environment which enable (afford) the object the ability to interact. In adaptation studies we refer particularly to textual and digital affordances.

allusion   an indirect or passing reference.

analogue   an analogous or parallel text.

analogy   a correspondence or partial similarity between text, motif or thing.

archetype   an original, a model or prototype. In literature this also refers to a recurrent symbol or motif.

bricolage   in a literary context, a collage or collection of different allusions, quotations and references in the context of a new creative work. Often associated with the work of structural anthropologists such as Claude Lévi-Strauss, who studied the transformations of myth (2001 [1978]), and with postmodernism (Barry 1995: 83). The term derives from the French for do-it-yourself (DIY).

citation   a passage cited or quoted, with the embedded legal sense of reference to works of authority.

convergence culture   referring to the idea of different forms of access to and consumption of media increasingly coming together and therefore blurring edges and boundaries between forms, including literature, film and the internet. (On the interactive and participatory audiences this fosters, see Jenkins 2006.)

defamiliarization   a term frequently deployed in Structuralist and Russian Formalist theory to describe the process of rendering something unfamiliar, especially in literature. Often used to describe the theatrical operations of Bertolt Brecht's theory of *Verfremdungseffekt* or 'alienation effect' (Counsell 1996: 103). Also links to Sigmund Freud's notion of *das Unheimlich*, the 'uncanny' or the 'strangely familiar' (1963 [1919]).

hybridity   in literature a term deployed to describe a blend, fusion or compound of influences at the level of both language and form. Often used by critical theorists to refer to intercultural encounters with both a positive and negative slant (see Bhabha 1995: 206–9).

hypertext   Gerard Genette's term (1997 [1982]: ix) for the appropriative or adaptive text (see also 'hypotext').

hypotext   Genette's term (1997 [1982]: ix) for the source text of any appropriation or rewriting (see also 'hypertext').

imitation   a copy; a counterfeit. In music, this term carries the wider sense of the repetition of a phrase in a different pitch. In classical and early modern culture the term was used in a non-pejorative sense, although in postmodern theory it can refer to the purely derivative.

improvisation   a composition or performance of music or verse without a script; in appropriation, the term is extended to a work that adapts in a free-form way a precursor or source text. On improvisation in a social and dramatic context, see Greenblatt (1980: 227–8).

intercultural   term used to describe texts and performances that seek to deploy strategies, references and/or techniques from cultures other than that of the originating artist.

intermediality   connections or interventions between different mediums and genres.

interpolation   the insertion of words, phrases, characters or plotlines into a text.

intertextuality   Julia Kristeva's term for the permutation of texts by utterances and semiotic signifiers deriving from other texts (1980). Now the term is used more widely to refer to the relationship between literary texts and other texts or cultural references (for a full discussion, see Allen 2000).

metonymy   specifically the act of substituting a word denoting an object or action for one denoting a property associated with it, but in its extended use a word or thing used as a substitute or symbol for another. Often opposed to metaphor.

mimesis   imitation or representation. The phrase is most commonly associated with Aristotelian theories of imitation and representation. See also René Girard's anthropology-inflected study of mimesis (1988).

montage   in film, the process or technique of selecting, editing or piecing together separate sections of film to form a continuous whole, particularly associated with the work of Sergei Eisenstein in the twentieth century, but in its more extended use a mixture, blend or medley of various elements; a pastiche. The term is also used to describe the appropriation of existent songs and music in hip-hop and dj-ing by means of 'cut 'n' mix' and sampling.

parody   a humorous, often exaggerated imitation of author, work or style (for a full discussion, see Dentith 2000).

pastiche   a term deriving from French, which in the musical sphere refers to a medley of references, a composition made up of fragments pieced together (Dentith 2000: 194). Central to accounts of post-modernist theory and practice (see Barry 1995: 83), in the wider domains of art and literature pastiche has undergone a further shift of reference, being applied most often to those works that carry out an extended imitation of the style of a single artist or writer.

proximation   Genette's phrase (1997 [1982]: 304) for an updating or the cultural relocation of a text to bring it into greater proximity with the cultural and temporal context of readers or audiences.

remediation   in conventional terms there is a notion of remedying or improving something but in adaptation theory it refers to something being actively translated into a new media form or new technology that is at stake (Bolter and Grusin 2000).

replication   the act of copying. In music, this means repeating a phrase one or more octaves above or below the given tone.

revision   the action or instance of revising, or revisiting, although the phrase is given a specifically feminist politics by Adrienne Rich as 're-vision' (1992 [1971]).

riff   a short or repeated phrase in jazz music, often as a basis for improvisation.

sampling   in musicology, the modification or reuse of part of one musical recording in the context of another. Particularly prevalent in the genre of hip-hop.

supplement   a thing or part added to a book. In *Of Grammatology*, Jacques Derrida debates the notion of supplementarity, since '*supplement*' in French can also mean replacement or substitute (1976: 141–57).

synecdoche   a figure of speech in which a part is made to represent the whole.

transformation   the act or instance of transforming; metamorphosis, change.

travesty   a grotesque misrepresentation or imitation of something.

variation   the act or instance of varying; a departure from a former or normal condition. In music, this refers to the repetition of a theme in a changed or elaborated form.

version   an account of a matter from a particular point of view; a form or variant of a thing as performed or adapted.

BIBLIOGRAPHY

Abbott, H. Porter (2002) *The Cambridge Introduction to Narrative*, Cambridge: Cambridge University Press.

Ackroyd, Peter (1983) *The Last Testament of Oscar Wilde*, Harmondsworth: Penguin.

Ackroyd, Peter (2002) *Dickens: Public Life and Private Passion*, New York: Hylas.

Ackroyd, Peter (2003 [1990]) *Dickens*, London: Sinclair-Stevenson.

Adorno, Theodor and Horkheimer, Max (1997 [1944]) *Dialectics of Enlightenment*, London: Verso.

Allen, Graham (2000) *Intertextuality*, London: Routledge.

Andreas, James R. Sr (1999) 'Signifyin' on The Tempest in Gloria Naylor's Mama Day', in Christy Desmet and Robert Sawyer (eds) *Shakespeare and Appropriation*, London: Routledge.

Andrew, Geoff (2001) 'Baz Luhrmann (I)', *Guardian*, 7 September.

Ashcroft, Bill, Griffiths, Gareth and Tiffin, Helen (eds) (1995) *The Postcolonial Studies Reader*, London: Routledge.

Atkinson, Kate (1997) *Human Croquet*, London: Black Swan.

Atkinson, Kate (2002) *Not the End of the World*, London: Doubleday.

Atkinson, Kate (2004) *Case Histories*, London: Doubleday.

Attridge, Derek (ed.) (1990) *The Cambridge Companion to James Joyce*, Cambridge: Cambridge University Press.

Attridge, Derek (1996) 'Oppressive Silence: J. M. Coetzee's Foe and the Politics of Canonisation', in Graham Huggan and Stephen Watson (eds) *Critical Perspectives on J. M. Coetzee*, Basingstoke: Macmillan.

Baker, Jo (2013) *Longbourn*, London: Transworld Digital [e-book edition].

Bakhtin, Mikhail (1984 [1968]) *Rabelais and His World*, trans. Hélène Iswolsky, Bloomington, IN: Indiana University Press.

Barry, Peter (1995) *Beginning Theory: An Introduction to Literary and Cultural Theory*, Manchester: Manchester University Press.

Barnes, Julian (1989) *The History of the World in 10½ Chapters*, London: Picador.

Barthes, Roland (1981) 'Theory of the Text', in R. Young (ed.) *Untying the Text: A Post-structuralist Reader*, London: Routledge.

Barthes, Roland (1988) 'The Death of the Author', in David Lodge (ed.) *Modern Criticism and Theory: A Reader*, London: Longman.

Barthes, Roland (1993 [1972]) *Mythologies*, trans. Annette Lavers, London: Vintage.

Basnett, Susan (2014) *Translation*, London: Routledge.

Bate, Jonathan (1993) *Shakespeare and Ovid*, Oxford: Clarendon.

Bate, Jonathan (1997) *The Genius of Shakespeare*, London: Picador.

Baudrillard, Jean (1981) *Simulacra and Simulation*, trans. Sheila Faria-Glaser, Ann Arbor, MI: University of Michigan Press.

Bazin, André (2000) 'Adaptation or the Cinema as Digest', in James Naremore (ed.) *Film Adaptation*, London: Athlone Press.

Beckett, Sandra (2008) *Red Riding Hood for All Ages: A Fairy Tale Icon in Cross-Cultural Contexts*, Detroit, MI: Wayne State University Press.

Beckett, Sandra (2009) *Recycling Red Riding Hood*, London: Routledge.

Beckett, Sandra (2013) *Revisioning Red Riding Hood around the World: An Anthology of International Retellings*, Detroit, MI: Wayne State University Press.

Beer, Gillian (1983) *Darwin's Plots: Evolutionary Narrative in Darwin, George Eliot, and Nineteenth-Century Fiction*, London: Ark.

Benjamin, Walter (2002 [1935]) 'The Work of Art in the Age of Its Techno-logical Reproducibility', in Howard Eiland and Michael W. Jennings (eds) *Selected Writings, Volume 3: 1935-1938*, Cambridge, MA: Harvard University Press.

Benjamin, Walter (2003 [1940]) 'On the Concept of History', in Howard Eiland and Michael W. Jennings (eds) *Selected Writings, Volume 4: 1938–1940*, Cambridge, MA: Harvard University Press.

Bennett, Arnold (2007 [1908]) *The Old Wives' Tale*, Harmondsworth: Penguin.

Bennett, Ronan (2004) *Havoc in Its Third Year*, London: Bloomsbury.

Bettelheim, Bruno (1975) *The Uses of Enchantment: The Meaning and Importance of Fairy Tales*, London: Thames and Hudson.

Bhabha, Homi K. (1995) 'Cultural Diversity and Cultural Differences', in Bill Ashcroft, Gareth Griffiths and Helen Tiffin (eds) *The Post-Colonial Studies Reader*, London and New York: Routledge.

Bigsby, Christopher (ed.) (1997) *The Cambridge Companion to Arthur Miller*, Cambridge: Cambridge University Press.

Bingham, Dennis (2010) *Whose Lives Are They Anyway?: The Biopic as Contemporary Film Genre*, New Brunswick, NJ: Rutgers University Press.

Bloch, Robert (2013 [1959]), *Psycho*, London: Robert Hale.

Bloom, Harold (1973) *The Anxiety of Influence: A Theory of Poetry*, Oxford: Oxford University Press.

Boehm-Schnitker, Nadine and Gruss, Susanne (eds) (2014) *Neo-Victorian Culture: Immersions and Revisitations*, London: Routledge.

Boitani, Piero and Mann, Jill (eds) (1986) *The Cambridge Chaucer Companion*, Cambridge: Cambridge University Press.

Bolter, Jay David and Grusin, Richard (2000) *Remediation: Understanding New Media*, Cambridge, MA: MIT Press.

Bonner, Frances and Jacobs, Jason (2011) 'The First Encounter: The Many Adaptations of the Lewis Carroll Alice Books', *Convergence* 17(11): 37–48.

Bouret, Jean (1968) *Toulouse-Lautrec*, London: Thames and Hudson.

Bowers, Maggie Ann (2004) *Magic(al) Realism*, London: Routledge.

Bowlby, Rachel (1997) *Feminist Destinations and Further Essays on Virginia Woolf*, Edinburgh: Edinburgh University Press.

Brahms, Caryl and Simon, S. J. (2000 [1941]) *No Bed for Bacon*, London: Akadine Press.

Brontë, Charlotte (1985 [1847]) *Jane Eyre*, Harmondsworth: Penguin.

Brown, Tom and Vidal, Belén (eds) (2013) *The Biopic in Contemporary Film Culture*, London: Routledge.

Bruhn, Jorgen, Gjelsvik, Anne and Hanssen, Eirik Frisvold (eds) (2013) *Adaptation Studies: New Challenges, New Directions*, London: Bloomsbury.

Bruns, Axel (2008) *Blogs, Wikipedia, Second Life and Beyond: From Production to Produsage*, New York: Peter Lang.

Bullough, Geoffrey (1957–1975) *Narrative and Dramatic Sources of Shakespeare*, 8 vols, London: Routledge.

Burnett, Mark Thornton (2012) *Filming Shakespeare in the Global Marketplace*, Basingstoke: Palgrave.

Burnett, Mark Thornton (2013) *Shakespeare and World Cinema*, Cambridge: Cambridge University Press.

Byatt, A. S. (1991) *Possession: A Romance*, London: Vintage.

Byatt, A. S. (2001) *The Biographer's Tale*, London: Chatto and Windus.

Calbi, Maurizio (2013) *Spectral Shakespeares: Media Adaptations in the Twenty-First Century*, Basingstoke: Palgrave.

Cardwell, Sarah (2002) *Adaptation Revisited: Television and the Classic Novel*, Manchester: Manchester University Press.

Carey, Peter (1985) *Illywhacker*, London: Faber.

Carey, Peter (1988) *Oscar and Lucinda*, London: Faber.

Carey, Peter (1997) *Jack Maggs*, London: Faber.

Carey, Peter (2000) *True History of the Kelly Gang*, London: Faber.

Carr, Helen (1996) *Jean Rhys*, Plymouth: Northcote House.

Carter, Angela (1967) *The Magic Toyshop*, London: Virago.

Carter, Angela (1990) *The Virago Book of Fairy Tales*, London: Virago.

Carter, Angela (1992) *Wise Children*, London: Vintage.

Carter, Angela (1994) *American Ghosts and Old World Wonders*, London: Vintage.

Carter, Angela (1995 [1979]) *The Bloody Chamber*, London: Vintage.

Carter, Angela (2001 [1988]) *Fireworks*, London: Virago.

Cartmell, Deborah and Whelehan, Imelda (eds) (1999) *Adaptations: From Text to Screen, Screen to Text*, London: Routledge.

Chaucer, Geoffrey (1986) *The Canterbury Tales*, in *The Complete Works of Geoffrey Chaucer*, F. N. Robinson (ed.), Oxford: Oxford University Press.

Chedgzoy, Kate (1995) *Shakespeare's Queer Children: Sexual Politics and Contemporary Culture*, Manchester: Manchester University Press.

Chevalier, Tracy (1999) *Girl with a Pearl Earring*, London: HarperCollins.

Clark, Sandra (ed.) (1997) *Shakespeare Made Fit: Restoration Adaptations of Shakespeare*, London: Everyman.

Clarke, Marcus (1997 [1885]) *His Natural Life*, Graham Tulloch (ed.), Oxford: Oxford University Press [World's Classics].

Coetzee, J. M. (1987) *Foe*, Harmondsworth: Penguin.

Collins, Jim (2010) *Bring on the Books for Everybody: How Literary Culture Became Popular Culture*, Durham, NC: Duke University Press.

Collins, Wilkie (1999 [1860]) *The Woman in White*, John Sutherland (ed.), Oxford: Oxford University Press [World's Classics].

Collins, Wilkie (1999 [1868]) *The Moonstone*, John Sutherland (ed.), Oxford: Oxford University Press [World's Classics].

Conan Doyle, Sir Arthur (2011 [1887]) *A Study in Scarlet*, Harmondsworth: Penguin.

Connor, Steven (1996) *The English Novel in History 1950–1995*, London: Routledge.

Coombe, Rosemary (1994) 'Authorizing the Celebrity: Publicity Rights, Postmodern Politics, and Unauthorized Genders', in Martha Woodmansee and Peter Jaszi (eds) *The Construction of Authorship: Textual Appropriation in Law and Literature*, Durham, NC: Duke University Press.

Cooper, Pamela (2002) *Graham Swift's 'Last Orders'*, New York and London: Continuum.

Corcoran, Neil (2010) *Shakespeare and the Modern Poet*, Cambridge: Cambridge University Press.

Counsell, Colin (1996) *Signs of Performance: An Introduction to Twentieth-Century Theatre*, London: Routledge.

Coupe, Laurence (1997) *Myth*, London: Routledge.

Cox, Philip (2000) *Reading Adaptations: Novels and Verse Narratives on the Stage, 1790–1840*, Manchester: Manchester University Press.

Crimp, Douglas (1982) 'Appropriating Appropriation', in Paula Marincola (ed.) *Image Scavengers: Photographs*, Philadelphia: Institute of Contemporary Art.

Cruz, Amada, Jones, Amelia and Smith, Elizabeth T. (eds) (1997) *Cindy Sherman: Retrospective*, London: Thames and Hudson.

Cunningham, Michael (1998) *The Hours*, London: Fourth Estate.

Darwin, Charles (1988 [1859]) *The Origin of Species*, Jeff Wallace (ed.), Ware: Wordsworth.

De Certeau, Michel (2013 [1984]) *The Practice of Everyday Life*, trans. Steven F. Rendell, 3rd edn, Berkeley, CA: University of California Press.

De Grazia, Margreta (1994) 'Sanctioning Voice: Quotation Marks, the Abolition of Torture, and the Fifth Amendment', in Martha Woodmansee and Peter Jaszi (eds) *The Construction of Authorship: Textual Appropriation in Law and Literature*, Durham, NC: Duke University Press.

De Groot, Jerome (2009) *The Historical Novel*, London: Routledge.

De Groot, Jerome (2015) *Remaking History: The Past in Contemporary Historical Fictions*, London: Routledge.

Defoe, Daniel (1985 [1724]), *Roxana*, David Blewitt (ed.), Harmondsworth: Penguin.

Defoe, Daniel (1986 [1719]) *Robinson Crusoe*, J. Donald Crowley (ed.), Oxford: Oxford University Press [World's Classics].

DeLillo, Don (1988) *Libra*, Harmondsworth: Penguin.

Dentith, Simon (1995) *Bakhtinian Thought: An Introductory Reader*, London: Routledge.

Dentith, Simon (2000) *Parody*, London: Routledge.

Deppman, Jed, Ferrar, Daniel and Gordon, Michael (eds) (2004) *Genetic Criticism: Texts and Avant-textes*, Philadelphia: University of Pennsylvania Press.

Derrida, Jacques (1976) *Of Grammatology*, trans. Gayatri Chakravorty Spivak, Baltimore, MD: Johns Hopkins University Press.

Derrida, Jacques (1985) *The Ear of the Other: Otobiography, Transference, Translation*, New York: Schocken Books.

Derrida, Jacques (1992) 'Aphorism Countertime', trans. Nicholas Royle, in Derek Attridge (ed.) *Acts of Literature*, London: Routledge.

Desmet, Christy (2014) 'YouTube Shakespeare, Appropriation and Rhetorics of Invention', in Daniel Fischlin (ed.) *Outerspeares: Shakespeare, Intermedia, and the Limits of Adaptation*, Toronto: University of Toronto Press [e-book edition].

Desmet, Christy and Sawyer, Robert (eds) (1999) *Shakespeare and Appropriation*, London: Routledge.

Di Pietro, Cary (2006) *Shakespeare and Modernism*, Cambridge: Cambridge University Press.

Dickens, Charles (1938) *The Letters of Charles Dickens: Volume 3*, Walter Dexter (ed.), London: Nonesuch Press.

Dickens, Charles (1994 [1861]) *Great Expectations*, Kate Flint (ed.), Oxford: Oxford University Press [World's Classics].

Dickens, Charles (1999 [1846]) *Oliver Twist*, Oxford: Oxford University Press [World's Classics].

Dillon, Janette (1993) *Chaucer*, Basingstoke: Macmillan.

Dillon, Janette (2012) *Shakespeare and the Staging of English History*, Oxford: Oxford University Press.

Dionne, Craig and Kapadia, Parmita (eds) (2008) *Native Shakespeares: Indigenous Appropriations on a Global Stage*, Basingtoke: Palgrave.

Duffy, Carol Ann (1999) 'Little Red-Cap', in *The World's Wife*, London: Picador.

Duncker, Patricia (2015) *Sophie and the Sibyl: A Victorian Romance*, London: Bloomsbury.

DuPlessis, Rachel Blau (1985) *Writing beyond the Ending: Narrative Strategies of Twentieth-Century Women Writers*, Bloomington, IN: Indiana University Press.

Dyas, Dee (2001) *Pilgrimage in Medieval English Literature, 700–1500*, Cambridge: D. S. Brewer.

Eagleton, Terry (1994 [1981]) *Walter Benjamin, Or Towards a Revolutionary Criticism*, London and New York: Verso.

Eliot, T. S. (1969) *The Complete Poems and Plays*, London: Faber.

Eliot, T. S. (1984) 'Tradition and the Individual Talent', in Frank Kermode (ed.) *Selected Prose of T. S. Eliot*, London: Faber.

Elliot, Kamilla (2003) *Rethinking the Novel/Film Debate*, Cambridge: Cambridge University Press.

Ellis, John (1982) 'The Literary Adaptation: An Introduction', *Screen* 23(1): 3–5.

Erickson, Peter (1996) 'Shakespeare's Naylor, Naylor's Shakespeare: Shakespearean Allusion as Appropriation in Gloria Naylor's Quartet', in T. Mishkin (ed.) *Literary Influence and African-American Women Writers*, New York: Garland.

Farquhar, George (1988 [1706]) *The Recruiting Officer*, London: Methuen.

Faulkner, William (1996 [1930]) *As I Lay Dying*, London: Vintage.

Ferris, David S. (ed.) (2004) *The Cambridge Companion to Walter Benjamin*, Cambridge: Cambridge University Press.

Fforde, Jasper (2005) *The Eyre Affair*, London: Hodder and Stoughton.

Fischlin, Daniel (ed.) (2014) *Outerspeares: Shakespeare, Intermedia, and the Limits of Adaptation*, Toronto: University of Toronto Press [e-book edition].

Fischlin, Daniel and Fortier, Mark (eds) (2000) *Adaptations of Shakespeare: A Critical Anthology of Plays from the Seventeenth Century to the Present*, London: Routledge.

Forster, E. M. (1985 [1910]) *Howard's End*, Oliver Stallybrass (ed.), Harmondsworth: Penguin.

Foster, Hal (1988) 'Wild Signs: The Breakup of the Sign in 70s' Art', in Andrew Ross (ed.) *Universal Abandon?: The Politics of Postmodernism*, Edinburgh: Edinburgh University Press.

Foster, Hal (1997) 'Death in America', in Colin MacCabe, with Mark Francis and Peter Wollen (eds) *Who Is Andy Warhol?*, London: British Film Institute.

Foucault, Michel (1979) 'What Is an Author', *Screen* 20: 13–33.

Foucault, Michel (1984 [1978]) *The History of Sexuality: An Introduction*, trans. Robert Hurley, Harmondsworth: Penguin.

Fowles, John (1996 [1969]) *The French Lieutenant's Woman*, London: Vintage.

Frayn, Michael (1999) *Headlong*, London: Faber and Faber.

Freud, Sigmund (1963 [1919]) 'The Uncanny', in Philip Rieff (ed.) *Studies in Parapsychology*, trans. Alix Strachey, New York: Collier Books.

Frow, John (1988) 'Repetition and Limitation – Computer Software and Copyright Law', *Screen* 29: 4–20.

Gaines, Jane M. (1991) *Contested Culture: The Image, the Voice, and the Law*, Chapel Hill, NC and London: University of North Carolina Press.

Gamble, Sarah (1997) *Angela Carter: Writing from the Front Line*, Edinburgh: Edinburgh University Press.

Garber, Marjorie (1987) *Shakespeare's Ghost Writers: Literature as Uncanny Causality*, London: Methuen.

Gates, Henry Louis Jr (1988) *The Signifying Monkey: A Theory of African-American Literature*, New York and Oxford: Oxford University Press.

Gay, John (1986 [1728]) *The Beggar's Opera*, Harmondsworth: Penguin.

Genette, Gérard (1997 [1982]) *Palimpsests: Literature in the Second Degree*, trans. Channa Newman and Claude Doubinsky, Lincoln, NE: University of Nebraska Press.

Geraghty, Christine (2008) *Now a Major Motion Picture: Film Adaptations of Literature and Drama*, New York and London: Rowman and Littlefield.

Geraghty, Christine (2009) 'Foregrounding the Media: *Atonement* (2007) as an Adaption', *Journal of Adaptation in Film and Performance* 2(2): 9–109.

Gere, Anne Ruggles (1994) 'Common Properties of Pleasure: Texts in Nineteenth-Century Women's Clubs', in Martha Woodmansee and Peter Jaszi (eds) *The Construction of Authorship: Textual Appropriation in Law and Literature*, Durham, NC: Duke University Press.

Gibson, James J. (2014 [1986]) *The Ecological Approach to Visual Perception*, London: Psychology Press.

Gilbert, Sandra M. and Gubar, Susan (2000 [1979]) *The Madwoman in the Attic: The Woman Writer and the Nineteenth-Century Literary Imagination*, 2nd edn, New Haven, CT: Yale University Press.

Girard, René (1988) *'To Double Business Bound': Essays on Literature, Mimesis, and Anthropology*, London: Athlone Press.

Gordon, John (1981) *James Joyce's Metamorphoses*, New York: Barnes and Noble.

Gosse, Edmund (1989 [1907]) *Father and Son: A Study of Two Temperaments*, Peter Abbs (ed.), Harmondsworth: Penguin.

Greenblatt, Stephen (1980) *Renaissance Self-Fashioning: From More to Shakespeare*, Chicago: University of Chicago Press.

Greene, Graham (2001 [1951]) *The End of the Affair*, London: Vintage.

Greer, Germaine (2008) *Shakespeare's Wife*, London: Bloomsbury.

Gross, John (ed.) (2002) *After Shakespeare: An Anthology*, Oxford: Oxford University Press.

Hall, Stuart (1972) 'The Social Eye of *Picture Post*', *Working Papers in Cultural Studies* 2: 71–120.

Hansen, Adam and Wetmore, Kevin (eds) (2015) *Shakespearean Echoes*, Basingstoke: Palgrave.

Hanson, Lawrence and Hanson, Elizabeth (1956) *The Tragic Life of Toulouse-Lautrec*, London: Secker and Warburg.

Hardie, Philip (ed.) (2002) *The Cambridge Companion to Ovid*, Cambridge: Cambridge University Press.

Hardy, Thomas (2008 [1874]) *Far From the Madding Crowd*, Linda Shires (ed.), Oxford: Oxford University Press [World's Classics].

Harrison, Nancy R. (1988) *Jean Rhys and the Novel as Women's Text*, Chapel Hill, NC: University of North Carolina Press.

Hassall, Anthony J. (1997) 'A Tale of Two Countries: *Jack Maggs* and Peter Carey's Fiction', *Australian Literary Studies* 18: 128–135.

Hawkes, Terence (1992) *Meaning by Shakespeare*, London: Routledge.

Head, Dominic (1997) *J. M. Coetzee*, Cambridge: Cambridge University Press.

Head, Dominic (2002) *The Cambridge Introduction to Modern British Fiction, 1950–2000*, Cambridge: Cambridge University Press.

Head, Dominic (2009) *The Cambridge Introduction to J.M. Coetzee*, Cambridge: Cambridge University Press.

Heilmann, Ann and Llewellyn, Mark (2010) *Neo-Victorianism: The Victorians in the Twenty-First Century 1999–2009*, Basingstoke: Palgrave.

Hermans, T. (ed.) (1983) *The Manipulation of Literary Studies in Literary Translation*, London: Croom Helm.

Hesmondhalgh, David (2000) 'International Times: Fusions, Exoticism, and Anti-racism in Electronic Dance Music', in Georgina Born and David Hesmondhalgh (eds) *Western Music and Its Others: Difference, Representation, and Appropriation in Music*, Berkeley, CA: University of California Press.

Hill, Geoffrey (2005) *Scenes from Comus*, Harmondsworth: Penguin.

Hoesterey, Ingeborg (2001) *Pastiche: Cultural Memory in Art, Film, and Literature*, Bloomington, IN: Indiana University Press.

Hofman, Michael and Lasdun, James (eds) (1994) *After Ovid: New Metamorphoses*, London: Faber.

Holderness, Graham (ed.) (1988) *The Shakespeare Myth*, Manchester: Manchester University Press.

Huang, Alexa and Rivlin, Elizabeth (eds) (2014) *Shakespeare and the Ethics of Appropriation*, Basingstoke: Palgrave.

Huggan, Graham (2002) 'Cultural Memory in Postcolonial Fiction: The Uses and Abuses of Ned Kelly', *Australian Literary Studies* 20:142–154.

Hughes, Robert (1988) *The Fatal Shore: A History of the Transportation of Convicts to Australia, 1787–1868*, London: Pan.

Hulbert, Ann (1993) 'The Great Ventriloquist: A. S. Byatt's *Possession: A Romance*', in Robert E. Hosmer Jr (ed.) *Contemporary British Women Writers*, Basingstoke: Macmillan.

Hulme, Peter and Sherman, William H. (eds) (2000) *'The Tempest' and Its Travels*, London: Reaktion.

Hutcheon, Linda (1985) *A Theory of Parody: The Teaching of Twentieth-century Art Forms*, London and New York: Methuen.

Hutcheon, Linda (1988) *The Poetics of Postmodernism: History, Theory, Fiction*, London: Routledge.

Hutcheon, Linda (2006) *A Theory of Adaptation*, London: Routledge.

Hutcheon, Linda (2013) *A Theory of Adaptation*, 2nd edn, London: Routledge.

Innes, Lyn (2008) *Ned Kelly: Icon of Modern Culture*, London: Helm.

Iser, Wolfgang (1971) 'Indeterminacy and the Reader's Response in Prose Fiction', in J. Hillis Miller (ed.) *Aspects of Narrative*, New York: Columbia University Press.

Iser, Wolfgang (1972) 'The Reading Process: A Phenomenological Approach', *New Literary History* 3(2): 279–299.

Iser, Wolfgang (2001) 'Interaction between Text and Reader', in Colin Counsell and Laurie Wolf (eds) *Performance Analysis: An Introductory Coursebook*, London: Routledge.

Isler, Alan (1996) *The Prince of West End Avenue*, London: Vintage.

James, Henry (1984 [1880]) *Washington Square*, Harmondsworth: Penguin.

James, Henry (2010 [1897]) *What Maisie Knew*, Christopher Ricks (ed.), Harmondsworth: Penguin.

Jenkins, Henry (1992) *Textual Poachers: Television Fans and Participatory Culture*, London and New York: Routledge.

Jenkins, Henry (2006) *Convergence Culture: Where Old and New Medias Collide*, New York: New York University Press.

Jones, Lloyd (2006), *Mister Pip*, London: John Murray.

Jones, Ross (2015) 'Sherlock Facts: 21 Things You Didn't Know', *Telegraph*, 25 April.

Joyce, James (1986 [1922]) *Ulysses*, Harmondsworth: Penguin.

Kaplan, Cora (2007) *Victoriana: Histories, Fictions, Criticism*, Edinburgh: Edinburgh University Press.

Kaplan, Fred (1988) *Dickens: A Biography*, London: Hodder and Stoughton.

Keen, Suzanne (2003) *Romances of the Archive in Contemporary British Fiction*, Toronto: University of Toronto Press.

Keneally, Thomas (1987) *The Playmaker*, London: Sceptre.

Kennedy, Dennis (1993) *Looking at Shakespeare: A Visual History of Twentieth-Century Performance*, Cambridge: Cambridge University Press.

Kidnie, Margaret Jane (2008) *Shakespeare and the Problem of Adaptation*, London: Routledge.

Knight, Stephen (2003) *Robin Hood: A Mythic Biography*, Ithaca, NY: Cornell University Press.

Krauss, Rosalind (1985), *The Originality of the Avant-Garde and Other Modernist Myths*, Cambridge, MA: MIT Press.

Kristeva, Julia (1980) 'The Bounded Text', in *Desire in Language: A Semiotic Approach to Literature and Art*, trans. Thomas Gora, Alice Jardine and Leon S. Roudiez, Leon S. Roudiez (ed.), Oxford: Blackwell.

Kristeva, Julia (1986) 'Word, Dialogue and Novel', in Toril Moi (ed.) *The Kristeva Reader*, trans. Sean Hand and Leon S. Roudiez, Oxford: Blackwell.

Ledent, Bénédicte (2002) *Caryl Phillips*, Manchester: Manchester University Press.

Lee, Hermione (2003), 'Someone to Watch over You', Review of Graham Swift's *The Light of Day*, *Guardian*, 8 March.

Leitch, Thomas (2007) *Film Adaptation and Its Discontents: From 'Gone With the Wind' to 'The Passion of Christ'*, Baltimore, MD: Johns Hopkins University Press.

Leitch, Thomas (2008) 'Adaptation Studies at a Crossroads', *Adaptation* 1: 63–77.

Leitch, Thomas (2009) 'Twelve Fallacies in Contemporary Adaptation Theory', *Criticism* 45(2): 149–171.

Leitch, Thomas (2013) 'The Ethics of Infidelity', in Christa Albrecht-Crane and Dennis Cutchins (eds) *Adaptation Studies: New Approaches*, Lanham, MD and Plymouth: Fairleigh Dickinson University Press.

Leray, Marjolaine (2011) *Little Red Hood*, London: Phoenix Yard Books.

Lessig, Lawrence (2008) *Remix: Making Art and Commerce Thrive in the Hybrid Economy*, London: Bloomsbury.

Levine, Jennifer (1990) 'Ulysses', in Derek Attridge (ed.) *The Cambridge Companion to James Joyce*, Cambridge: Cambridge University Press.

Lévi-Strauss, Claude (2001 [1978]) *Myth and Meaning*, London: Routledge.

MacCabe, Colin, Murray, Kathleen and Warner, Rick (eds) (2011) *True to the Spirit: Film Adaptation and the Question of Fidelity*, Oxford: Oxford University Press.

McCarthy, Tom (2011) 'My Desktop', *Guardian*, 24 November.

McClary, Susan (2001) *Conventional Wisdom: The Content of Musical Form*, Berkeley, CA: University of California Press.

McEwan, Ian (2002 [2001]) *Atonement*, London: Vintage.

McEwen, John (2008) *Paula Rego: Behind the Scenes*, London: Phaidon.

McKendrick, Walter M. (1998) 'The Sensationalism of *The Woman in White*', in Lynn Pykett (ed.) *Wilkie Collins: A Casebook*, Basingstoke: Macmillan.

McLuskie, Kate and Rumbold, Kate (2014) *Cultural Value in Twenty-First Century England: The Case of Shakespeare*, Manchester: Manchester University Press.

MacNeice, Louis (1966) *Collected Poems*, London: Faber.

Mahoney, Elizabeth (2010) 'Review of *The Red Shoes*', *Guardian*, 3 August.

Mantel, Hilary (2009) *Wolf Hall*, London: Fourth Estate.

Mantel, Hilary (2012) *Bring Up the Bodies*, London: Fourth Estate.

Marber, Patrick (1996) *After Miss Julie*, London: Methuen.

Marsden, Jean I. (ed.) (1991) *The Appropriation of Shakespeare*, Hemel Hempstead: Harvester Wheatsheaf.

Martin, Cathlena (2009) 'Charlotte's Website: Media Transformation and the Inter-textual Web of Children's Culture', in Rachel Carroll (ed.) *Adaptation in Contemporary Culture: Textual Infidelities*, London and New York: Continuum.

Martindale, Charles (ed.) (1988) *Ovid Renewed: Ovidian Influences on Literature and Art from the Middle Ages to the Twentieth Century*, Cambridge: Cambridge University Press.

Massai, Sonia (ed.) (2005) *World-Wide Shakespeares: Local Appropriation in Film and Performance*, London: Routledge.

Mathieson, Barbara (1999) 'The Polluted Quarry: Nature and Body in A Thousand Acres', in Marianne Novy (ed.) *Transforming Shakespeare: Contemporary Women's Re-visions in Literature and Performance*, Basingstoke: Macmillan.

Maurel, Sylvie (1998) *Jean Rhys*, Basingstoke: Macmillan.

Miles, Geoffrey (ed.) (1999) *Classical Mythology in English Literature: A Critical Anthology*, London: Routledge.

Miller, Arthur (2000 [1953]) *The Crucible*, Harmondsworth: Penguin.

Miller, J. Hillis (1990) *Versions of Pygmalion*, Cambridge, MA: Harvard University Press.

Milner, John (1988) *The Studios of Paris: The Capital of Art in the Late Nineteenth Century*, New Haven, CT: Yale University Press.

Miola, Robert (1992) *Shakespeare and Classical Tragedy: The Influence of Seneca*, Oxford: Clarendon Press.

Morris, Meaghan (1988) 'Tooth and Claw: *Tales of Survival* and *Crocodile Dundee*', in Andrew Ross (ed.) *Universal Abandon: The Politics of PostModernism*, Minneapolis: University of Minnesota Press.

Mullan, John (2003a) 'Elements of Fiction: Clichés', *Guardian*, 12 April, 'Review': 32.

Mullan, John (2003b) 'Elements of Fiction: Dialogue', *Guardian*, 5 April, 'Review': 32.

Mullan, John (2003c) 'Elements of Fiction: Interior Monologue', *Guardian*, 19 April, 'Review': 32.

Murray, Simone (2012) *The Adaptation Industry: The Cultural Economy of Contemporary Literary Adaptation*, London: Routledge.

Naremore, James (ed.) (2000) *Film Adaptation*, London: Athlone Press.

Naylor, Gloria (1992) *Bailey's Cafe*, New York: Vintage.

Naylor, Gloria (1993 [1988]) *Mama Day*, New York: Vintage.

ní Fhlathúin, Máire (1999) 'The Location of Childhood: *Great Expectations* in Postcolonial London', *Kunapipi* 21: 86–92.

Norbu, Jamyang (2000) *The Mandala of Sherlock Holmes: The Missing Years*, London: John Murray.

Novy, Marianne (ed.) (1999) *Transforming Shakespeare: Contemporary Women's Re-Visions in Literature and Performance*, Basingstoke: Macmillan.

O'Neill, Stephen (2014) *Shakespeare and YouTube: New Media Forms of the Bard*, London: Arden/Bloomsbury [e-book edition].

O'Rourke, James (2010) *Rethinking Shakespeare through Presentist Theory*, London: Routledge.

Oates, Joyce Carol (1993) *Black Water*, New York: Plumo/Penguin.

Oates, Joyce Carol (2000) *Blonde*, London: Fourth Estate.

Orlean, Susan (2000) *The Orchid Thief*, London: Vintage.

Ovid (1987) *Metamorphoses*, trans. A. D. Melville, Oxford: Oxford University Press.

Patterson, Annabel (1987) 'Intention', in Frank Lentricchia and Thomas McLaughlin (eds) *Critical Terms for Literary Study*, Chicago: University of Chicago Press.

Pang, Laikwan (2012) *Creativity and Its Discontents: China's Creative Industries and Intellectual Property Rights Offences*, Durham, NC: Duke University Press.

Pavis, Patrice (ed.) (1996) *The Intercultural Performance Reader*, London: Routledge.

Peterson, Kaara L. and Williams, Deanne (eds) (2012) *The Afterlife of Ophelia*, Basingstoke: Palgrave Macmillan.

Phillips, Caryl (1997) *The Nature of Blood*, London: Faber.

Phillips, Caryl (2015) *The Lost Child*, London: Oneworld.

Phillips, Helen (2000) *An Introduction to The Canterbury Tales: Reading, Fiction, Context*, Basingstoke: Macmillan.

Poe, Edgar Allen (1998 [1843]) 'The Gold-Bug', in David Van Leer (ed.) *Selected Tales*, Oxford: Oxford University Press [World's Classics].

Poole, Adrian (2004) *Shakespeare and the Victorians*, London: Thomson Learning/Arden Shakespeare.

Porter, Peter (1997) 'Jack Maggs', *Guardian*, 18 September.

Powers, Richard (1991) *The Gold Bug Variations*, New York: HarperCollins.

Powers, Richard (2001 [1985]) *Three Farmers on Their Way to a Dance*, New York: Perennial.

Powers, Richard (2014) *Orfeo*, London: Atlantic Books.

Putz, Adam (2013) *The Celtic Revival in Shakespeare's Wake: Appropriation and Cultural Politics in Ireland, 1867–1922*, Basingstoke: Palgrave Macmillan.

Price, Monroe E. and Pollack, Malia (1994) 'The Author in Copyright: Notes for the Literary Critic', in Martha Woodmansee and Peter Jaszi (eds) *The Construction of Authorship: Textual Appropriation in Law and Literature*, Durham, NC: Duke University Press.

Pullman, Philip (2001) *His Dark Materials*, 3 vols, London: Scholastic.

Pykett, Lyn (1994) *The Sensation Novel from 'The Woman in White' to 'The Moonstone'*, Plymouth: Northcote House.

Pykett, Lyn (ed.) (1998) *Wilkie Collins: New Casebook*, Basingstoke: Macmillan.

Rhodes, Kimberly (2012) 'Double Take: Tom Hunter's *The Way Home* (2000)', in Kaara L. Peterson and Deanne Williams (eds) *The Afterlife of Ophelia*, Basingstoke: Palgrave.

Rhys, Jean (1985) *Letters, 1931–1966*, Francis Wyndham and Diana Melly (ed.), Harmondsworth: Penguin.

Rhys, Jean (1987 [1966]) *Wide Sargasso Sea*, Harmondsworth: Penguin.

Rich, Adrienne (1992 [1971]) 'When We Dead Awaken', in Maggie Humm (ed.) *Feminisms: A Reader*, Hemel Hempstead: Harvester Wheatsheaf.

Ricoeur, Paul (1991) 'Appropriation', in Mario Valdes (ed.) *A Ricoeur Reader*, London: Harvester Wheatsheaf.

Ridout, Nicholas (2009) *Theatre and Ethics*, London: Routledge.

Roe, Sue (1982) *Estella, Her Expectations*, Hemel Hempstead: Harvester Wheatsheaf.

Roemer, Danielle M. and Bacchilega, Cristina (eds) (2001) *Angela Carter and the Fairytale*, Detroit, MI: Wayne State University Press.

Rothwell, Kenneth (1999) *A History of Shakespeare on Screen*, Cambridge: Cambridge University Press.

Rushdie, Salman (1991) *Imaginary Homelands: Essays and Criticism, 1981–1991*, New York and London: Granta.

Rushdie, Salman (1998 [1988]) *The Satanic Verses*, London: Vintage.

Sage, Lorna (1994) *Angela Carter*, Plymouth: Northcote House.

Said, Edward (1983) 'On Originality', in *The World, the Text, and the Critic*, Cambridge, MA: Harvard University Press.

Said, Edward (1993) *Culture and Imperialism*, London: Vintage.

Sale, Roger (1978) *Fairy Tale and After: From Snow White to E. B. White*, Cambridge, MA: Harvard University Press.

Sanders, Julie (2001) *Novel Shakespeares: Twentieth-Century Women Novelists and Appropriation*, Manchester: Manchester University Press.

Sanders, Julie (2011), 'Preface: Dynamic Repairs: The Emerging Landscape of Adaptation Studies', in Tricia Hopton, Adam Atkinson, Peta Mitchell and Jane Stadler (eds) *Pockets of Change: Adaptation and Cultural Transition*, Lexington, KY: Lexington Books.

Sanghera, Sathnam (2014) *Marriage Material*, London: Windmill Books.

Sanjek, David (1994), '"Don't Have to DJ No More": Sampling and the "Autonomous" Career', in Martha Woodmansee and Peter Jaszi (eds) *The Construction of Authorship: Textual Appropriation in Law and Literature*, Durham, NC: Duke University Press.

Savory, Elaine (1998) *Jean Rhys*, Cambridge: Cambridge University Press.

Schumacher, Thomas G. (1995) '"This Is a Sampling Sport": Digital Sampling, Rap Music, and the Law in Cultural Production', *Media, Culture, and Society* 17: 253–273.

Sears, Djanet (2000 [1997]) *Harlem Duet*, in Daniel Fischlin and Mark Fortier (eds) *Adaptations of Shakespeare: A Critical Anthology*, London: Routledge.

Sellars, Susan (2001) *Myth and Fairytale in Contemporary Women's Fiction*, Basingstoke: Palgrave.

Shakespeare, William (1998) *The Complete Works*, Stanley Wells and Gary Taylor (gen. eds), Oxford: Oxford University Press.

Showalter, Elaine (1991) *Sister's Choice: Tradition and Change in American Women's Writing*, Oxford: Oxford University Press.

Sim, Stuart (ed.) (2001) *The Routledge Companion to Postmodernism*, London: Routledge.

Smiley, Jane (1992) *A Thousand Acres*, London: Flamingo.

Spivak, Gayatri Chakravorty (1990) 'Reading The Satanic Verses', *Third Text* 11: 41–60.

Spivak, Gayatri Chakravorty (1991) 'Theory in the Margin: Coetzee's *Foe*. Reading Defoe's *Crusoe/Roxana*', in Jonathan Arac and Barbara Johnson (eds) *Consequences of Theory*, Baltimore, MD and London: Johns Hopkins University Press.

Spivak, Gayatri Chakravorty (1997 [1989]) 'Three Women's Texts and a Critique of Imperialism', in Catherine Belsey and Jane Moore (eds) *The Feminist Reader: Essays in Gender and the Politics of Literary Criticism*, 2nd edn, Basingstoke: Macmillan.

Squires, Claire (2002) *Philip Pullman's 'His Dark Materials' Trilogy*, New York and London: Continuum.

Stam, Robert (2000) 'Beyond Fidelity: The Dialogics of Adaptation', in James Naremore (ed.) *Film Adaptation*, London: Athlone Press.

Stam, Robert (2005) *Literature through Film: Realism, Magic and the Art of Adaptation*, Oxford: Blackwell.

Stam, Robert and Raengo, Alessandra (eds) (2009) *Literature and Film: A Guide to Theory and Practice of Adaptation*, Oxford: Blackwell.

Stoppard, Tom (1990 [1967]) *Rosencrantz and Guildenstern Are Dead*, London: Faber.

Swarup, Vikas (2005) *Q & A*, London: Black Swan.

Sweeney, Susan Elizabeth (2003) 'The Magnifying Glass: Spectacular Distance in Poe's "Man of the Crowd"', *Poe Studies/Dark Romanticism* 36: 3–17.

Swift, Graham (1983) *Waterland*, London: Picador.

Swift, Graham (1992) *Ever After*, London: Picador.

Swift, Graham (1996) *Last Orders*, London: Picador.

Swift, Graham (2003) *The Light of Day*, London: Hamish Hamilton.

Teale, Polly (2003) *After Mrs Rochester*, London: Nick Hern.

Terry, Philip (ed.) (2000) *Ovid Metamorphosed*, London: Chatto and Windus.

Teverson, Andrew (2013) *Fairy Tale*, London: Routledge.

Thième, John (2001) *Postcolonial Con-Texts: Writing Back to the Canon*, New York: Continuum.

Thorpe, Michael (1990) 'The Other Side: *Wide Sargasso Sea* and *Jane Eyre*', *Ariel* 8: 99–110.

Thorpe, Vanessa (2009) 'Margate's Shrine to Eliot's Muse', *Observer*, 12 July.

Tiffin, Helen (1987) 'Postcolonial Literatures and Counter Discourse', *Kunapipi* 9: 17–34.

Todorov, Tzvetan (1990) *Genres of Discourse*, trans. Catherine Porter, Cambridge: Cambridge University Press.

Tóibín, Colm (2004) *The Master*, London: Picador.

Tomalin, Claire (2012 [1990]) *The Invisible Woman: The Story of Nelly Ternan and Charles Dickens*, Harmondsworth: Penguin.

Tournier, Michel (1984 [1967]) *Friday; Or, the Other Island*, Harmondsworth: Penguin.

Tudge, Colin (2002) *In Mendel's Footnotes*, London: Vintage.

Ue, Tom and Cranfield, Jonathan (2014) *Fan Phenomena: Sherlock Holmes*, London: Intellect.

Updike, John (2000) *Gertrude and Claudius*, New York: Alfred Knopf.

Vidal, Belén (2013) 'Introduction', in Tom Brown and Belén Vidal (eds) *The Biopic in Contemporary Film Culture*, London: Routledge.

Virgil (1983) *The Eclogues and The Georgics*, trans. Cecil Day-Lewis, Oxford: Oxford University Press.

Wallace, Christopher (1998) *The Pied Piper's Poison*, Woodstock and New York: Overlook Press.

Warner, Marina (1992) *Indigo, or Mapping the Waters*, London: Vintage.

Warner, Marina (1994) *From the Beast to the Blonde: On Fairy Tales and Their Tellers*, London: Chatto and Windus.

Waters, Steve (2015) *Temple*, London: Nick Hern.

Waters, Steve (2015) 'Interview on Temple', *Independent*, 16 May.

Waugh, Patricia (1995) *The Harvest of the Sixties: English Literature and Its Background 1960–1990*, Oxford: Oxford University Press.

Webb, Diana (2000) *Pilgrimage in Medieval England*, London and New York: Hambledon Continuum.

Webb, Diana (2002) *Medieval European Pilgrimage, c. 700–1500*, London: Palgrave.

Weimann, Robert (1983) 'Appropriation and Modern History in Renaissance Prose Narrative', *New Literary History* 14: 459–495.

Weimann, Robert (1988) 'Text, Author-Function, and Appropriation in Modern Narrative: Toward a Sociology of Representation', *Critical Inquiry* 14: 431–447.

Wertenbaker, Timberlake (1991 [1988]) *Our Country's Good*, London: Methuen.

Wheeler, Michael (1994) *English Fiction of the Victorian Period, 1830–1890*, 2nd edn, London: Longmans.

White, Gareth (2013) *Audience Participation in Theatre: Aesthetics of the Invitation*, Basingstoke: Palgrave.

White, Hayden (1973) *Metahistory: The Historical Imagination in Nineteenth-Century Europe*, Baltimore, MD: Johns Hopkins University Press.

White, Hayden (1987) *The Content of the Form: Narrative Discourse and Historical Representation*, Baltimore, MD: Johns Hopkins University Press.

Widdowson, Peter (1999) *Literature*, London: Routledge.

Willett, John (ed. and trans.) (1992 [1964]) *Brecht on Theatre: The Development of an Aesthetic*, New York: Hill and Wang.

Williams, Tennessee (2001 [1957]) *Orpheus Descending*, in *'The Rose Tattoo' and Other Plays*, Harmondsworth: Penguin Modern Classics.

Wilson, James (2001) *The Dark Clue: A Novel of Suspense*, London: Faber.

Woodcock, Bruce (2003) *Peter Carey*, 2nd edn, Manchester: Manchester University Press.

Woodmansee, Martha and Jaszi, Peter (eds) (1994) *The Construction of Authorship: Textual Appropriation in Law and Literature*, Durham, NC: Duke University Press.

Woolf, Virginia (1981) *The Diary of Virginia Woolf: Volume 2, 1920–24*, Anne Olivier Bell (ed.), Harmondsworth: Penguin.

Woolf, Virginia (1988 [1923]) 'Mr Bennett and Mrs Brown', in Andrew McNeillie (ed.) *The Essays of Virginia Woolf: Volume 3, 1919–1924*, London: Hogarth Press.

Woolf, Virginia (1992 [1925]) *Mrs Dalloway*, Claire Tomalin (ed.), Oxford: Oxford University Press [World's Classics].

Woolf, Virginia (1998 [1941]) *Between the Acts*, Frank Kermode (ed.), Oxford: Oxford University Press [World's Classics].

Worton, Michael and Still, Judith (eds) (1990) *Intertextuality: Theories and Practices*, Manchester: Manchester University Press.

Wullschlager, Jackie (2008) 'Not So Happily Ever After', *Financial Times*, 20 December.

Young, Tory (2003) *Michael Cunningham's 'The Hours'*, London and New York: Continuum.

Zabus, Chantal (2002) *Tempests after Shakespeare*, Basingstoke: Palgrave.

Zipes, Jack (1979) *Breaking the Magic Spell: Radical Theories of Folk and Fairy Tales*, London: Heinemann.

Zipes, Jack (1983) *Fairy Tales and the Art of Subversion: The Classical Genre for Children and the Process of Civilization*, London: Heinemann.

Zipes, Jack (1994) *Fairy Tale as Myth: Myth as Fairy Tale*, Lexington, KY: University of Kentucky Press.

FILMS

Adamson, Andrew and Jenson, Vicky (dirs) (2001) *Shrek*.

Adamson, Andrew, Asbury, Kelly and Vernon, Conrad (dirs) (2004) *Shrek 2*.

Almereyda, Michael (dir.) (2000) *Hamlet*.

Blake-Nelson, Tim (dir.) (2001) *'O'*.

Boyle, Danny and Tandan, Loveleen (dirs) (2008) *Slumdog Millionaire*.

Branagh, Kenneth (dir.) (1996) *Hamlet*.

Branagh, Kenneth (dir.) (1999) *Love's Labour's Lost*.

Camus, Marcel (dir.) (1959) *Black Orpheus (Orfeo Negro)*.

Chan-Wook, Park (dir.) (2003) *Oldboy*.

Cheah, Chee Kong (dir.) (2000) *Chicken Rice War*.

Cocteau, Jean (dir.) (1945) *La Belle et la bête*.

Cocteau, Jean (dir.) (1950) *Orphée*.

Coppola, Francis Ford (dir.) (1979) *Apocalypse Now*.

Cuarón, Alfonso (dir.) (1998) *Great Expectations*.

Daldry, Stephen (dir.) (2002) *The Hours*.

Diegues, Carlo (dir.) (1999) *Orfeu*.

Fiennes, Ralph (dir.) (2013) *The Invisible Woman*.

Greenaway, Peter (dir.) (1991) *Prospero's Books*.

Heckerling, Amy (dir.) (1995) *Clueless*.

Henríquez, Leonardo (dir.) (2000) *Sangrador*.

Henson, Brian (dir.) (1992) *The Muppet Christmas Carol*.

Hitchcock, Alfred (dir.) (1960) *Psycho*.

Hughes, Ken (dir.) (1955) *Joe MacBeth*.

Jarman, Derek (dir.) (1979) *The Tempest*.

Jonze, Spike (dir.) (2002) *Adaptation*.

Kurosawa, Akira (dir.) (1954) *The Seven Samurai*.

Kurosawa, Akira (dir.) (1960) *The Bad Sleep Well*.

Kurosawa, Akira (dir.) (1961) *Yojimbo*.

Lee, Spike (dir.) (2013) *Oldboy*.

Leigh, Mike (dir.) (2014) *Mr Turner*.

Leone, Sergio (dir.) (1964) *A Fistful of Dollars*.

Leone, Sergio (dir.) (1965) *A Few Dollars More*.

Luhrmann, Baz (dir.) (1996) *William Shakespeare's 'Romeo + Juliet'*.

Luhrmann, Baz (dir.) (2001) *Moulin Rouge*.

Lumet, Sidney (dir.) (1959) *The Fugitive Kind*.

Lyne, Adrian (dir.) (1987) *Fatal Attraction*.

McGehee, Scott and Siegel, David (dirs) (2012) *What Maisie Knew*.

McQueen, Steve (dir.) (2008) *Hunger*.

McQueen, Steve (dir.) (2013) *Twelve Years a Slave*.

Madden, John (dir.) (1998) *Shakespeare in Love*.

Marshall, Rob (dir.) (2014) *Into the Woods*.

Miller, Chris and Hui, Raman (dirs) (2007) *Shrek the Third*.

Miller, George (dir.) (1979, 1981, 1985) *Mad Max 1–3*.

Olivier, Laurence (dir.) (1948) *Hamlet*.

Powell, Michael and Pressburger, Emeric (dirs) (1944) *A Canterbury Tale*.

Powell, Michael and Pressburger, Emeric (dirs) (1948) *The Red Shoes*.

Reilly, William (dir.) (1990) *Men of Respect*.

Robbins, Jerome and Wise, Robert (dirs) (1961) *West Side Story*.

Rozema, Patricia (dir.) (2000) *Mansfield Park*.

Schepisi, Fred (dir.) (2001) *Last Orders*.

Schlesinger, John (dir.) (1967) *Far From the Madding Crowd*.

Sidney, George (dir.) (1953) *Kiss Me Kate*.

Stone, Oliver (dir.) (1986) *Salvador*.

Stone, Oliver (dir.) (1991) *JFK*.

Stone, Oliver (dir.) (2006) *World Trade Center*.

Sturges, John (dir.) (1960) *The Magnificent Seven*.

Van Sant, Gus (dir.) (1991) *My Own Private Idaho*.

Van Sant, Gus (dir.) (1998) *Psycho*.

Vinterburg, Thomas (dir.) (2015) *Far from the Madding Crowd*.

Welles, Orson (dir.) (1966) *Chimes at Midnight*.

Winterbottom, Michael (dir.) (2001) *The Claim*.

Wright, Joe (dir.) (2007) *Atonement*.

Zeffirelli, Franco (dir.) (1990) *Hamlet*.

TELEVISION

Maher, Brendan (2006) *Wide Sargasso Sea*, BBC.

Moffatt, Steven and Gatiss, Mark (2010) 'A Study in Pink', *Sherlock*, BBC, Series 1, Episode 1.

MUSIC

L'Arpeggiata and Christina Pluhar, *All'Improvviso: Ciaccone, Bergamasche, et un po' di Follie* ..., Alpha 512.

Ellington, Duke (1999 [1957]) *Such Sweet Thunder*, Sony/Columbia Legacy CD CK 65568.

Gould, Glenn (2002) *A State of Wonder: The Complete Goldberg Variations 1955 & 1981*, Sony Classical CD, SM3K 87703 [sleeve notes by Tim Page].

Quadriga Consort (2003) *Ground: Ostinate Variationen*, HARP Records CD, LA73002 [sleeve notes by Elisabeth Kurz].

Wood, Hugh and BBC Symphony Orchestra (2001) *Symphony and 'Scenes from Comus'*, NMC D070.

INDEX